5/05

PEREGRINE FALCON

Number Sixty
THE CORRIE HERRING HOOKS SERIES

PEREGRINE

FALCON

Stories of the Blue Meanie

BY JIM ENDERSON

ORIGINAL ART BY ROBERT KATONA

University of Texas Press AUSTIN

Designed by Ellen McKie

LIBRARY OF CONGRESS CATALOGING-IN-PUBLICATION DATA

Enderson, James.
Peregrine falcon : stories of the Blue Meanie / Jim Enderson ; original art by
Robert Katona.—1st ed.
p.   cm. — (The Corrie Herring Hooks series ; no. 60)
Includes bibliographical references and index.
ISBN 0-292-70590.(cloth : alk. paper) — ISBN 0-292-70624-3 (pbk. : alk. paper)
1. Peregrine falcon. I. Title. II. Series.
QL696.F34E54   2005
598.9'6—dc22   2004017365

For Betty, Anne, Carrie, Cathy, and Ritt

CONTENTS

ACKNOWLEDGMENTS

It has been much easier to write this book because of help from many friends. Several reviewed all or part of the text, including Tom Mauch, Jack and Vicki Stoddart, Barry Watson, Lloyd Kiff, Kent Carnie, Dan Berger, Morgan Berthrong, Tim Gallagher, and Hal Webster. Much of the historical information has not been recorded. I relied on conversations with Pete Widener, Bob Berry, Joe Alston, Frank Bond, Will Shor, Madison Haley, Bill Heinrich, Jerry Craig, Tom Cade, Ralph Rogers, and the late John Campbell because their experiences were a part of that history.

My wife, Betty, was very encouraging and was always available for helpful criticism. Dan O'Brien gave useful advice early on, when it mattered. I am grateful to Lloyd Kiff for his critical review and special interest.

From the very beginning, even before he saw crude drafts of the early chapters, Robert Katona wanted to create the illustrations. I am delighted his work can show the peregrine in many different settings in this book, and I am in his debt.

PEREGRINE FALCON

INTRODUCTION

On a chilly spring morning in 1978, Joe Alston settled behind his spotting scope and peered at Haystack Rock. He had come to Dinosaur National Monument as a temporary wildlife biologist for the Colorado Division of Wildlife. Through March and early April, he had seen no peregrines and his work had been uneventful. On 8 April that was to change.

On that day, Joe's wife, Judy, accompanied him to the field. Much of the spectacular six-hundred-foot cliff was hidden from their position on the top. They moved a few tens of yards to the side for a better look. A scattering of piñon pines and junipers still blocked the view. Only the very edge of the precipice provided a panorama of the gorge of the Yampa River, on its way to the Colorado in the blue haze below.

Time passed slowly in the cold wind. They had seen a battered blue pickup on the two-track road to the cliff, and now wondered who else had ventured to such a lonely place. Tourists seemed unlikely, given the remoteness of the site and the early season. They decided to call it a day, and on the way out found the pickup gone. Alston noticed what appeared to be trash at the cliff edge near where the truck had been parked. Expecting a case of illegal dumping, he found instead a gruesome scene.

On top were rags, some wire, and a gas can. Below on a ledge a few scores of yards from the top were a tire, burned brush, and the weathered body of a woman in a plaid shirt. Alston hurried for help and soon returned with a deputy sheriff. After confirming there had indeed been a crime, the deputy and Alston scouted the area and found the pickup. It was abandoned. Armed with the deputy's rifle, he went the way of the suspect and found a man lying calmly under a piñon, smoking a cigarette. Alston, untrained in lawman things, went up to the poor man and said, "Excuse me, may I talk with you." It turned out the man was armed, but his gun was broken. Before long the deputy returned and the villain was taken away. Four months later the remains of a second woman were found at the bottom of the cliff.

How bad can luck be? Little did the murderer know, returning to burn the body that had failed to fall to the bottom of the cliff a few months before, that Haystack Rock was one of only a few places in temperate North America where peregrines still nested. The murderer had chosen poorly. He dumped the remains of his victims over one of the most carefully watched cliffs in North America. For all his effort he ended up in Wyoming Prison. Alston eventually became superintendent of Grand Canyon National Park.

Alston's experience is one of the true stories that make up this collection of tales of the peregrine falcon in the twentieth century. Peregrines have a history of a few thousand years on the gloves of falconers. These falcons became highly celebrated as hunters. Based on falconry alone, this creature might have remained obscure to the public in general. However, in the last half of the previous century the big blue falcon became almost a household word, a flagship of conservation, and a species most people knew was somehow very important. This notoriety grew because the falcon had suffered a widespread catastrophic population collapse, largely owing to the unanticipated toxic side effects of persistent chlorinated insecticides. The peregrine became a metaphor that undermined widely held assumptions about the invulnerability of the natural world.

My purpose is not to dwell on what has already been told by other writers. Instead, these accounts, often based on my own experiences, are intended to provide a kind of binocular view of the special people, the peculiar events, and the remarkable response of the peregrine that have driven its phenomenal

An adult female peregrine seen on the cliffs of the Colorado National Monument.

history in the last eight decades. Here and there I have also sought to explain the more special biological attributes of peregrines.

There is a vast popular and scientific literature dealing with this bird, which now is surely one of the best-studied wild animals on the planet. One of the main goals of this book is simply to explain why this wild bird deserves its popularity. Excellent sources of further information on the peregrines include a pair of conference reports, both with the main title of *Peregrine Falcon Populations*. The first was edited by Joe Hickey and published by the University of Wisconsin Press in 1969. The second was edited by Tom Cade and others and was published by the Peregrine Fund, Boise, in 1988. Derek Ratcliffe's *The Peregrine Falcon*, published in 1993 (2nd edition) by Academic Press in San Diego, provides deep insight regarding the falcon in Britain. In 2002, a very comprehensive summary of the bird by Clayton White and others appeared in the *Birds of North America* series (No. 660) produced by the Cornell Laboratory of Ornithology and the Academy of Natural Sciences. In late 2003 *Return of the Peregrine*, a wonderful anthology written by people involved in the rescue effort, was published by the Peregrine Fund, Boise.

Thousands of people came to save the peregrine from extinction. They were business people, students, biologists, and bureaucrats, and they were from both sides of the Atlantic. They cooperated in friendship and common resolve on an unprecedented scale. Among them were many falconers, the varied men and women who held the bird on the glove. Whoever they were, those who came to help were deeply changed by the big blue bird with "dispassionate brown eyes."

The cost of recovery easily exceeded $50 million, and if all indirect accounting were done, the figure might well approach twice that amount. Taxpayers paid only part of the bill. Private individuals and foundations donated millions Motives were as varied as the people, but their goals were the same: rescue the peregrine.

In 1939, Paul Mueller, a Swiss chemist, synthesized a new kind of molecule, DDT. Chemically, this substance was simply a couple of rings of carbon atoms. Chlorine atoms were used to replace a few outlying hydrogen atoms. The entirely new substance had several properties including extreme durability and solubility in fat, which taken together should have raised red flags. But at the time, its promise as an insecticide was compelling. DDT wrecked the way nerves work in insects.

DDT was used by the Allies to delouse people in World War II because it effectively killed the parasites but did not harm humans. The chemical was soon put to more noble uses, killing insect pests in the countryside and in homes and businesses. Mueller was awarded the Nobel Prize in 1948 for his work at the time the peregrine began its global decline. From 1947 onward, in the two decades that followed, thousands of tons of DDT were dumped on forests, marshes, and crops, first in Eurasia and North America, and later nearly everywhere else.

Then the strangest thing happened. The "wonder insecticide," which was almost indestructible, unexpectedly attached itself to fat molecules in small animals such as insects that became food for larger animals. The chemical accumulated in each larger animal and was passed on when that animal was eaten in turn. DDT rode the successive levels of animals up the food chain. Birds of prey high up in the food chain loaded up. Once in the top birds (especially those that ate fish or other birds), DDT, mainly changed to DDE, interfered with the gland that forms shells on eggs. Many raptors were in trouble. Poor shells meant broken shells, broken shells meant less hatching, less hatching resulted in fewer young, and fewer young meant fewer new adults to replace older adults that were lost in ordinary ways. Peregrines took the hit, and they took it hard.

The falcon disappeared from major parts of North America and Europe by the 1960s. Other kinds of raptors were affected, but usually less severely. Peregrines, and a few other birds of prey including bald eagles, tended to feed mainly on prey high in the food chain. The stage was set for falcon rescue. This book is partly about that endeavor.

Stories of the peregrine must also include its legacy in twentieth-century falconry. After all, falconers were among those who knew the bird best. They knew where it could be found, when and where it disappeared, and how it should be handled in captivity. They understood best the potential for managing eggs or young in the eyrie to ultimately increase the number of young fledged. They imagined what might be required to breed captives in a loft. They were closest to understanding, from the outset, how the species could be put back into its world. Falconers provided much of the energy that drove the recovery efforts. As a falconer and biologist, I cannot resist revealing a bit of my part in what happened.

What about the name *blue meanie*? So far as anyone knows, the name was first given to the peregrine by my friend Grainger Hunt, who knew of the villains in *Yellow Submarine*. Birds of prey, often called raptors, include mainly hawks, eagles, owls, vultures, and falcons. Some owls, some hawks and eagles, and most kinds of falcons are strongly aggressive by nature. The falcons are wonderfully alert birds that win food by boldly chasing down other birds in the open. Often prey escape, but some meet an untimely end.

Some raptors attack large intruders—including people—at their nests, the better to protect their young. Adult peregrines, gray-blue on the topside, are powerful predators and very defensive at their cliff-side nests, called eyries. From the view of prey or intruder, peregrines are very nasty. They are, in fact, meanies—big blue meanies.

The story of the peregrine falcon is a story of searches. Only a few months ago, at a hearing on peregrines held by the Colorado Wildlife Commission, a woman bird-watcher from a local Audubon chapter testified, hand on her heart, that she had watched birds for years and had seen but one peregrine. She concluded from this that they are very rare. Of course, peregrines are not as common as crows or robins, but they are no longer rare. To see a peregrine, one must set out to the most likely haunts. The quest often leads to big country and open sky. And now in many cities, you must search among skyscrapers and tall bridges. Peregrines love high places and because of this are often beyond easy range of human vision.

In another sense, what people did on behalf of this stricken species a few decades back were also searches. These were not so much scientific studies to learn the details of falcon biology as massive crash inquiries into the cause of the population sickness on two continents, and trial-and-error discoveries of ways to reverse the decline and to return the bird to places from which it had vanished. The people won in their searches. The great renewal of this bird, set in motion over thirty-five years ago, continues. The blue meanies are back.

I » THE NATURE OF THE FALCON

SPEED   All birds are ugly without feathers. It follows that feathers in their form and color "make" any bird, for better or worse. In the case of the peregrine, a fair share of its enormous appeal is due to its plumage. No feather on the falcon is the same as another. Of course each feather on one side of the falcon is the mirror image of its counterpart on the other side. Each feather is curved in its own way to cause it to lie in concert with those nearby. Body feathers overlap immediately to the sides and rear. In flight, feathers are usually pressed to the body by the airflow. That pressure may alert the bird to its speed. Feathers on the topside of the body seem stiffer than those underneath, the better to hold them tight. Turbulence on top, especially in slow flight or sharp turns, is greater than underneath.

In a high-speed dive, the bird deliberately assumes different shapes to precisely alter the forces caused by the potent slipstream. Just the right shape is critical to minimize friction with the air. Less friction pushes up the speed limit. Feathers are the clean shape of the falcon.

The effect of compactness is crucial at high speed. Loose feathers tend to vibrate, creating a slower, noisier, and distracted hunter. Even though blue meanie feathers are pretty stiff and lie tight in flight, some vibration is inevitable. In a high-speed dive, a telltale buzz, like canvas tearing, is unmistakable. Buffeting of thin trailing edges of wing and tail feathers probably causes much of the noise.

Peregrines are renowned for speed in flight. Just how fast are they? And why should they be fast at all? Most other kinds of birds, even raptors, do well at a slower pace. A few years ago, Vance Tucker of Duke University invented a remarkable instrument to find out how fast falcons fly. The machine was essentially a surplus artillery range finder wired to a laptop computer. The operator aimed the device at a diving falcon, kept it in focus, and moved the instrument on its tripod to track the bird. The computer simultaneously performed the complex calculations based on range, windage, and elevation. A printout showed the path of the falcon in time and space, each position calculated twice per second.

For its maiden trial, I urged Tucker to bring the rig to Mount Princeton in the upper Arkansas River Valley in Colorado. The falcons nested on a huge

Alpha, the first temperate North American peregrine bred in captivity, showing tight feather overlap.

cliff, the top of which is more than a thousand feet above the valley floor. The highest point on the cliff-top was a twenty-foot cross built of logs, placed there by owners of a local church camp. The male peregrine routinely sat on the cross, launching into near-vertical unholy dives at passing jays, blackbirds, swifts, and the like.

Dozens of hunting dives, called stoops, were tracked and their speeds computed. Even now, the results are not complete, but a few of the fastest speeds recorded approached ninety yards per second. Not even a Heisman quarterback can hurl a football so fast. Ninety yards per second converts to about 184 miles per hour.

What is the advantage of so much speed in a stoop? Of course, many of the birds that falcons eat are swift in their own right. The falcon often first sees its prey at a great distance, sometimes a half-mile or more, in this case from an old rugged cross. The faster the falcon can race to its prey the better, before things change for the worse. A flock of potential meals might make good its escape. Blinding speed suddenly places the falcon within reach of its prey. Prey that first saw the meanie as a distant speck in the sky, now an instant later find him in their midst. If peregrines were simply to chase prey on the level, only about seventy or eighty miles per hour could be attained, not enough for a crucial surprise advantage.

I have scoped the big cliffs of crumbling white granite on Mount Princeton in the springtimes of many years, looking for blue meanies. Once, a Rocky Mountain goat concealed herself in a cliff-side boulder field where only a goat could go. Within an hour she stood up, and then walked through the rocky rubble followed by a brand new kid, umbilical cord trailing. In moments she moved from my view, the youngster keeping pace with its mother.

The last year we tracked the falcons, we watched through spotting scopes in helpless disbelief when two boys from the church camp appeared at the cross atop the cliff. After glancing about, perhaps to be sure no one was watching, they uprooted the huge cross and toppled it over the precipice. As in the Haystack Rock incident (see Introduction), villains should not expect to remain undetected in their mischief at cliffs inhabited by peregrines.

Obviously, such great flight speed requires lots of room. This is the underlying reason that peregrines are often found on high cliffs, endless coastal beaches and storm wash flats, in the open sky above forests, and on the tundra. But peregrines are more than just fast. They can soar for hours on long wings held rigid, riding thermal updrafts or winds deflected up by the land. Perhaps by chance encounter they first learn where the best lift can be found.

In the early morning, before level ground has warmed, a falcon sails back and forth a few feet from the face of the white, sun-warmed Mount Princeton cliffs. The bird is steady in flight, but its shadow dances over uneven surfaces. Without a wingbeat, each pass results in a gain of several feet. The careful observer often sees the shadow first, recognizes its distinctive shape, and then finds the peregrine.

THE WEAKER SEX   Male peregrines usually weigh about two-thirds the weight of the two-pound females, and are easy to tell from females when the two are in the air together. Males usually seem obviously smaller and more slender. Persian and Arab falconers, who had experience only with migrants and not with nesting falcons, long held that the larger sex was the male. This is perhaps not surprising, given regional attitudes. It turns out that males are smaller than females in many raptors. A few other types of birds, such as the gull-like predatory jaegers, also show the difference. This is the reverse of the usual case in birds, and in many mammals, where males are more massive.

Satisfactory explanation for the smaller size of males in certain raptors has been elusive. At least a score of different theories float about in the literature. Now, my former student Zach Jones and I think we can explain the backward sizes based on what we have seen in peregrines.

The ideas are simple to follow. Peregrines eat mostly birds caught in flight. Most of the birds they catch are in the size range of blackbirds and swallows. Birds in that size range are easy to carry to the young falcons compared to larger prey. When blue meanies kill birds much heavier than pigeons, they must eat them where they fall.

It turns out that small animals, birds included, are more agile and better at dodging than large animals. This is because small animals are stronger *for their weight* than big animals. For example, tiny hummingbirds are strong enough to hover easily in calm air, a difficult task for an eagle. Thus small hawks hunt hummingbirds. It follows that a peregrine can be a better hunter of smaller birds if it is as close to the size of the prey as possible, the better to match their agility.

This is not to say that small birds are absolutely stronger than large ones. It is only that they are stronger relative to their weight. In effect, less of their muscle strength need be used to just move great mass and can be used instead for faster acceleration and maneuvering.

It is also true that there are many more *kinds* of small birds than big ones, and small birds tend to live at higher densities. For these reasons small prey birds are generally encountered more often than big prey. Why then have peregrines remained fairly big themselves? Would it not be better to be small and eat even smaller birds?

The difficulty is this. If peregrines were too small they would be unable to subdue larger prey outside of the nesting season, when food transport is less important. If there are no nestlings to feed, heavy birds like ducks can be eaten where they fall. Excessive downsizing would eliminate the option of catching large birds. (Downsizing might also place blue meanies in unfortunate competition with small hawks and falcons.)

By remaining fairly large, blue meanies enjoy access to a wide range of food sizes, the better to avoid hunger. So it is good to think of the peregrine as a general bird predator, able to catch many kinds of small birds, but big enough to eat larger ones, such as pigeons, crows, or ducks, when the getting is good.

But why is the *male* smaller than the female, and not the other way? It is because the female lays the eggs. In the few weeks prior to egg laying, female peregrines grow heavier and sit about a great deal. A few days before egg laying, females seem unable to fly with legs held up in the normal way, so large are their bellies.

Further, high-speed chases for prey are surely risky. Prey must be hit or grasped at high speed. There is always the risk of damage from collision. Delicate eggs in her big abdomen might be damaged. So the male does the hunting, providing for the female. The female sits and waits. She waits in the period of her confinement for the male to cater in the food. When he arrives, she flies out and begs, wings held downward.

Peregrine with prey. Large birds are eaten where they fall.

Aerial prey transfer.
The smaller, more agile male provides most of the food for female and brood.

After the eggs are laid, the female relies on the same strategy that worked when she was heavy and sluggish, filled with developing eggs. The bigger, powerful female relies on her lesser mate to feed her. She incubates the eggs much of the time, the male accepting that task only to relieve her so she can exercise and rest.

It all works well. She is larger, the better to cover and heat three or four big eggs. And when the young hatch, the more massive and powerful female works well in keeping them warm in the cold, shaded in the heat, and dry in the wet. Further, if it comes down to fending off would-be predators, the young are better off with the more formidable female at home.

If size difference between mates in certain raptors works so well, why haven't more kinds of birds adopted the system of a small male and a large female? Jones and I have a tentative explanation for this question as well. Many nonraptorial birds generally eat much smaller and less agile animals than do raptors. In fact, many kinds of birds feed their nestlings only tiny things such as insects. For those birds, food comes only in *small* packages, and only a few can be carried to the nestlings in one hunting trip. Worse, the tiny packages are often difficult to find because they are scattered or hidden. It takes time to round up a beakful. In many species finding enough rations for the young is too much of a job for one adult alone, especially when the nestlings are larger. Both adults must cooperate in finding enough to eat. For peregrines, food comes in much bigger bundles. One jay is a full-course meal. A few successful hunts by the male each day are usually enough to feed all the family.

The small male/large female system is beautifully adaptive. The casual observer may conclude the male does all the work. In reality, the sexes share the tasks of raising youngsters, and both are the winners.

There is one place in the world where blue meanies seem to push the limit in regard to small food packages. Bill Mattox and his coworkers have spent many summers with the peregrines in western Greenland. Indeed, one cannot reflect on Greenland falcons without thinking of Mattox. His fluency in Danish enabled him to arrange Greenlandic studies with the authorities in Copenhagen. He knows the arctic peregrine as well as anyone.

In western Greenland, blue meanies nest widely on the many cliffs in the ice-free area between the coast and the inland ice cap. The astounding fact is that the falcons raise their young on only a few kinds of songbirds. Pipits, longspurs, redpolls, snow buntings, and wheatears form the main menu. They are all more or less the size of sparrows.

Where food comes in such small tidbits, imagine the task for the male of feeding three big hungry youngsters, his mate, and himself. Each day, the three young might devour nine or ten, the female would consume two or three, and the poor working male surely would need the same. In all, perhaps a dozen tidbits are needed, requiring as many successful hunts each day. The midnight sun helps make the time-consuming foraging feasible. Females sometimes contribute, occasionally pouncing on young redpolls and long-spurs seen from the eyrie.

Ian Newton, the British ecologist, has studied the problem of size differ-ence between the sexes in raptors. The difference is greatest in those species that catch alert, fast, and elusive animals, intermediate in those that eat a mix of agile prey and sluggish, unwary prey, and least in raptors that eat prey that are totally unsuspecting. The latter includes prey such as mice, amphib-ians, reptiles, and insects. California condors and the New World vultures, which nearly always have the patience to wait for their prey to die before they seek it, show no size difference at all between the sexes. Incidentally, owls also show little or no size difference between the sexes. These observa-tions seem to underscore the value of small males if the favored prey is fast and agile.

In a way, male and female peregrines are distinct kinds of birds. Males are much quicker and more aerial. They tend to be away hunting when people visit eyries. In defense, males tend to go higher and dive farther at intruders, but they seldom attack as close as females. Females may land on the nest ledge and walk right up to an intruding human, ready for battle. We have actually caught females by hand in this way.

Peregrines are usually aggressive in nest defense. Blue meanies in Britain are an exception. There, they seem to keep their distance from people. Gamekeepers have killed peregrines at eyries for more than 150 years. The goal was to protect red grouse, the icon of upland bird gunning. Falcons now nesting on the highland crags are the descendants of those that kept away from people and lived to nest another day. So a different peregrine culture was established and maintained.

WHY PEREGRINES ARE NATURALLY SCARCE   The above notions on body size and prey abundance might seem to lead to another puzzle. If blue meanies are scaled in size to best use small birds, and occasionally larger ones, and if this makes available a greater supply of prey, then why are peregrines not more abundant than they are? Seldom are peregrine nests spaced less than a couple of miles apart, and many nest sites are spread far more thinly on the land. In western Colorado, for example, there are only a few places where several eyries are packed to a separation of a couple of miles. The others in the region, several dozen or so, are scattered widely.

Surely there are billions of small and midsized birds. There is a great deal of potential meanie food around, enough to feed nearly unlimited numbers of broods of young falcons. Why, indeed, had the lady from the local birdwatcher club not seen many peregrines over the years, instead of just one?

First off, this is not ultimately an issue of how many nestling peregrines are reared each year, or of how many peregrines die each year. At first blush, it might seem that the faster a species reproduces, or the less often individuals die, the larger the population will be.

Consider first the matter of making new falcons. Any species that has been around very long has come around to making new individuals as fast as it can. Of course each offspring must be of good quality so that it will have a fair shot at making youngsters itself one day. Selection focuses on making lots of quality young. Individuals who failed to make a strong showing in reproduction long since lost out to neighbors that did. Peregrines alive today are descendants of ancient winners in baby making. The same can be said of us all.

A similar argument can be made in the case of dying. Creatures that have been around for untold generations have become really proficient at staying alive as long as possible. This is to say that peregrines today are the descendants of individuals who on average escaped early death, lived longer, and produced more new falcons because they did. Those not so skilled at survival lived less long on average, and in turn counted fewer descendants. And because survival skills and falcon-making skills are inherited, we have now a world of creatures that are professionals in regard to surviving and reproducing. The amateurs left no enduring legacies.

But what, then, limits peregrine numbers and keeps them scarce? The well-known raptor ecologist Grainger Hunt, and Ian Newton, have independently helped unravel this knot. Their explanations are also easy to follow. The comparison is with a piggy bank whose owner puts coins into the bank as fast as coins become available, and takes coins from the bank as slowly as possible. If the latter is slower than the former, in the end the wealth of the owner is limited by the *size of the bank*. In the case of falcons, habitat is the "bank." The limit is set by the supply of things falcons need to exist. Coins need space to be stored, but living things need not only space, but food, a place to hide, and so on. These needs may change in the long run through centuries, but change little from generation to generation.

Imagine what peregrines must have. Food is crucial. Prey birds seem to be nearly everywhere. But not all kinds of birds in the right size range are equally exposed to falcon attack. Some species are more secretive and keep to the safety of cover. Prey birds of many types also have their own ups and downs by place, by season, and by year. The deeper question is whether or not peregrines can be so numerous in a region as to actually create a food shortage, limiting the numbers of falcons. You can imagine it is difficult to know when and where, or even whether, the availability of food works to limit peregrines.

Other things that peregrines need include places to roost at night safe from predators, places to avoid severe weather, and secure places to nest. It turns out that blue meanies chose wisely in regard to the latter when they first appeared on the planet. They mainly chose cliffs. With that choice, they at once satisfied the other needs.

Peregrines are birds of the open, the better to use speed in sudden attack. They are built for speed instead of agility. Streamlining owes to slender wings and smooth, compact plumage. The bird is heavier than it looks because of tight plumage. All these things work against the falcon in forests. Peregrines found it better to nest on cliffs, and now that lofty behavior is written on their genes.

Peregrines in most places have a mindset that cliffs are where they must nest. Formerly, that behavior limited the bird to more or less rough country. In North America the species now often nests on tall buildings and large bridges. This is really in keeping with cliff nesting. Cliffs are great places to nest because they are difficult for mammal predators that eat young falcons. Further, cliffs often have caves or ledges where eggs are protected from the weather. Only in a few regions, such as Australia and central Europe, does this falcon nest extensively in trees as well as on cliffs. Other exceptions to cliff nesting occur in the Arctic, and in Scandinavian bogs, where nests are sometimes on the ground.

A major problem is that cliffs are often rare on the landscape, even in otherwise rugged country. Newton found that peregrines in Scotland nest on nearly all the good cliffs. But they must be far enough apart to prevent neighbors from squabbling. When all the good and sufficiently isolated cliffs have owners, a few less fortunate pairs may nest on poor cliffs or on the ground. Most pairs unable to obtain cliffs presumably fail to nest at all. In this way nesting pairs would seem to be limited by the number of cliffs. This is also why non-nesting adults are sometimes seen trespassing in the territory of an established pair. These unattached adults apparently drift about the countryside, and this is why they are called "floaters."

If all the useful cliffs are occupied, nesting pairs reach their limit. Grainger Hunt argues that the limit is relentless. In his view, when pairs are unable to find big vacant cliffs, the falcons may settle for smaller, poorer cliffs (or cliffs in poorer habitat). Smaller crags may give less protection to eggs and young than big cliffs. In the end, too few young are made at poor sites to replace the old birds that were forced to use them. Poor cliffs remain in use because the overall supply of new adults exceeds the availability of good cliffs. Peregrines forced to settle for poorer sites are doomed to produce fewer youngsters. In the end, falcons attempting to make do with poor cliffs must be continually replaced by some of the offspring of those using good cliffs. Future biologists face a challenge to confirm the ways these things work.

You would think that the scattering of escarpments in most regions of the world determines the scattering of peregrine eyries. This seems likely in many places. But what of places where cliff lines are continuous for many miles, as they may be on coasts or along major rivers? Why don't the falcons accept near neighbors instead of demanding separation of at least a mile or more? The species seems to be genetically programmed to exclude near neighbors. Male peregrines, especially, have a major role in spacing because they are out and about and no doubt are aware of neighboring males. They drive them away when they are too near. In these aerial dogfights, the combatants race across the sky under full power, the resident falcon seeking to force a retreat from the other. This display is bird flight at its very best.

PEREGRINES EVERYWHERE   Although peregrines do not often nest where cliffs, bluffs, or tall buildings are absent, the falcon wins the gold medal for world distribution. It is far easier to say where they do not breed than where they do. They nest nearly everywhere except Antarctica, Iceland, Africa north of the Sahara, New Zealand, islands in the middle and eastern

An intruding male provokes
an attack in a territorial dispute.

Pacific, and the humid, tropical parts of Africa and the Americas. Because of their far-flung distribution, with small chance for mixing, birds from different regions look different.

Clayton White, a professor at Brigham Young University, has studied these subtle distinctions. More than three decades ago he described the distinct type that nests in arctic America (the subspecies *tundrius*). In all, about twenty variants are recognized. Spanish peregrines are known for their big feet, Australian birds for their black heads, and Aleutian falcons for their great size. For most of us, the differences in color patterns and proportions are too minor to consider.

Perhaps most unusual is the peregrine from southern South America, where normal-colored peregrines live with nearly white ones. The pale birds were called "pallid falcons" and were long thought to be a separate species, but a United States Fish and Wildlife Service (FWS) biologist found that blond falcons mate with ordinary peregrines. Broods may include normal and pale birds, peregrines all. The phenomenon is like that of leopards: spotted or black, they are the same breed of cat.

Perhaps the least abundant forms of blue meanie, much less than a hundred pairs each, are the races on the Fijian islands and on the Cape Verde Islands off the west coast of Africa. I believe the most numerous peregrine subspecies nests several thousand pairs strong across the tundra of Greenland, Canada, and Alaska. In winter and in migration, peregrines have probably been everywhere on the planet, except perhaps Antarctica. There have even been several sightings on Hawaii, but none have bred there. Extremes in migration are best revealed in the case of falcons from northern Greenland that may winter in Argentina, a flight of seven thousand miles.

BROWN MEANIES AND BLUE MEANIES   "Pastel" best describes the colors of peregrines. The upper surfaces are blue-gray, the better to blend, smoke-like, with the soft earth tones of their cliff homes. Subtle bars across all upper feathers seem to relax the border between bird and rock surface. The underside of the adult is barred charcoal over off-white. Again, touches of gray, and sometimes exceedingly thin amber, cast as pastels, create the delicate tones. In overhead lighting, the darker back of the bird is lightened and the paler chest and belly are set in shadow so that the whole bird tends to be neutral.

Further concealing the motionless bird is the sharply contrasting head and body. Black mask and white throat and ear patches boldly set the head disjunct from the rest. Humans, of course, quickly learn the association of the head and body, but a passing eagle might fail to put the two together.

Peregrines are not always blue. The first set of feathers, after the down of nestlings, lasts until the birds are yearlings. It is dark pastel brown on the back and streaked underneath with dark brown on the tan chest and belly. Why are juvenile peregrines so distinctive? Other kinds of falcons show only slight differences in the two plumages. Other birds such as gulls have distinctive plumages as juveniles. Perhaps the brown plumage of young peregrines serves as a signal and blocks the aggression adults show other adult peregrine intruders in their airspace. I have seen resident adults markedly limit their hostility toward visiting brown yearlings.

Because peregrines in defense attack at such great speed, the really distinct subadult plumage may allow recognition of the juveniles by adults at a distance, and prevent youngsters from getting hurt by their own parents in the weeks after the young learn to fly. Such protection could last all year.

In fact, when a brown yearling female trespasses in the territory of an adult male, she may pair with him if he is otherwise unmated. Twice in Colorado since 1975 such pairings have produced young. Normally falcons are at least two years old before nesting.

In western North America, prairie falcons are widespread in peregrine country. Prairies are brown on top, but the brown is pale compared to that of young peregrines. Up close, the color differences between the two kinds of falcons are obvious, but both are about the same size, so in the field there is plenty of confusion. Adult peregrine males apparently distinguish between brown peregrines and brown prairie falcons; they sometimes pair with the former, but only extremely rarely with the latter.

The true aficionado learns to distinguish prairies and peregrines by flight pattern alone. Prairies seem lighter on the wing, more buffeted by air currents. The late R. L. Meredith, in his recent posthumously published book on early American falconry, had clearly picked up on the difference. He said peregrines "always looked as if they were going some place" and that prairie falcons, unless in pursuit, "seemed a little less definite about it." With a bit of practice, you can verify Meredith's Law.

Even in a soar, which has been perfected by both species, the two can be distinguished. Peregrines tend to hold their wings slightly downward, with only the outboard half horizontal; prairies hold their wings straight out, horizontal from the wing-root. And the wings of the blue falcon usually appear more swept back.

GREAT-FOOTED FALCON   Peregrines have especially big feet, a characteristic shared with the bird-eating orange-breasted falcon of tropical America. John James Audubon called peregrines in the eastern United States "great-footed hawks," but he was certain these were the same as peregrines in the Old World. The usual excuse for the long toes is that such outrageous feet are better at reaching small birds as falcon and prey pass each other in a millisecond. Surely, longer toes do reach farther.

In their style of hunting, falcons must not actually ram their prey. At such high speeds even the hunter would surely be injured. Peregrines must arrange very near misses with precision, day after day. They must judge small distances instantaneously, passing by their prey just within reach. It seems unlikely falcons need long toes to make the hit. If the length of reach is critical, why aren't the legs also long? Perhaps long toes simply enable the foot to more fully encircle birds caught, the better to prevent prey from fluttering free.

Big feet do serve really fast-diving falcons in another way. In our dive speed study at Mount Princeton, we noticed the attacking falcon always slowed markedly in the last twenty to thirty yards before impact. Speed was lost because big feet were lowered into the airflow. Reduced speed at the end

of the dive may allow peregrines more precision in catching fast and agile birds. If so, the outrageous feet of peregrines more than make up for the awkward way they walk, each step a test to avoid tripping over one's own toes.

RANGEMASTER   One great advantage of speed in the sky, beyond the capture of food, is that swift hunters can push back the horizon in search of prey. In the early 1990s my students put tiny but powerful transmitters on peregrines at cliffs along the Front Range in Colorado. The observers climbed to mountaintops daily to track the signals from five adults as they went about the business of finding food for their young. Hunting ranges proved enormous. In the course of three months, the five birds hunted in areas averaging 340 square miles.

The hunting grounds of neighboring falcons greatly overlapped, but they probably saw each other only rarely in the vast gulf of air. The students radio-tracking the birds actually saw a falcon but once, even with the advantage of knowing when the meanies were near. So few falcons in such a great area underscores how thin peregrines are on the land compared to their prey. It follows that the chance of any individual prey bird being caught by those big feet is exceedingly tiny.

It is amazing how powerful the miniature transmitters really are. When the receiver was carried in my airplane, we were actually able to find a female hunting near cottonwoods and willows beside a creek almost twenty-five miles from her brood of nearly grown young. The closer we approached the louder became the signal. Finally we flew over the source, and the signal began to fade. Doubling back a few hundred feet off the ground we beagled about until we spotted her perched on a power pole. If only she could have known that the tiny package attached to her tail led us to her.

A brown-headed cowbird surprised in the open may escape only by dodging.

Marcy Cottrell Houle with Chimney Rock female prior to release with transmitter, 1977.

Perhaps it is better birds can know none of these things. But one of my early students felt differently. Marcy Cottrell was concerned that the transmitter we attached to the female at Chimney Rock near Mesa Verde in southwest Colorado, the first we placed on any wild peregrine, would somehow "rob the bird of its wild nature, reducing its free spirit." Apparently that did not happen, at least not to a significant degree. The bird roamed at least eleven miles from her eyrie, bringing home food for her fledged young trip after trip. Years later, Marcy Cottrell Houle wrote *Wings for My Flight* based on her sojourn with peregrines in Anasazi country.

VISION AND CURVED FLIGHT   Peregrines, like all raptors, have super vision. The wide head allows for huge eyes that nearly touch at the centerline, separated only by a membrane. Unlike human eyes, only the iris and pupil are in view between the eyelids. Because of this, falcon eyes seem much smaller than they really are. Great eye size makes for better clarity, just as more pixels result in sharper digital pictures.

But the air through which the light passes limits the clarity possible even with the best eyes. In the speed trials at Mount Princeton we noticed that on sunny days long dives often ceased by eleven o'clock in the morning. "Heat waves" are caused by the mixing of air heated by the ground to different temperatures and densities. This shimmering haze was easily seen with binoculars. Coastal falcons may have fewer problems; heat haze is usually less over water.

Heat haze or not, peregrines face a potentially serious problem in high-speed stoops. The surfaces of their eyes are exposed to the slipstream. The risk is that of flash drying the surface, so fast is the airflow. All birds have a thin third eyelid that can be flicked to the rear, wetting the eye surface. Meanies must use this membrane like a high-speed windshield wiper or hold it in a protective position as needed. It can only be a nuisance, but critical to the lifestyle. No one knows how much the membrane interferes with visual acuity.

The Mount Princeton work pointed to another strange aspect of peregrine vision. Unlike the eyes of mammals, which are able to look directly at only one object at a time, the eyes of most birds are able to look at *two* objects simultaneously, one object *ahead*, the other *to the side*. The view to the side is apparently seen more sharply, because falcons peer sideways at small, distant objects using one eye, but ahead with both eyes if the thing is near. Looking ahead, both eyes view the object at once, resulting in depth perception.

Imagine a falcon launching an attack at a tiny distant bird. The side view is best, given the distance. But the peregrine must hold its head perfectly in line with its body for the sake of streamlining. As a result, it flies *indirectly* toward the prey. Flying straight at the target would prevent use of the critically acute side vision. The falcon starts off the attack in a direction that seemed to us at first a ploy, an indirect approach. It was as if the falcon was trying to fool the prey, disguising an actual attack.

But the falcon was simply watching the target in the best way. The closer the falcon hurtled the more it turned toward the prey. Again and again, Tucker measured the male diving in tightening curved paths to his prey. Only in the last dozen yards or so did the meanie fly directly at the target, using both eyes straight ahead, the better to make a good hit. The Mount Princeton male usually curved to the right, but a male on the Front Range of Colorado started off using his left eye.

HUNTING   If peregrines are such fine and practiced hunters, why do attacks often fail? Surely by now meanies should have gotten it right. A small bird has no hope of outrunning the falcon's stoop. The only way to save itself is to jinx and dodge. But this is an imperfect art; some zig when a zag would have been better. A small bird does not get too many chances to perfect its skill in its attempt to save its only life. Prey must just try harder. But the falcon is after only one meal. An unsuccessful falcon can find some other food to attack. When falcons really try, they can be very good. In the mid-1980s, Larry Hays, a naturalist at Zion National Park, saw a female with big hungry youngsters catch several swifts in less than an hour.

Even more interesting is what happens when prey is hit. One notion is the falcon hits with its chest, delivering a stunning blow. Many others claim the hit is with clenched feet, like a fist. Steve Herman, a professor at Evergreen State College, made ultra-slow-motion films of falcons and prey. The pictures showed that prey was attacked with an open foot. In nature, the action is far too brief for the eye to follow.

Prey may be held, or the grip may be lost because of the great speed difference. If the struck bird is not held, peregrines wheel up and over in a tight loop, and return before the prey has recovered or fallen far. Sometimes the loops seem less than thirty feet in diameter and the time to get around only a second or two. So fast does it happen that a distant observer sees only a flash of light in the sky as the meanie goes over the top of the loop, upside down, sunlight reflecting from its pale underside.

Seen through a spotting scope, wings are bent up, bearing the huge load of centrifugal force. Why do the bones not break? The force must be limited in some way. Perhaps wing area is automatically made smaller by closing the wings as the load increases, so the breaking point is never reached. Maybe flight feathers bend to limit the load, or air escapes between the wings and the body.

First-year peregrines have wing and tail feathers that are about half an inch longer than those of the adults. Thus young birds learning to fly have greater wings and tails, which make for relatively more lifting force. The advantage comes in the days of clumsy flight as the youngsters learn to fly, and in the weeks ahead as they learn how to exploit updrafts. More area of wings and tail also makes possible slower, safer landings.

Even with more wing area, it takes time to get it right when landing. Old falcons have learned to land into the wind, and to bleed off excess speed in a direct, graceful, upward glide before touchdown. Unlike young birds, adults decide on the perch ahead dozens of yards before arrival. Departures usually begin with a slow launch and a shallow dive to gain flying speed. The exception involves hunting flights. From the very beginning the style of the departure announces the hunting falcon is in a hurry on strong, fast, deep wingbeats.

OVERVIEW   The falcon revealed in this account is a superlative aeronaut. It stands distinct from all other falcons. Great diving speed is its trademark. Speed is used as a weapon in the assault on prey. Prey birds high in the open

Male peregrine in the start of a high-speed loop to recover a falling Steller's jay.

sky are ordinarily immune to attack by nearly all kinds of raptors, but not by peregrines. Most kinds of falcons are fast, but this super-predator uses its speed in spectacular steep dives targeting faraway prey. The speed strategy works almost everywhere in the world. Few birds or mammals, except humans, have a broader distribution.

The roles of males and females in the long breeding season are separate, their tasks made easier by difference in body size. The smaller, more maneuverable male mainly provides for the family. Food that comes in large packages, compared to the food of insectivores, makes that possible. The much more massive female carries the large eggs before they are laid, and then keeps them warm. She is the force that would-be predators at the nest fear most.

The great weight of this falcon, coupled with wings that are partly folded except when soaring, results in a direct, steady flight. A smooth pitch upward to a perch when landing and a short dive at takeoff define its grace. The first is a way to slow down, the second a way to gain flying speed. Long, lightning stoops in the hunt, usually too far and too fast for observers to follow, are this falcon's hallmark. But amazingly, although built for dives and powerful level flight, the extended long wings and spread tail provide superior soaring ability.

Peregrines are thin on the land, even where food may seem plentiful. They are held in check in most places by a limited number of suitable nesting cliffs, by an unwillingness to accept near neighbors, and perhaps at certain times and places by a scarcity of prey in the open where it can be caught. Because blue meanies in many regions are closely linked to cliffs (or tall human-made structures) for nesting, that is where you must go to see them in spring and summer. Your trek will often be to big country where the views from cliff-tops are awesome. That is partly why we search for peregrines.

11 » MY EARLY SEARCHES

BEGINNINGS   Surely the pattern of one's life is set at an early age. My early years were in rural Iowa, rich in the sights and smells of cottonwoods in the creek bottoms, and mud and frogs. There was a pond behind the house beside the shiny tracks of the Rock Island Line Zephyr. The railroad right-of-way was a wildlife oasis in a desert of cornfields. I found it impossible to keep my hands off the robin eggs in the nest in our little cherry tree.

McNatton, the wonderful man next door with a pipe and brown-stained teeth, knew how to click the telegraph key at the railroad depot. More fascinating, he put the mail in a canvas bag held by a pole beside the tracks. The Zephyr would snatch it up without slowing. That speaks loads for the village of Fernald. One hot summer evening, McNatton shot a skunk in his chicken house with a very big shotgun. I never did see the skunk, but I heard the gun and smelled musk, both of which are not unpleasant to this day.

Only a boy would be foolish enough to chase a badger into a newly plowed field. It had very white teeth and I kept my distance. And then it began a new hole in the black soil and slowly sank from view. I learned that day that a badger is able to out-dig a boy with a shovel. In 1943 we left that place, but an attraction to animals was in my blood.

In 1951, I spent the summer on an uncle's farm in northwest Iowa. Uncles and aunts had a special place in the scheme of things. They were surely less authoritarian than parents, but by gentle persuasion, and open encouragement, they made their mark.

One evening, my uncle sent me to the grove of cottonwoods to drive the cows up for milking. *Killy, killy, killy*—a hawk dove at me again and again. I ran all the way to the milk shed, shouting for my uncle to bring a gun. He said that I should do the shooting and handed me the big old double-barreled gun and two red shells. I ran back down to the spot in the big cottonwoods. It was false bravado: I was afraid to shoot because of the inevitable pain from the recoil. *Killy, killy, killy.*

Suddenly the head of a small falcon appeared from an old woodpecker hole. The hole was in a huge broken-off tree, twenty-five feet from the ground. This was a nest, the reason for the anxious parent. Dark eyes, nearly hidden by narrow black masks extending from the top of the head down the cheeks, stared down at me.

The author with first kestrel, 1951.

The thick rough bark had fallen from the trunk, which was no less than four feet through the center. It was as smooth and slippery as silk. Worse, there was no branch anywhere. A ladder, I needed a ladder. But the tallest ladder was only twenty feet. The grain elevator, used to put corn in the crib, was tall enough. We towed it to the grove with the big red tractor and cranked it up, and I climbed the step-like blades to the hole. In went my hand; the cavity was empty. How could that be? This was surely the hole with the falcon.

Then Uncle Joel, patient as always, pointed to a lower branch nearby. Hanging from the branch, holding on for dear life, was a brand new kestrel that had made its first flight only minutes before we arrived with the elevator. Its nest-mates had fledged earlier and were scattered higher up out of reach. The kestrel became a pet, and although it was not apparent then, my course was set. Birds of prey and falconry would forever be compelling.

And how strange to learn later that the tree with the kestrel, only one hundred yards from the bank of the Raccoon River, was no doubt growing there when the geographer John Wesley Powell passed by in 1868. His task was to map this branch of the Des Moines River. In 1869 he became famous for his adventures on the Colorado River and its tributaries, the Green and the Yampa. Many years later, I would learn firsthand that the Colorado River country is a sanctuary for falcons.

NOTIONS OF BIRDS OF PREY   This chapter concerns events leading to the discovery of the catastrophic impact of pesticides on raptors on several continents. At the time of the kestrel episode in 1951, the mold had already been cast. Paul Mueller had been given his prize three years before in Stockholm. DDT was on the ground and in the wind. In those days there were very few folks interested in the biology of birds of prey.

Actually, most of the popular attention shown birds of prey dealt with how to get rid of them. Ammunition ads in outdoor magazines asserted, amid illustrations of hawks carrying off chickens, that their bullets were hawk bullets. The old U.S. Biological Survey in the Department of Agriculture actually did study raptors, or rather their stomachs, to learn how grievous was the damage done to farmers. With great chagrin I admit being a participant, as seen in my first reaction to the kestrel in the Iowa grove.

In my high school and junior college years in northern Illinois, birds of prey became increasingly important to me. Part of the appeal no doubt was the distraction they provided someone not too committed to schoolwork. In 1939, Frank and John Craighead had published *Hawks in the Hand*. I found the book in the school library. The volume appeared unopened. It was an account of how they used hawks to avoid schoolwork as well. Actually, they were keen naturalists and talented photographers; the wonderful black-and-white pictures of the brothers on cliffs and in trees, visiting these savage hawks and falcons, served to spur me onward.

Emulating what the Craigheads had done fifteen years before, Ralph Swanson, Larry Roder, and I pooled our money and bought a camera. We built a blind of smelly war-surplus canvas near red-tailed and red-shouldered hawk nests. Another uncle who was a telephone lineman gave us a set of cast-off pole climbers. They were a great help in ascending trees when there were no branches low down. We mastered the trick of stabbing the gaff into the tree rather than our legs. We pooled our funds and bought one hundred feet of half-inch-thick hemp rope. It made getting down from tall trees easier.

One day after school my friends lowered me over the side of the three-story Masonic Temple so I could peer into the nest of kestrels in a rusted-out cornice. The rope held. In the end, no photo of an adult hawk at the nest was obtained. We gained a new level of respect for the awesome photos obtained by twin brothers from Washington, D.C., Frank and John Craighead.

Through the early 1950s we sometimes kept kestrels and red-tailed hawks as pets. Despite much talk about falconry we had no real notion of how to go about it. We had jesses, swivels, and leashes, which are necessary to tether a hawk safely. But that was as far as it went. There was no way to move ahead, no mentors to help us learn more about raptors.

In that time, we worked out only the rudiments of hawk keeping. Unknown to us, help was only an hour's drive away. Three men, who would one day become central figures in raptor work, and now esteemed colleagues, lived nearby. They were Dan Berger, Jerry Swartz, and Jim Weaver. One day, our paths would cross.

The mid-1950s was a low point in my life with birds of prey. The whole thing might have gone the other way. The normal demands on one's time, part-time jobs, and college classes threatened to derail my connection with raptors. Minor events kept it going: the finding of a very improbable stuffed prairie falcon in the junior college biology lab; a clipping from the Des Moines newspaper showing Bob Elgin actually flying a peregrine falcon to a lure; and a gift of a magnificent copy of *The Art of Falconry* by Frederick II, Emperor of the Holy Roman Empire in its waning years in the thirteenth century. All these reminders of falconry stand clear, even today. In 1956 I enrolled in the University of Illinois at Urbana.

UNKNOWING MENTORS   I loaded up on zoology classes and took a part-time job cleaning opossum cages at the Illinois Natural History Survey. Apparently opossums do not contract rabies, and Carl Mohr was hoping to discover if this was really so. My next position at the Survey was with a chap named Milton Sanderson who had an inordinate fondness for beetles.

My task was to keep fresh alcohol in the thousands of jars of beetles on his shelves. Now and then he would hand me a bottle of beetles and tell me to soften them up. This required a different solution. When it had worked its wonders, Dr. Sanderson could pull out the skeletal parts of their reproductive members. The male and female parts fit together like lock and key. Naturally, only members of the same species have locks and keys that match. If key and lock were mismatched then no mating was possible. Almost every week Dr. Sanderson described a new species of beetle from the thousands he had brought from Sinaloa, Mexico.

One day a tall, slender man named Dick Graber came to the lab with a report he wanted Sanderson to read. He looked much like a cowboy just off the range; sunburned, unshaven, and uncombed, truly a modern Will Rogers. He *was* just off the range, finishing a bird study on the Black Mesa where Oklahoma adjoins Colorado. I told him I was interested in birds of prey. Graber showed me how to trap kestrels in winter using a mouse as bait. Once again I had a falcon for a pet. I would not be without a falcon again. One day Graber asked where I was going to graduate school. Up to that time the thought had not crossed my mind.

The lasting lesson at the university was that people there were following their passions. This made credible my work of finding out about birds of prey. I spent more and more time in the library, searching articles for the whereabouts of nesting peregrines. On my shelf today is a green metal recipe box filled with cards, each with directions to a peregrine cliff. Most locations are in the Appalachian Mountains or in California. All of that searching was in complete ignorance of the fact that by then, 1957, most of the eyries in the green box were vacant.

The scientific ornithological journals of the time actually held few reports dealing solely with birds of prey. A wonderful exception was a 1942 article on the duck hawk (the quaint old misnomer for the peregrine) in the eastern United States by Joe Hickey. Formerly a businessman, Hickey decided to follow his heart in middle age and study wildlife. His paper was followed, in 1946, by a summary on peregrines in the western United States by Richard Bond. That article was understandably the less thorough of the two, given the size of the West and the paucity of observers. At the time it hardly mattered; the two papers stood alone on the topic.

Heinz Meng finished a thesis on Cooper's hawks in 1951 in upstate New York, and the Craigheads published an entire book on the ways in which a variety of hawks and falcons live on the land and exploit their prey. Their work was done from 1941 to 1949, including an annoying recess for World War II. The fascinating aspect was that part of the account was set in the Yellowstone country.

The studies by Meng and the Craigheads were proof it was okay to study raptors. In southern California a graduate student by the name of Tom Cade had studied how kestrels react to near neighbors in the nesting season. The report appeared in 1955. When I found the paper in 1958, Cade was in Alaska floating down rivers, studying peregrines and gyrfalcons. He was to have a major impact on my career.

FAILED SEARCHES   One article from the 1940s caught my eye. An embryologist at Vanderbilt University in Tennessee had discovered a few pairs of peregrines nesting in cavities in trees at Reelfoot Lake in northwestern Tennessee. Sinking of the area during an earthquake had recently formed a basin. Flooding by a tributary of the Mississippi River created the lake. The man's name was Walter Spofford. In some of his visits to the nests, a young boy by the name of Tom Butler assisted Spofford. Many years later, Butler learned about electronics and would help me master the techniques of tracking wild falcons by means of small radios.

Reelfoot Lake is only two hundred miles from Urbana. Off I went in spring break, 1957, my first real quest for the blue meanic. How difficult could it be to find peregrines? Actually, very difficult when one is uninformed. Of course, I had never seen a peregrine, so there was the nagging question of identification. How much different could a peregrine be from a kestrel? So I looked for giant kestrels. Despite four days in a flat-bottomed boat with a special motor for shallow water, no falcon was seen. Severe sunburn called for thick layers of Noxema.

In the spring of 1958, on a tip from Richard Brewer, a graduate student at Urbana, I drove southwest to the cliffs at Wolf Lake on the Mississippi River a few miles upstream from Cape Girardeau, Missouri. Peregrines had been seen there in 1957. I could not find a falcon. Looking back, I think that failure, and the one at Reelfoot, simply created a greater imperative to succeed.

The Wolf Lake cliff, on the Illinois side of the river, is made of magnificent white limestone with lots of wide ledges. No wonder falcons were attracted to it. No other big outcrop occurs farther downstream on the Mississippi, and this was likely the southernmost eyrie on a cliff in the entire drainage. A few tree nests had been reported in the region, similar to those in the Reelfoot swamps. Upstream on the Mississippi, good cliffs appear at the Illinois-Wisconsin border, and northward. Duck hawks were once widespread on the river bluffs there.

In the fall of 1958 fate took another turn. A guest lecturer from the University of Minnesota gave a seminar at Illinois. His topic concerned the use of song patterns in warblers as a means of finding close relatives among the many species. His name was Harrison Tordoff. People called him Bud. Graber told me that Tordoff, a World War II fighter ace, was interested in raptors, and introduced us. Tordoff talked of prairie falcons, and I pumped him for all he knew. Finally he said, "If you drive all day long in western Kansas in winter, you should see a prairie."

Within two weeks my first wife, Dayle, and I were in a shabby motel in Wakeeny, Kansas. We had no idea where western Kansas began, but the land looked pretty flat. We had kestrel traps and two live mice in the car. How difficult could it be to catch a prairie falcon? The next morning was overcast but the wind was calm. We drove out of town, headed for the first country road we came to, clueless as to what it takes to find a prairie falcon. Of course, we had never seen a prairie falcon. We would watch for a giant kestrel.

The road resembled the one in the Hitchcock movie *North by Northwest* where a crop duster buzzes Cary Grant. Except for a simple roadside power line, the wheat stubble fields were utterly featureless. Now and then we flushed a hawk from its perch on a power pole. Some I did not recognize. Suddenly, well up ahead a big bird dropped swiftly from a pole, picked up speed, and pumped straight away a few feet above the ground, resembling for all the world a duck with no neck, a big round head, and a long tail. A prairie falcon!

We drove for three days and saw three prairies. Tordoff had been right. We had seen a falcon a day. Unlike kestrels, prairies were very wary, and there was no chance of getting a trap out before they bolted and raced away. Their speed and power were unforgettable.

Early in 1959, I got wind of peregrines just downstream from Lansing, Iowa, on the Mississippi. Richard Brewer said the local game warden had seen the birds the previous year. Spring break of 1959 I drove up, like a hound after a hare, through the beautiful, rolling hills of glaciated country around Dixon, Illinois. A fresh tint of green was on the fields and oaks. This place marks the full southern extent of the Pleistocene ice.

I drove into Lansing late at night. In my excitement I could not keep from calling the warden. The dimly lighted phone booth in that little town is still vivid in my memory, "No, they are not here this year, I was along the railroad tracks under the cliff last week. Sorry." What a blow! I simply could not find a peregrine. Three strikes and you're out. What kind of field person was I? The question would not have been so painful had I known that Dan Berger, who had watched the upper Mississippi eyries for years, was unable to find peregrines in the region in 1959. The birds were not just temporarily absent from the warden's cliff. They were mysteriously gone for good.

(At this writing, I cannot keep from revealing that in the year 2000, big blue meanies once again nested on the Lansing cliff.)

KESTRELS AND THE PILOT BLACK   There was plenty to do back at Urbana. Graber had convinced me to study the numerous nesting kestrels in the countryside near the university. He arranged for me to use an ancient Ford pickup truck, kept by the Natural History Survey to haul trash. It was a great field vehicle. The work involved catching every bird I could and cutting small holes in wing feathers so that the bird could be recognized if seen again. Many kestrels stayed in the study area in spring, found trees with holes for nesting, and reared young. I followed the marked birds all summer in the old truck, and was finally able to map the hunting range of each falcon. An area a bit less than a square mile had enough mice to feed a kestrel family.

The work involved a lot of tree climbing. I knew how from high school days. The young birds in every kestrel nest had to be counted. As I came down from a brood of youngsters in a hole in a monstrous sycamore, a great black snake moved slowly, in smooth undulations, toward the tree I was descending. The creature was about six feet long.

The black rat snake, or "pilot black," is special. Most individuals are gentle and easily handled. I reminded myself of this as I reached the six-foot level and dropped to the ground. The snake was indeed gentle, but once in my hands, it looped coil after coil around my arms and shoulder. Damn! How would I get this thing back to the campus?

This is what the trunk of a car is for. The plan came quickly. Peel the snake off myself, toss the fellow into the trunk, and then slam the trunk lid shut. The first part I finally accomplished with difficulty, and the slamming of the lid seemed instinctive. An hour later I drove up to the little house in Urbana that Dick and Jean Graber called home. Jean came out. "I have a big snake in the trunk you might like." I opened the trunk of my old Plymouth—no snake!

A quick inspection revealed a snake tail hanging from where the trunk and the headliner of the passenger compartment met. The snake had crawled into the tiny space between the steel roof and the liner over the backseat. Without the slightest hesitation, Jean climbed into the trunk, slid her skinny arm along the scaly tail, found a good place to grasp, which is like any other place on a snake, and then asked the important question: "What kind of snake is this?"

(Her greatest skill, however, was to skin small birds for perfect museum specimens, and to use the small remnant bodies for delicious hamburger.)

The pilot black eventually ended up in the care of Hobart Smith, herpetologist at Illinois. Years later Dr. Smith joined the faculty at the Air Force Academy and we would talk of the pilot black.

WYOMING PRAIRIE FALCONS   "There is no future in birds of prey" was the counsel of my advisor, Charles Kendeigh. He hoped I would stay at Illinois and work on energy requirements of sparrows. Not hardly! There were prairie falcons in the west, and they had barely been studied. Kendeigh agreed to call a former student of his who was then a professor at the University of Wyoming at Laramie. "Yes, there are prairie falcons here," and "Yes, you can send what's-his-name to work on them," he said. It was as simple as that.

The week after we arrived in Laramie in the unwilling blue Plymouth, the Air Force Academy showed up to play football in the opening game of the 1959 season. The academy mascot was a prairie falcon. During the halftime, I got the first close-up look at the bird I had come to study. I was shocked. Imagine that you had spent years handling fox terriers without ever seeing a bigger dog, and then one day someone walks up with a chocolate lab on a leash.

My expectation was that prairies were like kestrels, simply magnified in every feature. But prairies were not just kestrels put in a photographic enlarger. The proportions were very different. Compared to kestrels, the bigger falcon was not only nine times heavier, but had relatively smaller wings and tail for its weight. The legs were relatively much shorter, and the toes much longer. The whole scale was different. Kestrels have relatively bigger feathers covering the head; those on prairies are smaller and lie more tightly.

At a glance one could see the two falcons would perform differently, just as do terriers and labs. The larger falcon would not be buoyant and maneuverable. Surely it would not be able to hover in calm air on beating wings, motionless in space. Hovering is the forte of the kestrel. The big falcon would not be able to "jinx," following the erratic flight of an insect. Perching on wires would be done only with much difficulty, not worth the trouble.

As it turns out, change in size demands change in scale. The scaling of structures, in turn, enables the more massive falcon to do certain things well, but prevents it from doing others at all. In the world of falcons, the jack-of-all-trades model is a myth. The fun would come in seeing how prairie falcons are special in their own way.

No one at the university knew anything about falcons. Further, the professor who approved my application to Wyoming suddenly took a yearlong sabbatical leave to Afghanistan. I fell in with a couple of other professors, George Baxter and Ken Diem. They gave me free rein and loads of encourage-

Cadet R. W. Arnold with prairie falcon mascot at football game,
University of Wyoming versus Air Force Academy, 1959.

ment. A quaint old-timer by the name of Warren Higby lived in Laramie. He
had learned the basics of falconry from a friend who had known the Craigheads in the 1930s. Higby taught me how to trap the big prairies and how to
make and use a falcon hood.

The hood, custom fitted for each individual, made possible easy handling
of wild prairies. Of course you can handle a fresh-caught prairie without a
hood if you do not mind the sight of your own blood. The big falcons bite
pretty hard. Higby also coached on the subtleties of training falcons. All-
important was control of the bird's weight so that it was neither too hungry
and weak, nor too fat and indifferent to the lure.

The lure, a leather bag the size of your hand, is swung on a line. Falcons
soon learn to fly to it, their attraction reinforced by the attached meat. The
lure is the major way a lost falcon is recovered. A falcon can see the lure from
a great distance—much farther than the falcon can be seen by the falconer.

A university freshman in Laramie by the name of Dick Burnside was
interested in falconry; he kept a big hawk, and later caught a prairie falcon.
He had a war-surplus jeep, and it was in the mountains around Laramie that
I learned from him the art of getting stuck in mud and snow, and getting
unstuck. We still talk of it.

ROPE TRICK   The more serious lessons in graduate school concerned the use of a rope to reach falcon nests on tall cliffs. The first lesson is most memorable. The mountaineering club at the university held a class in rappelling at a small cliff in the hills near town. A woman volunteer was first. She put on a diaper-like sling made of nylon webbing and attached two steel rings called carabiners in tandem, each with a steel crossbar. A nylon line, ten times the strength of our hemp rope in Illinois, was threaded over the bars and tied to a tree on top of the cliff.

She was carefully coached: "The hand controlling your descent is the one holding the rope *below* the bars; the upper hand, holding the rope in front of your face, only steadies you." By wrapping the rope around one's rump with the lower hand, one could increase friction still more. Coupled with the friction provided by the bars, enough drag could be obtained to provide slow progress down the rope.

She backed off the forty-foot cliff with her feet wide apart, braced against the rock, in the proper style. The first ten feet of the descent went as planned. Then she looked down (the usual mistake of a novice) and lost her presence of mind. She forgot which hand controlled the friction. She let go with the hand creating friction on the rope over the bars, and grabbed the rope above her head with *both* hands. It was the natural thing to do. Even had she been wearing gloves, not nearly enough friction could result from a grip on the smooth slender line. Down she went in what was only a little slower than a free fall. Fortunately, the cliff was not tall, but her hands were badly burned.

EARLY RAPTOR PEOPLE   The three years with prairie falcons in Wyoming raced by. I never saw a peregrine in that time, even though some of the country was suitable for nesting. Once, in the spring of 1961, I saw a falcon high overhead that seemed somehow different. Maybe it was a blue meanie, a kind of ghost.

The first honest-to-goodness peregrine I saw was a captive in Denver in 1961. A group of falconers met from as far away as Alaska to form the North American Falconers Association. Several people brought their hawks and falcons to fly. The duck hawk was brought from Duluth, where it was trapped in migration. There was even talk that I might have the handsome male, but that did not happen. No doubt money changed hands, sealing a deal. By that time, I was set against the marketing of raptors even though they were not protected and cash exchanges were legal.

I took my prairie falcon to the meeting. She sat hooded on the back of the front seat of the car. That was where she always rode. As I entered the café at the motel where the falconers were staying, a voice said, "Whatcha got in the car, a chicken hawk?" I turned to see a big ruddy-faced farmer sipping coffee in a booth by the window. Completely taken in, I began the standard lecture on the misnomer "chicken hawk" and that prairie falcons were really noble hunters of the great American plains. The character in overalls, who was actually an accomplished falconer, let me keep right on talking. "Birds of prey are really very beneficial to farmers because they eat mice and . . ." A mischievous grin stopped me short. "My name is Don Hunter and I have come from South Dakota to join these characters who fly chicken hawks." Forty years have passed; Hunter died this year. We remained fast friends since that meeting in the café.

The Denver gathering in 1961 was held at the new home of Hal Webster. Construction was nearing completion. A small, wiry, intense man sat at the rock fireplace. He was sketching the head of a peregrine on the hearth with a piece of charcoal. His name was Frank Beebe, artist for the Provincial Museum in Victoria, British Columbia. He had recently published a paper on the biology of maritime peregrines on Canada's Queen Charlotte Islands.

At about the same time, Cade published his study of peregrines and gyrfalcons in Alaska. Those two papers, along with the earlier two by Hickey and Bond, completed the general information on peregrines on the continent. Of course the four studies did not cover the falcon everywhere in North America. Vast regions including northern Canada, the Rocky Mountains, the Southwest, and Mexico remained to be explored for peregrines.

INDIAN FROM THE AIR   In the spring of 1962, my time at Wyoming was coming to an end. In April, a friend and classmate, Mayo Call, dressed me up in an Army uniform and smuggled me into the rear seat of a military Cessna L-19 he flew for the National Guard. We were intent on finding nesting prairie falcons. Small, isolated cliffs dot the expanse of the Laramie Plains, and we checked them one by one, looking for telltale "whitewash" dropped by the falcons at favorite perches.

"Whoa!" I shouted. Mayo horsed the little olive-colored machine around for another pass. Sure enough, staring up at us from a small cave on the smooth vertical face of red sandstone was a snow-white human skull. The cliff, perhaps eighty feet tall, was miles from any road. We had no rope to get down to the cave.

Back at the airport, we loaded rope and sling into the plane and were off again. This time Mayo eased onto the prairie a few hundred yards from the cliff. Access to the ledge was straight down. Fortunately, the entrance to the cave was not overhung by the cliff. Down I went, no doubt the first human there since the burial. The skull was beside a flat rock that had been placed to cover the chest area. Beads, bracelets made of copper wire, and thin brass discs littered the sand around the skeleton. Perhaps this had been an Arapahoe, or a Shoshone. Very little tissue remained on the bones. The remnants were dried black and very hard.

In the opinion of the university anthropologist, the remains we found were those of a young woman. She had clearly been lowered to the cave, arms arranged across her chest, and covered by the big flat rock. Was she placed there by family or by friends? The woman was clearly held in great regard. Burial at a site so rare and inaccessible suggests she was special. The beads were of the type used in trade with the whites, dating to the mid-1800s.

She had been in the burial cave for a century. But she was not always alone. There was a good deal of old falcon whitewash splashed just above the floor at the back of the cave. I have often wondered how many broods of young prairie falcons grew up beside her white bones.

My desk at the university was in the zoology museum. The setting was somewhat similar to the office of Indiana Jones in the popular movies. The best parts were the massive windows. The glass, made before the turn of the century, scrambled ever so slightly the images of the distant Snowy Range. The tall ceiling seemed to absorb smoke from my cigars when I worked on my thesis.

One morning in May 1962, the phone rang in the museum. "Jim Enderson, this is Donald Victor Hunter." It was the South Dakota farmer from the café in Denver. "How would you like to go with me and Frank Beebe to the Queen Charlotte Islands to find peregrines?" My search for the big blue falcon had taken a momentous turn.

HINDSIGHT   Only twelve years separated the discovery of the kestrel hanging helplessly from the branch in the cottonwood in the floodplain of the Raccoon River and Hunter's invitation to paradise. How different it might have been had the kestrels in the cottonwood failed to hatch. I might have taken a job in the university bookstore instead of the Natural History Survey. What if Tordoff had given his warbler-song lecture at Michigan State instead of Illinois? What if, by simple chance, no prairie falcon had been seen on the Kansas prairie in winter? A major component in the events of those twelve years had been plain good luck.

Of course, the people were the main part of it. Uncle Joel, Swanson and Roder, Graber, Brewer, Baxter, Diem, Burnside, and Higby all enabled my intoxication with birds of prey to deepen. They had greased the skids. The trend toward good luck and good people was to broaden.

III » FIRST WILD PEREGRINES

QUEEN CHARLOTTE ISLANDS: FLIGHT TO PARADISE This was Hunter's plan. He would fly his plane to Laramie from his farm in southeastern South Dakota and pick me up, and then we would fly on to Boise for the night, reaching Victoria on Vancouver Island the next day. The following day, weather permitting, would see us up to the east side of the island and northwest over the 250 miles of open ocean to Sandspit in the Charlottes, not far from the southernmost islands of Alaska. This was to be a peregrine search an order of magnitude greater than any I had imagined, a free ride on a flight to paradise.

After a week of hurried packing, and last-minute visits to prairie falcon nests under study, I was ready. Hunter showed up right on time. We spent the night in Boise with Morley Nelson, a bullet-riddled veteran of the Italian campaign in 1945 with the Tenth Mountain Division (the ski troopers). Nelson was excited about our trip and we talked deep into the night. Two decades later, Nelson would become a crucial player in the odyssey of the peregrine by promoting the establishment of the Peregrine Fund's breeding center for endangered raptors in Boise.

I was fascinated by Nelson's passionate interest in falconry. He told of leaving his hospital bed in Italy, where he was recovering from wounds suffered in the Alps, to crawl up to a cliff. He had seen falcons there from his bed. A colonel chewed him out for leaving the hospital, in effect disobeying orders. Nelson, then a captain, responded by saying he had been near death twice, and if he now had "the strength see a falcon eyrie again," he damn well would.

The next morning we left Nelson and rode Hunter's little V-tailed Beechcraft over the Cascades, up Puget Sound, and on to Victoria. At that time Victoria seemed as if it had been dislodged from coastal England and set down, in its entirety, on the south end of Vancouver Island. The town was complete with little red telephone booths, each with a domed roof and dozens of tiny panes of glass. There, a shilling was still a shilling. People spoke with a deep British accent. I imagined that even the smell was British. Actually it was only the smell of the ocean, which I had not experienced before.

Morning found us in a major quandary. Beebe had invited, unexpectedly, a young friend to go along to the Charlottes. The four of us, and all the duffle and equipment, and tanks full of fuel, exceeded the load limit of the airplane. "We are too heavy by 5 percent," Hunter said. "Not too much for a Fortress, but too much for the Beech." I wondered what he meant.

I sorted through my belongings. What could be left behind? Sleeping bag no, air mattress yes, raincoat no, rubber boots yes; the load was lightened. We were still too heavy. "Leave the climbing line." The two-hundred-foot-long nylon rope weighed about twenty-five pounds. Without it we would not be able to move about on the cliffs. I was especially concerned because it was now clear only one of us knew how to rappel—me. "We can surely find a rope in the village on the island; fishermen always have good ropes," Beebe said. Famous last words.

We taxied to the runway. I was in the backseat with the kid Beebe had inconveniently invited. Duffel bags were wedged between us. The excitement of finally being under way offset the concern that we should have felt. The window beside me hinged outward for ventilation. I unlatched it and opened the Plexiglas to the limit. After everything was checked and we were ready for takeoff, Hunter looked over his shoulder and muttered, "Close the window."

The takeoff roll seemed to be longer than ordinary, especially considering we were at sea level, where performance is best. I began to wonder, as many had wondered before, if airplanes were really meant to fly. Finally, with the view of the end of the runway becoming spectacular, Hunter calmly eased back on the wheel, and off we went. Bang! The roar was deafening. What had happened? The window beside my head had popped open. I was scared witless. Hunter responded. "Close the window." Unfortunately, the airflow would not allow the window to latch. Our only alternative was return to the airport for another try. The second attempt was without mishap.

On the northern tip of Vancouver Island the fuel tanks were topped off at a Coast Guard station. Good move, I thought, because we would soon be out of sight of land over the inhospitable expanse of open ocean. Water temperature was about forty-four degrees Fahrenheit. And there was only a single engine on that airplane, just one "fan" up front, according to Hunter. It was best not to think of it.

An hour later we slipped between cloud layers as conditions slowly worsened. We lost radio contact with the station behind us on Vancouver Island. In a few long minutes, the station ahead at Sandspit, the only strip in the Charlottes, advised of acceptable weather for landing.

There had been little need to worry. I was soon to learn that Hunter, less than twenty years before, had piloted B-17 Fortresses in raids to Europe. After victory there, he piloted B-29s from Tinian Island to Japan, and was twice awarded the Distinguished Flying Cross. Hunter was no stranger to open ocean.

"THE PLACE WHERE TIME BEGAN" (HAIDA LEGEND) Captain Wilson was full-blooded Haida. He agreed to take us southward to the lee islands of the group, a hundred miles from the coast of British Columbia. His fishing trawler was big enough to deal with pretty rough water. There were no bunks, but we could roll out bags on the benches in the small cockpit. Anyway, sleep was not of interest. I wanted to see a blue meanie in the wild.

There was practically no way to miss. These islands nurtured the densest population of peregrines reported up to that time, and Beebe was with us. Small seabirds were there in colossal numbers, and good nesting ledges were everywhere around the rugged islands. The moderating effect of the Japan Current keeps the whole region, even out to the Aleutians, relatively mild in winter. At least it is mild enough so that seabirds there need not migrate; they feed on the rich fauna of the ocean, mainly small shrimp-like creatures.

We set off in the evening, crossed a channel two miles wide, and then motored twenty miles down the lee side of Moresby Island. The obvious anchorage for the night was in a small cove on the east (lee) side of a small islet. Captain Wilson knew it well. Protection from the swells was critical. The windward west side would have been impossible. In the morning we would find peregrines. Sleep was elusive. At that latitude, fifty-five degrees north, there is no darkness in summer. A soft, diffuse glow bathed the land, the water, and the gigantic trees. My sleeping bag provided no cushion from the hard bench.

Don Hunter (left) and Frank Beebe with the half-inch hemp rope on the way to the Queen Charlotte Islands, 1962.

We had another problem. Try as we did, the best piece of climbing rope we could find at Sandspit was ninety feet of *one-half-inch hemp*. Both the short length and the strength were marginal. The climbing-into-nests part of this expedition was going to be sketchy. We were now no better equipped than I had been in the early days in Illinois.

Captain Wilson was a quiet man who spoke good English. He was broadly built and his skin was a handsome dark red. His people had been on these islands for several thousand years, but they were probably not a part of the first dispersal of humans into North America more than eleven thousand years ago.

Whatever their origins, the Haida, the totem pole people, barely survived the smallpox epidemic brought upon them by the fur traders. Villages were totally eradicated, and disposing of the dead became impossible. This was my first encounter with a true Native American (before the term was politically correct). I watched him and was awestruck. How could his people have lived in this wilderness before steel hooks, nylon nets, and fuel oil? Now the totem pole builder was guiding us to the blue meanies.

I awoke to the start of the diesel engine. Hunter and the Haida had us under way. I was no more than dressed when we rounded the south end of the island. *Cack, cack, cack*—the hoarse, staccato alarm call of a peregrine. And there it was, flying straight away toward a rocky buttress projecting from a wall of Sitka spruces. The falcon landed on a dead snag within fifty feet of the outcrop. Surely it had young there; falcons without eggs or young are seldom so defensive.

We lowered the dinghy and Hunter and I rowed to the shore. Captain Wilson lay off with the trawler, engine idling, because the depth at this place was greater than the length of the anchor cable. The dinghy was round-bottomed, like a canoe. It was very unstable. The tide was out, exposing massive, slippery boulders. I stepped for a foothold that was awash between waves. Fortunately it was covered with barnacles the size of half-dollars and their shells provided traction. I pulled up, hemp rope over my shoulder, and searched for another foothold on the steeply sloping face of the boulder.

There was none. I tested the floor of a little crevice, but it was too narrow for my boot. Hunter had pulled back a few yards to avoid damage to the dinghy on the rocks. I was holding on, more and more tired with each moment. The leg supporting all my weight on the barnacles began to suffer from fatigue. It commenced to tremble like a sewing machine, clear warning the muscles were about to give up. I was headed for a swim before breakfast. Suddenly Beebe yelled from the trawler, "The starfish, the starfish!" The rock I clung to was the home of several big bright-orange starfish. I grabbed the rough back of a near one and found it firmly attached to the rock. They were living anti-skid steps. It turned out to be a four-starfish rock by the time I gained the top.

*A Peale's peregrine falcon (the type in the maritime Northwest)
comes out to defend his eyrie.*

First Wild Peregrines   « 43

Father to the rescue: a Peale's falcon disrupts an attack by an eagle on a youngster.

The forest came right down to within fifty feet of the upper limit of the tide. In this setting, ocean spray is not great. The forest floor was a foot-thick mat of moss, and in all directions the only color was green. Rainfall here exceeds two hundred inches a year. The eyrie was about a hundred feet above the shore, and it was easy to crawl to a place opposite the ledge, which was actually a hole under the exposed roots of a spruce. The soil under the roots had fallen away, forming a shelf three feet deep on top of the underlying bedrock.

On the ledge in full view, forty feet away, were three half-grown meanies. Below the ledge, littering the shallow ravine leading to the shore, were dozens of more-or-less complete skeletons of little seabirds. Many had most of the flight feathers remaining, but always the chest was missing. Food was so plentiful in these islands that peregrines dined mainly on breast of auklet, abandoning the rest for another auklet, or perhaps breast of petrel.

Both Hunter and Beebe wanted to capture a pair of nestlings. Needless to say, I very much wanted a peregrine for falconry. These young were too small to take; we could always stop off here on the return to Sandspit. The difficulty of seeking older young was that they might fly prematurely at the sight of my climbing onto their ledge. The result might be a splashdown in the ocean or a crash in the trees.

BALD EAGLES AND MONSTER TREES   In the next few days we found about a dozen pairs of peregrines, including two that had lost their young. The usual suspects in those cases were bald eagles. Eagles eat more than fish in the Charlottes. Young falcons were already on the wing at a few sites. One clumsy juvenile female struggled across a narrow channel two hundred feet in the air. A bald eagle came out of nowhere, and in a flash it was closing on the helpless peregrine. At the very last moment, the eagle suddenly rolled upside down, feet in the air. The hunter had become the hunted. The adult male peregrine flashed by, inches from the eagle's upheld talons. In the ensuing melee the blue meanie, in keeping with his name, dove again and again. Every time the eagle rolled to defend against the onslaught from above it lost speed and altitude. Meanwhile the young falcon made good her escape in the branches of the nearest spruce.

These things have worked well over the centuries. Contests such as this serve both eagles and peregrines in the long run. The adult peregrine was the latest edition in a long lineage of its kind that had the right stuff in the face of eagle talons. And on the other side, the eagle was the latest benefactor in a heritage of prudent eagles. What good is a meal in your talons if your wing is splintered?

Down through antiquity, eagles that fell to the sea with a broken wing or a cerebral concussion were slowly sorted out by meanies, just as eagles sorted out the young of timid peregrines. The Haida knew nothing of these things, but they were fully a part of the same relentless process. In the end, all creatures in those islands were right for that place.

On the third day out, Captain Wilson anchored off a big, low island covered with monster trees. "We need to have a bath now," he said. We unloaded by dinghy to the island, then followed him into the forest. A faint trail from the shore led into the cool, moist, dark-green forest.

Moss and lichens were knee-deep, and taller ferns were like a veil above the carpet. We climbed up a small steep hill and then kept to an arrow-straight ridge for 150 feet before dropping back to the forest floor. I stopped and looked back. We had just walked on much of the trunk of a giant fallen tree, limbs rotted away. It was covered with the same living mat of vegetation as the rest of the place.

More remarkable than the size of the dead giant itself was that it was covered with dozens of little spruce seedlings. Seedlings were otherwise uncommon on the forest floor. They were like parasites on the big tree, except real parasites take what they need from living, productive things, and that is why so many people are disgusted by their lifestyle.

In the case of this forest, the world is water-rich. This enabled trees to make wood in astronomical amounts. Eventually the nutrients in the forest floor were severely depleted. Nearly all the goodies were tied up in the wood of the magnificent trees. Now, when a tree finally dies and begins to rot, the treasure is unlocked. Seeds are everywhere, but only those that come to lie on a dead mammoth strike it rich.

I hurried on. There was shouting ahead in the direction of Captain Wilson, Hunter, Beebe, and the kid. When I found the four of them, they were buck naked, sitting in a big tin tank, up to their chins in clear, warm water. The tank was fed by a thermal spring. Ignoring my natural aversion to steeping in other people's juices, I jumped in. It was a hot tub to end all hot tubs.

SHANE   Toward the south end of the Queen Charlotte Archipelago the islands are smaller and lower, the expanses of water wider and rougher. I could only guess what the Pacific side must be like. Surely the surf was unmanageable, not to mention riptides, roaring like whitewater rivers between the islands.

We slowly sailed along the lee shore of a low island. Unlike many of these shores, here there was a narrow beach of coarse gravel. Behind the beach was a vertical, deeply irregular seawall. In a crevasse not more than thirty feet above the waterline was a white ledge. The white was feather down, recently shed by a brood of peregrines. In fact, a glance through binoculars revealed a completely feathered youngster standing on the shelf in full view.

Further glassing disclosed three more young sitting on top of the wall along the beach; they had already flown from the nest. We quickly devised a plan in the way that thieves come together before a robbery. Hunter would row me ashore to find out how well these birds could fly. The others would remain in the big boat, engine running, in case a flight should end up in the ocean. The most likely loot was the bird on the nest ledge.

I peered up at the ledge from the mouth of the narrow rift in the wall. The dark young female took one look at me and launched into flight. She passed ten feet over my head, flopped out over the shoreline, and turned for the beach. She barely made it to dry land. Before she could regain composure, I was there. She spun around, wings out, feathers on her neck and crown raised. The lessons of the ages had deemed it better to face your foe and fight than to turn, run, and become an easy meal, caught defenseless from behind. I grabbed for her quickly to lift her up. That was a mistake.

By that time I had handled many prairie falcons and should have known I would pay dearly. Quick as a blink, at least five of her eight talons were in my hands. Worse, the talons on one foot were embedded in at least one finger on each hand, so that they could not be separated. I was handcuffed by a brown meanie. After what seemed like ages, Hunter came to my rescue. Ever so carefully, so as not to break a talon off in my hand, he helped her let go of me.

Hunter had a hood, which he placed gently on her head. He then held the bird while I rowed us to the big boat. There seemed little chance any of the other three youngsters could be caught, because they had most likely flown several times and would be strong on the wing. "Let's give it a try," I said. Same plan as before might work. The boat would lie offshore a hundred yards, ready to fish a falcon from the water if need be.

We beached the dinghy at the same place as before. A very dark male was visible a little less than two hundred feet down the shore. I made for him. Young falcons are fairly naïve about danger, and he let me approach to the base of the wall beneath him. Then he gazed off at the ocean, hesitated a moment, and departed.

He went right out to sea. Hunter yelled to those on the boat to watch him and mark the place where he would hit the water. Damn! I had not come here to drown peregrines. The falcon would surely float for a few moments, perhaps long enough for Captain Wilson to motor to the spot. But salt water has a peculiar wetting effect. I feared the bird would quickly be soaked and chilled.

The bird grew smaller and smaller. Of course my binoculars were on the boat. "Damn!" again. Just as the fledgling was about to vanish, the speck moved to the right, seemed motionless for a few seconds, and then grew *larger*. He was headed back. Of all things, the bird flew directly to the crevasse with the nest and disappeared from sight.

Naturally, I raced back along the beach to the place, hoping he would be too tired to fly again. Not so. Out he came like a slow-pitched softball. As he was about to pass overhead, I jumped up and caught his body. He was magnificent, his dark brown eyes staring into mine.

Little else of the expedition is memorable. I had my peregrine and everything focused on caring for it. We had six falcons by that time, and food for them became a problem. Beebe had mentioned that Haida boys kept a pet peregrine, feeding it nothing but salmon heads, same as the dogs. The falcon was apparently maintained in full health by this totally foreign diet. We could see lots of fish below us in the clear water but had no way to catch them.

Captain Wilson saved the day. He shot a small harbor seal that had become trapped in a shallow tidal pool. I removed all the muscle from the carcass. The meat was very dark red, almost black, so great was the iron pigment. In that way, diving mammals store enough oxygen in their muscles to remain submerged for several minutes. We wrapped the meat in plastic and stored it in the bottom of the hull where the cold sea kept it chilled.

Eventually I named the peregrine Shane, after the character played by Alan Ladd in the movie of the same name. In the film, the boy played by Brandon DeWilde runs after Ladd, calling, "Come back, Shane." My peregrine flew out of sight on its first test flight on the Laramie Plains; hence the name. Despite his wayward tendency, I was to hunt with him for five years before he was lost.

The maritime peregrines of the Charlottes surely remain etched in the memories of those who have seen them. My visit was like time-travel to a younger, wilder world where neither prey nor predator nor forest had disappeared. How had these falcons avoided the fate of those at Reelfoot and on the bluffs along the Mississippi? One day, we would know.

IV » FIRST SURVEYS

FALCONRY CONNECTIONS   Today, folks interested in raptors are encountered everywhere. This was not so in 1962. There were only a few and they were widely scattered. Sometimes they met in strange ways. After World War II, Don Hunter studied law at Georgetown in Washington, D.C. He found the nest of a Cooper's hawk in the woods in nearby Virginia. While he was watching the nest, two men came up and wondered what Hunter was doing. They chatted for a while and then introduced themselves. They were the Craighead brothers. The encounter charged Hunter with renewed enthusiasm. One day he would have a major role affecting peregrines and raptors in general. In 1966 he co-founded the Raptor Research Foundation, the major organization of biologists studying birds of prey.

It is interesting that both Hunter and the Craigheads used the Library of Congress as a first source of information about falconry. The Craigheads and their lifelong friend Morgan Berthrong were isolated in their falconry interests and used the Library of Congress in 1936–1939, before World War II. Hunter was postwar. In those days the basics on training falcons had to come from old English books such as *The Badminton Library on Coursing and Falconry* (1892) and Michell's *The Art and Practice of Falconry* (1900).

In the late 1930s, both Walter Spofford and Richard Bond were at Woods Hole Marine Biological Laboratory in Massachusetts. Bond had a captive peregrine at the time. One afternoon, a young man, a graduate of Swarthmore, saw Bond with the falcon on his glove. "I have got to have one of those," he said, noticing that the falcon in public drew considerable attention. The young man was Bob Stabler. He was tall and square-jawed, and had a prominent brow and a small nose. He might have passed for Ernest Hemingway.

The very next week, Spofford and Bond took Stabler to the famous peregrine eyrie on Mount Tom in Connecticut. It was there the budding parasitologist obtained his first duck hawk. Years later, Spofford told me the trip to Mount Tom to obtain a falcon for Stabler was Bond's idea. Then and now, the unwritten code in falconry insists newcomers must first train a "lesser" bird, such as a kestrel, before they handle a duck hawk. In any case, decades later, Stabler would discover the cause and cure of a killer parasitic disease in falcons called frounce.

I learned of Stabler while studying at Laramie. My major professor had met him at a meeting at Colorado College, and he remembered Stabler was interested in falcons. Stabler actually knew little of the biology of prairie falcons and suggested I contact a chap named Harold Webster in Denver. Webster was a great help in the early days of the prairie falcon work. Mainly, he knew where the birds nested, and where they could be found in winter.

It turned out that Stabler, who had been teaching at Penn, had not heard of Colorado College before 1942. When he was living in Glen Mills, Pennsylvania, a young Navy officer on duty in Maryland paid him a visit. At the time, Stabler had edited a few issues of *The American Falconer*, the journal of a new, short-lived falconry club. The Navy officer was none other than Webster, budding falconer and erstwhile student at Colorado College.

In the spring of 1962, our time at Laramie was nearing its end. I began a search for honest work. I mailed countless letters of inquiry. One letter went to Stabler, then head of the zoology department at Colorado College. On returning from the Queen Charlotte trip I found a simple postcard. It announced, in Stabler's own longhand, that there would be an opening at the college. They were seeking an assistant professor of biology, and would I come *tomorrow* for an interview? I drove from Laramie the next day and was hired that afternoon.

There was a deeper falconry connection. A math professor, Tom Rawles, had arranged Stabler's appointment to the college in 1947. Rawles was tall, lean, white-haired, and precise. He had been a crony of Meredith's in Washington, D.C., before World War II when both were Army officers. Rawles liked the idea of another falcon man on campus. So did I.

Meredith had become an Army pilot not long after World War I. A propeller accidentally struck him, ending his flying career. In his travels in Europe following the war, he grew interested in training falcons. He kept peregrines and gyrfalcons far into his retirement. To this day he is considered the founder of North American falconry.

Despite the rarity of falconers in the early 1960s, a few were becoming insiders in my peregrine searches. In less than two years I had come to know many of the old-timers. They would graciously help in future quests for blue meanies.

LIL   The last major event in that summer of 1962 would be of great importance in later years. In summer, prairie falcons gather on the Laramie Plains when they finish the hard work of nesting. They come hundreds of miles from lower elevations to the cool high steppe, a prey-rich short-grass prairie. There, they regain their strength on horned larks and Richardson's ground squirrels. Part of my thesis work described this wonderful gathering.

On the last trip of my study, I stumbled upon a big dark falcon at dawn on the open prairie. I could hardly believe my eyes. It was a peregrine. Surely this was no misidentification. Only weeks before I had seen dozens of brand new peregrines in the Charlottes. The discovery of a peregrine on the Laramie Plains in summer was, and still is, a very unlikely event. No eyrie was known in the entire region.

The big chocolate-brown female had been on the wing for only a few weeks. From my speeding Chevy I tossed a pigeon equipped with a vest covered with nylon nooses. The falcon attacked in a flash, grappling with the doomed pigeon. Her long toes pulled tight two nooses and she was caught. A long line kept her from carrying the dead pigeon away. Her name was to be Lil, and she would join Shane, the male from the Queen Charlottes, in the move to Colorado.

PEREGRINE PEOPLE   The first year in Colorado was memorable. Rawles died of a heart attack in the fall. We lived in the cottage on their sprawling property and had become good friends. Although Rawles had no longer kept falcons, he loved having mine on the premises. The day he died, a female student ended her life in the zoology lab, a participant in an affair with another professor. That scholar was fired immediately, and I ended up teaching not only my classes, but his as well. There was little time to think of duck hawks.

One of the students I inherited was a tough Italian hockey player from Hibbing in northern Minnesota. Mike Minelli was probably better on the ice than in the zoology lab. But we hit it off. Birds of prey caught his fancy. I helped him catch his first kestrel. The hockey player eventually turned to teaching biology. Recently, Minelli bred goshawks in captivity, no feat for amateurs. We have remained dear friends all these years.

I did manage to get my thesis on the prairie falcon ready for publication. In the late spring it went off to the editor of the *Auk*, the journal of the American Ornithologists' Union. In a few weeks comments arrived from two referees. Referees are peers in the field of study who judge the merit of papers submitted for publication. In those days referees remained anonymous. One of my referees typed his review (fortunately favorable), suggesting improvements for the paper. Across the bottom of the stationery was printed "Lyman Hall." I wondered who the reviewer might be. Perhaps it was a chap by the name of Hall. Two years later I corresponded for the first time with Tom Cade. At the bottom of the second page of his letter appeared "Lyman Hall," the zoology building at Syracuse where he was then a professor.

In the fall of 1962, a high school kid by the name of Jack Stoddart showed up at Stabler's place with a young female peregrine shot through the wing by a bullet. Stoddart and his friends had learned a schoolmate had wounded the bird west of Denver and was keeping it as a pet. They had raided the poor lad's house and seized the falcon. The wing bones were shattered, but perhaps they would mend. Here was living proof of the presence of blue meanies in Colorado.

I kept the injured peregrine for several weeks, hopeful for signs the wing was growing more useful. No improvement was apparent. Finally, I destroyed the poor falcon, a very difficult task indeed. I clearly remember her last shudder. The loss of the big falcon seemed to renew in me the need to see more of these great predators. It was time for a new literature search, this one to be centered on the Rocky Mountains. Perhaps a letter-writing campaign, contacting people who might have information, would be productive. Meanwhile, I was off to the Colorado College library.

Then came a major break, one that would have enduring effect. Stabler's sister-in-law, Pinky Hamilton, also taught in our department. While a graduate student at Johns Hopkins in the 1930s she had dated a dapper chap named Joe Hickey. I think she still held a torch for him then, thirty years later. You could hear it in her voice. The name Hickey rang a bell. He was the Hickey who had written the article on duck hawks in the eastern United States back in 1942.

I contacted Hickey, telling him of my plans to survey the Rocky Mountain region for peregrines. By *the next day's mail* appeared a notebook dated 1942. It contained all of the eyrie locations Hickey learned of in the region from the Mississippi westward to the Continental Divide. Why was he so interested in my forthcoming search? What was in the wind?

ROCKY MOUNTAIN MEANIES   In the last half of the nineteenth century, naturalists came to the Rocky Mountains from universities and museums in the East. Ornithologists did their bird-watching with a shotgun. The limiting perimeter of their observations was surely influenced by the trajectory of lead pellets. These people were otherwise nearsighted. Field glasses and telescopes of the day were miserable instruments, and were used mostly to find birds to shoot.

When the collectors returned to Philadelphia, or New York, or Washington, D.C., they published long, dreary lists of birds encountered, but with vague notes on the locations. This was what the times required of them. Surely no one would desire to retrace their steps. We can now only speculate on the lost world that they so inadequately described. Compared to the many records of duck hawks in the eastern United States I had gleaned from the university library in Illinois six years earlier, records from the Rocky Mountains were appallingly few.

It did not occur to me the few far-flung locations where peregrines had been seen, then set in stone in libraries, would fix the pattern of my field search in the spring. I found the 1917 record from New Mexico, where Alexander Wetmore shot a peregrine at its eyrie, only to lose it in the sagebrush below. The shooting took place at Stinking Lake.

In 1911, A. A. Saunders, passing the time of day, fired his big Winchester repeating rifle at a cliff on the Gallatin River in Montana, flushing a peregrine from its nest. T. A. Taverner published a report, *Birds of the Red Deer River*, in 1919. He mentioned peregrines frequently. The Red Deer would be a port of call. My atlas revealed its location in southern Alberta, Canada.

Reports of historical eyries trickled in. I coveted each as if it were the discovery of a diamond mine. The geologist Bill Fischer, a colleague at Colorado College and an expert on the 1959 Yellowstone Park earthquake, told me of a pair he saw at Osprey Falls in the park in 1961. A falconer from Albuquerque, Tom Smylie, wrote of eyries at Los Alamos and the adjacent Jemez Caldera country. Smylie had played football at the University of New Mexico; the absence of his upper incisors amounted to a permanent record of that fleeting effort. Webster told of a pair he had seen near the Anasazi ruins at Mesa Verde.

Although I was unaware of it at the time, my inquiries were sometimes in bad taste. Falconers jealously guard nest locations, especially if they feel young falcons might be stolen. There is the well-known story of a falconer from Maryland, Al Nye, who visited Stabler in Pennsylvania. Nye was on his way to obtain a nestling peregrine further north. Stabler showed him two new birds he had just acquired. Nye said he was headed to a certain site on the upper Susquehanna River. Stabler wished him well, but failed to mention that his two new birds had just been taken from that very site. He knew the eyrie was empty.

In a daring move, I contacted Frank Craighead in Jackson, Wyoming. I wrote at the suggestion of the Craigheads' friend Morgan Berthrong, then chief pathologist at the main hospital in Colorado Springs. Berthrong was also a friend of Rawles's and Stabler's, and still kept two peregrines.

Craighead answered my letter. There was the usual reluctance to mention exact localities, but he wrote of a pair that nested on the Yellowstone River upstream from Billings. He said I might also check the defunct site at Livingston, Montana, "right across the street from the Dairy Queen."

Exact locations of abandoned eyries proved easier to obtain than those of current pairs. Better still, Craighead suggested I write Bob Elgas, whose eccentric hobby was the breeding of native ducks and geese. Elgas lived at Big Timber, Montana, on the Yellowstone. He pointed out three places where he had seen peregrines in the previous decade. His openness was refreshing.

My inquiry to a professor at the university in Edmonton, Alberta, provoked a three-page response. The letter was as vague as it was long. Apparently there had been a scuffle over peregrines and goshawks. The issue was between the professor, a wildlife photographer, and a game farm owner by the name of Al Oeming. My translation of the professor's letter, reading between the lines, suggested peregrines were still to be found on the rivers of Alberta east of the mountains. But his letter was full of caution, no doubt to put me off. "There is only a low likelihood even extensive river trips here would be successful." I was certain a search in Alberta should be by boat.

Most fortunate was my letter to Luff Meredith. Before his retirement, Meredith had been commander of Malmstrom Air Base in Great Falls. In that part of Montana, the Missouri River cuts deep, cliff-studded valleys through the high prairie. Meredith wrote of pairs he had found at the falls near the air base. The same falls provided much trouble for Lewis and Clark in 1805. Meredith mentioned a pair on the Marias River, a tributary of the Missouri below the Great Falls.

Then his letter shifted topics, and he wrote of the great *migration of peregrines* on the Gulf Coast of Texas, near where he lived. Meredith unknowingly set the stage for my future studies of peregrines in fall and winter on those warm beaches and wash flats of south Texas. Finally, Meredith's letter talked of falconry, revealing how he and the "old guard" disagreed with the open, high-profile approach taken by younger advocates of the sport. He did not say it, but I suspected his fear was that riffraff would be attracted to falconry. Perhaps he meant me.

Clayton White, a graduate student in Utah, wrote of nesting locations in the Green River area of northwest Colorado. He had finished a bird survey there just before the new Flaming Gorge Dam flooded vast areas of the Green River floodplain in Utah and Wyoming. White, who was studying peregrines in Alaska, wanted to see them in migration on the Gulf Coast. The migration in Texas was also included in my grandiose plans for the 1964 survey.

Glance at a map of North America. Appreciate how much country lies between central Alberta and central New Mexico. I naïvely threw in a fall count of falcons in south Texas for good measure. It should have been obvious. One person could not hope to mount anything like a complete search for blue meanies in the Rocky Mountains in one breeding season.

In all, my prize was sixty nest locations, wrested from sometimes reluctant informants, or gleaned from old journals. The task seemed simple. I would check as many as possible and see if peregrines were present. The search began in spring break, 1964.

The first lesson concerned "springtime in the Rockies," which is not like spring elsewhere at this latitude. In fact, it is not really spring at all. April and May are the wettest months in many of the places where I wanted to be. Often the wet would be in the form of snow. The plan was to begin in New Mexico and work northward, ready for Montana and Alberta as soon as school let out for the summer.

OFF TO THE FIELD   The first place to check was Wetmore's 1917 eyrie at Stinking Lake, accessible by three miles of dirt (not gravel) road. Access turned out to be a forced march in three miles of mud owing to the snow-melt. Mud in Mancos shale country is like mud nowhere else. "Gumbo" best describes the footing. Three or four pounds of gray mud clung to each boot, and each step required several times the normal effort. When I reached the site, it was very clear the walk out would be a problem. My leg muscles, soft from standing in a classroom, were spent. There was nothing to do but to watch for birds. In five hours, not a bird was seen. A wet snow began to fall. It was time to flee.

My legs were weak. Each step was a major effort. The slower the pace, the more the mud stuck to the boots. I had to go on. My jacket, now soaked, would be little protection in the quickly approaching darkness. I could see in my mind's eye the headline in the college student newspaper: BIOLOGY PROFESSOR DIES IN THE MUD IN NEW MEXICO. As it turned out, I was crippled for two days because of damaged muscles. The mountain passes were closed because of deep snow, so I slept in the car most of the first day. The drive home was sketchy. To lift a foot to the brake pedal required, literally, a helping hand.

Despite the sobering beginnings, mishaps were few. Lesson number one had been "Do not walk in the mud." Lesson number two was "Do not drive off with your spotting scope on top of the car." While loading gear into the venerable station wagon near a cliff on the Conejos River in southern Colorado, I set the scope on the roof to better manage the tripod and camp chair. Ten miles down the road came the light. But it was too late. I retraced my route. Two miles before I reached the spot, a truck came hurtling the other way, no doubt with my scope in the front seat. What motorist would not slam on the brakes, pick up a treasure lying in the road, and then rocket away before its stupid owner realized his blunder? More lessons were to come.

Chimney Rock is a 150-foot monolith of Mesa Verde sandstone perched on the tip of a shale mountain. The rock is near the Ute Indian Reservation in southwest Colorado and is the most prominent landmark between Durango and Pagosa Springs. Alfred Bailey and Robert Niedrach of the Denver Museum reported peregrines at this ancient Anasazi lookout in 1947. Nearby, Companion Rock is less of a landmark, but is even more interesting. Its base is littered with kivas, lodges, and the stonework of the cliff dwellers. The view of the Piedra River country is panoramic. A log from the roof of one of the buildings has been dated by its growth rings to the year 1038. Then, as now, people there looked up to the call of peregrines.

I pulled off the highway a mile from the rock and clamped my new spotting scope to the half-opened window. This was as close as I could drive until the snow melted. Before long, a passing truck slowed, stopped, and backed up. A slender middle-aged cowboy got out and walked to my open window. "What you lookin' at, folks climbin'?" I replied that I was bird-watching. This is my standard answer; most people are completely comfortable with that response. They usually throw a glance in the direction the scope is pointed, and then walk away satisfied.

This chap persisted. "My buddy used to climb that rock. He went up between the main rock and a spire by wedging himself in." The cowboy admitted to being too scared to climb very high. "Funniest thing, there was a big blue hawk that used to dive at us up there."

I kept my eye to the scope, always a good move to be rid of spectators. A few moments after he uttered the words *blue hawk*, an adult peregrine flew past the spire and landed on Companion. I nearly gasped aloud. But, gaze fixed firmly through the scope, I said I did not see a spire beside the main rock. "Oh, it fell off a few years back, glad I wasn't there." He wished me well and drove away.

Why had I not told him what I had seen? Was it because the word of peregrines on the rock might spread, and someone might steal the young, or shoot the adults? The friendly cowboy surely wasn't that kind of threat. Whatever the reason, I had become like so many who know of peregrines. I had become secretive, hoarding eyrie locations. Searching for blue meanies had become like a search for gold.

Stoddart called in May. He was the kid who had confiscated the wounded duck hawk from a classmate the previous year. A week later I peered over the edge of a big cliff on the Front Range. To the east, disappearing into the haze, sprawled the Denver Basin. Stoddart had seen a falcon there ten days before, and he knew they were what I was looking for.

The cliff of highly fractured granite overlooked a stream far below that flowed in a deep gorge to the gray-green prairie. I leaned out and examined the cliff face. Over the eons, water had seeped into fractures in the rock and had frozen. The enormous force caused by the expanding ice in the cracks loosened the whole cliff face. Pieces eventually fell away, creating many nooks, crannies, and ledges. Here and there, under places where a big bird could perch, were unmistakable streaks of fresh whitewash, telltale evidence falcons were using the cliff.

WHITEWASH Whitewash, the excrement of birds, is partly a suspension of tiny crystals of uric acid (mammals normally make urea, and uric acid in the case of gout). When dry, the chalklike marks are very helpful in ascertaining whether a cliff has been in use by falcons or other birds. With a bit of experience, one can tell whether the bird was a falcon, and roughly the age of the dropping.

Eagles and hawks splash their whitewash; ravens dribble here and there.

The whitewash of turkey vultures appears like that of falcons, except that there is always too much of it, especially where vultures gather in groups to roost at night. Falcon whitewash is special. It is dropped straight down in sufficient amounts to run vertically several feet on smooth sandstone.

Interpretation of whitewash is not an exact science. Of course, rough surfaces intercept flowing whitewash, and the streaks are shortened. But they are always straight down in the case of falcons, allowing for the different slopes of the surfaces. If the whitewash is under a protecting overhang, it may persist for several seasons, turning faint yellow, or sometimes very pale pink. On some deep ledges it surely persists for centuries, accumulating year after year. In fact, Kurt Burnham collected excrement from the floor of a gyrfalcon eyrie in Greenland and found through radiocarbon dating that some of it was about twenty-five hundred years old. On exposed ledges, the streaks may last only a few weeks, especially in rainy weather. As they wear away, the streaks become slightly broken; later they are obviously discontinuous.

Advanced whitewash analysis is less exacting. Prairie falcons tend to have a few favored perches, and these become very conspicuous as the nesting season dribbles on. Peregrines tend to sit in many different places on the cliff, a bit of white here, a bit there. And blue meanies often sit in dead trees (snags), except of course on the tundra. The thorough observer must carefully scope the upper surfaces of lower branches for telltale whitewash that had fallen from a falcon perched above.

It might seem that the search for peregrines really boils down to a search for bird droppings. The difficulty is that some pairs seem to hide their whitewash. An entire nesting season can elapse with very little showing. Only when the young are off the ledge, sitting about, does the rock become marked. Incidentally, the nest ledge itself rarely shows much white until the young are big enough to walk about and drop theirs over the side.

One glance at the cliff face near Golden, Colorado, was enough. "There are falcons here," I whispered to Stoddart. "I know that, I just saw them here a few days ago." How embarrassing for me to restate the obvious. Before long, a big blue meanie swung by and saw us. Then came the attack. Sometimes peregrines hit people. The impact is like that of a softball covered with protruding nails. This bird simply stooped at us and screamed.

By mid-June I had checked the New Mexico and Colorado locations on weekends. It was time to head for Yellowstone and points north.

SEARCH TO THE NORTH   The Indian wars in Wyoming were drawing to a close in the 1870s. The first naturalists to arrive, even before the country was safe for whites, were looking for fossils, not birds. I was able to find only a handful of nesting accounts of peregrines in the old journals or by word of mouth. But what the locations lacked in number was more than offset by their splendor. In early June, my wife, Dayle, our one-year-old son, Ritt, and I set off with a folding canoe atop the station wagon.

There was great satisfaction in knowing that this trip was not just a vacation, but honest-to-goodness research. Those who decide about tenure and promotion would, of course, take research into account. I wondered what they would think if they found out what great fun it was.

Gros Ventre Butte lies a few miles north of Jackson in full view of the spectacular Teton Range. A student of mine who knew the Craigheads had seen peregrines on the bluff in the late 1950s. There were actually two cliffs on the butte, both overlooking the bird-filled marshes of the National Elk Refuge. Neither rock showed signs of use.

Further north in Yellowstone, the site in the deep yellow canyon below the falls was also vacant. But the pair that Fischer reported at Osprey Falls was still in residence. A blue adult circled above a defunct osprey nest a few hundred yards downstream, and the faint wail of another peregrine could be

Eyrie on a dirt bank,
Red Deer River, Alberta.

heard over the roar of the falls. The noise masked the shuffling footfalls of a big, shiny black bear. Motion to the side caught my attention. There he stood, twenty feet away, peering into the canyon as if to confirm my observations. I leaped to my feet and he bolted off into a dense thicket of lodgepoles.

We were full of hope that Montana would be rich in blue meanies. It was not to be. We checked ten historical eyrie locations, including three shown to us by Bob Elgas, the waterfowl man. All ten appeared vacant, except for one bird in the place where A. A. Saunders had fired his Winchester fifty years before. We also sat on a picnic bench at the Dairy Queen in Livingston, contemplating the cliff across the highway that no longer echoed with the calls of Craighead's peregrines.

We crossed the border into Alberta. There, the major rivers cut deep coulees in the soft sediments as they meander eastward. One stream, the Rosebud, was too small to float a canoe, so I walked the railroad twenty miles to the next road where my wife could pick me up. The rivers were mostly gentle, and wildlife was abundant. And there were blue meanies. They required a new mindset. Instead of big cliffs, the nests were on dirt banks, generally less than forty feet tall.

PEREGRINES BY CANOE   The Red Deer River is the most important stream between Calgary and Edmonton. It flows in a coulee two hundred feet below level farmland. All that country was aspen parkland before settlement a century ago. An old man, Kerry Wood, had lived in Red Deer since the 1920s and knew falcons, but he could not bring himself to help. He claimed falconers had learned of the duck hawks in central Alberta and now came great distances to rob his nests. His letter amounted to a struggle to avoid rudeness without being dishonest. Finally, he wrote, "I must ask you not to visit me when you come to Alberta, I have not been too well."

There was no fast water on the river from the town downstream. The sides of the river valley were well forested, as they must have been centuries before. In the forty-mile section below Red Deer, there were perhaps half a dozen dirt banks that were tall enough for peregrines. And three were indeed occupied by falcons, two by prairie falcons, and one by peregrines. All the eyries contained tiny young birds.

But the rivers in that region are not always gentle. I chose rivers to float on the basis of how they looked on the map. Streams that meandered were probably flowing in wide valleys with sides too low for cliffs or tall dirt banks. The upper McLeod looked good. All set to put in the water, I noticed a man sitting on the porch of a house among the aspens across the road. It wouldn't hurt to check, so I walked over. "Is this a pretty good river to float?" I asked. "No one's made it yet," was the reply. He related how the river makes a couple of tight turns, at the same time plunging twenty feet over a couple of outcrops of bedrock. From then on, my policy was to seek information about a river before departure. I moved to a more gentle section of the stream.

The lower Pembina was mild—too mild, in fact. I got an early start at sunup. Soon the country flattened, and the current became nearly imperceptible. I fished around in the bottom of the canoe and pulled out a tiny gas outboard motor. It was all of three-quarters horsepower. I clamped it to a board behind my seat. At full throttle the whole works moved at about seven miles an hour.

The map showed only about thirty miles to the road crossing where Dayle and little Ritt would be waiting. The distance by water was surely more than twice that, given the tortuous river course. It would be near dark before I reached the crossing. The river flowed mainly through a mixed aspen and poplar forest. The trees were completely without leaves even though it was late June. A horde of moth caterpillars had created the illusion of late fall.

The Pembina valley slowly grew deeper. As the sun was getting low, I motored around a bend and saw a remarkable multilayered dirt bank not far ahead. The whole thing was of yellowish clay. The upper vertical part was about twenty-five feet tall. As I approached, whitewash came into view. Then came the rapid cacking call of a peregrine. Fifteen minutes later I was sitting in the eyrie with three big downy duck hawks. Two had the usual gray-green feet typical of youngsters, but the third had bright yellow feet like its parents.

As I finished clamping the last leg band in place on the unruly trio I heard the wail of the arriving father. He had not yet seen me. In he came. Imagine the sight. He was carrying a completely intact Franklin's gull, a bird nearly his size, if not nearly so heavy. The peregrine and the gull were a huge flying array of black and white.

Job done, I climbed to the top of the valley above the eyrie in hopes of seeing the road crossing downstream. To my shock, I climbed directly into the outskirts of a village, barking dogs and all. So much for the notion peregrines nest only far from human settlement.

Exploring rivers in peregrine country was great fun, even without the thrill of whitewater. But even smooth rivers have the power to terrify. The McLeod is one such stream. The section I floated was unruly from the start. The river had cut into its banks in many places the previous spring, and as the top of the bank fell over, trees growing at the edge fell out over the water. Often they hung there, horizontally, a foot off the surface. Such trees, extending sometimes sixty feet out from the bank, were called "widow-makers."

The proper strategy was to keep to the middle of the river. There were of course other subtleties, such as "Never pull out of the river above a widow-maker; you will be swept into it when you put in again." So there I was in the middle of the river, no doubt complacent in the correct technique.

Folding canoe used to visit eyries in Alberta, 1964.

The current had become fairly brisk. I rounded a bend, and behold, in the middle of the river was an island with a huge logjam on the upstream end. It was too late to go left or right. My canoe was carried broadside against the logs and pinned by the swift water. In a flash the canoe started to fill as the river rushed over the upstream side. In a moment the canoe would be swamped and I would be rolled to certain doom beneath the logs.

Fear was a great incentive. I threw myself upward and backward out of the sinking canoe onto the logs. Safety! With a lesser load, the craft raised up. The filling stopped. Slowly I grabbed all of the equipment I could reach and threw it onto the logs piled behind me. Finally, the canoe was light enough to drag up from the water. Once turned bottom-up and emptied of water, it could be dragged downstream over the logjam to safer water.

LOOKING BACK   At the end of the 1964 survey I had visited more than fifty places where blue meanies once nested. Only thirteen pairs of falcons were present. Surely, more nest sites should have been in use had the birds lived up to their reputation for great fidelity to eyrie and mate.

There were nagging doubts. Did I really know how to find these birds? Had I spent enough time at each place, and had the river searches been slow enough? The country was so immense. Was I spread too thin? I wondered how many peregrines had sat unseen, watching this comparatively blind human stumble by.

On the other hand, if there were lots of peregrines, I should have found more. I had discovered dozens of pairs of prairie falcons. Surely they were not much easier to find than blue meanies. A few pairs of peregrines still used cliffs where they had been reported decades earlier, underscoring the notion that finding falcons would be made easier by knowing where they used to be.

But at some point back then, I accepted the inevitable. It is nearly impossible to show beyond doubt that a site is vacant. Searchers cannot watch long enough or well enough to be dead certain no falcon was present that season. When a pair is discovered using a cliff, further proof is unnecessary. But a seemingly vacant cliff today may have a pair tomorrow, or may have had one yesterday. This is relentlessly frustrating to those who seek blue meanies.

v » DISASTER DECADE

The ten-year period, 1964–1973, following my first search for peregrines in the Rocky Mountains was marked by bad news and anxious pessimism concerning duck hawks. This chapter focuses on the remarkable resiliency of the bird and the cooperative resolve of people who were simply unwilling to settle for anything less than a happy ending. They would not let the blue meanies be gone. Never before had so many people worked so well together to see a species return. They were heroes all. Some were superheroes.

THE WISCONSIN CONFERENCE   In 1964, Hickey sent Dan Berger and Chuck Sindelar to survey some two hundred historical peregrine sites in the expanse from northern Alabama to Maine. Hickey convinced Kathleen Herbert, widow of Richard Herbert, who kept track of the Hudson River pairs, to fund the inquiry. The mission was to repeat Hickey's earlier survey. Hickey reported more than two hundred pairs of blue meanies in his 1942 landmark study. Berger and Sindelar found not a falcon, not a single blue feather. The duck hawks had vanished.

A year before, Hickey had sent me his old notes on nest locations he found when preparing for his 1942 study. The gift of notes was his way to encourage my quest in the Rockies for the disappearing falcon in the same year as the Berger and Sindelar survey. Something was up.

At the end of August 1965, a group of falcon folks were summoned to the University of Wisconsin in Madison to talk to each other about peregrines. Joe Hickey drew up the guest list. My invitation was in his precise and graceful handwriting. Hickey's purpose was to know what was wrong with peregrines. He had been in touch with Derek Ratcliffe, an Englishman who had just learned of widespread eyrie abandonment throughout England and Scotland.

About sixty people were guests at the Madison meeting. It was a strange and unlikely mix. There were falconers and anti-falconers, bird-watchers and gun hunters, professors and museum people, and there were business folks and students. There were Canadians, Finns, Frenchmen, Englishmen, a Swiss, and a West German.

The cold war was on; two East Germans were denied travel to the United States by their government. Had they come, we might have permanently gained two new falcon biologists. The foremost Russian expert was not allowed to travel for fear he might defect. Hickey used funds earmarked for the Russian to bring Tom Cade back from a field study in South Africa.

All of us loved peregrines, and we wanted to know what was wrong. I knew very few of the invitees—actually only Nelson, Hunt, White, and Beebe. Other names were synonymous with birds of prey: Spofford, Hamerstrom, and Cade. In all, about fifteen falconer types were invited. Some of these were more like pet keepers. Of course there were the usual wildlife experts and observers. As it turned out, the falconers were the most knowledgeable about what was happening to birds of prey in the wild.

No conference on wildlife, before or since, has had such a lasting effect. For some of us it would set in concrete the paths of lifetime careers. One by one, the people told their stories. The emerging pattern was not a simple one. Several raptors were involved. Peregrine numbers were crashing in the warmer parts of North America and in the colder parts of Europe. Cooper's hawks were scarce in Pennsylvania, but goshawks there were okay. Ospreys were way down in New England, but migrants from the north seemed to be holding strong. Bald eagles along the eastern seaboard were far fewer, but those in British Columbia were fine. For each species there seemed to be a "safe island." My thoughts went back to the magnificent Queen Charlotte peregrines, somehow secure in the Pacific on the western edge of North America.

What had gone wrong? Had some unknown disease or parasite been the cause of the disappearance of these raptors? These notions were soon discarded. How could such a thing have happened in this strange pattern? The conferees went so far as to consider the extinction of the passenger pigeon as the cause for peregrine losses in the United States. The pigeon was surely a blue meanie favorite, just the right size. But the timing was very wrong. The pigeon vanished six decades before peregrines started down. Further, it was obvious these falcons are not dependent on any one kind of food.

Morley Nelson suspected long-term drought was involved in the decrease of duck hawks. He had seen downward trends in mountain snowpack, runoff water in spring, and smaller lakes and ponds over recent decades. He suggested this trend toward a drier world, especially in the western United States, might be a cause. I doubted this novel and interesting idea. The New Mexico duck hawks I had seen were dry-proof. A few pairs nested dozens of miles from permanent lakes or streams.

As the discussions wore on, similarities emerged among peregrine populations that were in trouble here and abroad. There was a common pattern in the timing. First, reports of the disappearance of eggs were common, not just an egg at a time, but often whole clutches of eggs. Sometimes eggs vanished at an eyrie year after year. The pattern of disappearance was too widespread to have been caused by egg collectors. Next, many pairs stopped laying altogether.

Adults showed up in the spring, but for some reason, seemed not to lay eggs. Lone unmated adults occupied many cliffs. Last, after a few years of failure, eyries no longer held peregrines at all. In some regions, all eyries reached that final stage and fell into disuse. This clearly happened in the eastern United States, northern Germany, much of Finland, and southeastern England. In other places, such as Scotland and southern Germany, a few pairs persisted. I hoped the Rocky Mountain birds were no worse off than this last group, and would not continue the slide into oblivion.

THE CHEMICAL CONNECTION   In 1965 the accidental poisoning of wildlife by chemicals used to control insects was well known. Perhaps the most notorious catastrophe was the loss of hundreds of waterbirds called grebes at Clear Lake in California. Chemicals had been sprayed around the lake to kill biting flies. Another case, closer to the conference, was the poisoning of gulls in Wisconsin.

Gulls ate fish from Lake Michigan. The fish had accumulated chemicals from plankton they had eaten. The microscopic plankton had gathered pesticides from lake-bottom sediments bearing chemicals from hundreds of inflowing streams. More than energy and nutrients was served up the food chains. Poison was flowing up to the top predators.

Hickey had been thoughtful enough to invite chemists who knew of such things. Foremost were Lucille and Bill Stickel, a husband-and-wife team from the federal wildlife labs in Maryland. Another was Don Spencer, an employee of the research branch of the United States Department of Agriculture. Spencer would later sell his soul to the pesticide manufacturers and lobby against the eventual restriction on DDT. Anyway, it was ironic that the chemists were not of much help. This was because most of the testing of pesticides on birds up to that time used ducks and chickens. The idea was that toxic chemicals might kill bird embryos or adults directly, the dead bird being then clear evidence of the effect. Tests had mainly sought to find out how much insecticide could be fed to test birds before they succumbed. DDT turned out to be a relatively poor duck or chicken poison.

In fact, test animals had been fed a lot of nasty pesticides and they did not die unless the amounts of the poisons were much greater than usually found in wild birds. Just as baffling was the news that toxic chemicals are naturally converted by animals into a variety of milder substances. Even if it turned out one insecticide was suspect, any one or more of several chemical by-products might actually be the problem. Or did certain chemicals act in some hidden combination?

The Stickels pointed out that ducks and fowl could reproduce with lots of DDT in their bodies. They had also found that "a little" DDT in eggs was not a problem in the hatching of chicks. Another diversion was the report that when test birds had eaten enough pesticide to block reproduction, it was also enough to kill the bird itself. Perhaps some kind of stress, short of full-blown poisoning, was the problem.

A book detailing the conference was published in 1969. It won great reviews. The chapter on toxic chemicals was understandably short, given the state of knowledge at the time. But here and there were the seeds of ideas that would break the case wide open. Cade cautioned that whatever was amiss, it was an insidious, unnatural factor. He argued that peregrines had a rich and vigorous past, even in the face of much direct persecution by humans. We could only hope their future would someday be restored.

Scattered in the conversations about chemicals were suggestive comments. "DDT is made into DDE by organisms that get it inadvertently in food." "The effects of DDE alone are not sufficiently studied." DDE was by then "quite widespread." Fran Hamerstrom's husband, "Hammy," a well-respected wildlife biologist, said, "There may be more pieces to the puzzle than we know yet." The pieces would prove to be those of broken eggshells.

AFTERMATH   The "great meeting" in Wisconsin became history in a heartbeat. Looking back, it is difficult to overstate how suddenly perspectives changed. My narrow focus had been to find falcons. The mission had grown from the disappointments of the Mississippi River sites and Reelfoot, the glorious success in the Queen Charlottes, and the exhausting survey in the Rocky Mountains.

For me personally, the conference was bedazzling. I was a would-be peregrine expert called before the gods. I was to tell them all about the status of the bird I loved. Never mind that my experience spanned only a few months and involved only a tiny part of the quickly vanishing range of the species. Tiny as it was, too much area had spread me thin. But now was the time to vanquish dragons. The dragons were pesticides.

Dan Berger and I became friends at the meeting. His dry humor was incessant. His objectivity reminded one of Spock in *Star Trek*. If only there were a way to find out whether pesticides were really a hidden menace to birds of prey. We asked the Stickels, and a Brit, Ian Prestt, to counsel us before they left Madison. We invented two schemes. In the spirit of true scientific investigation, Berger and I would test the effects of dieldrin, perhaps the nastiest dragon of all, on wild prairie falcons to see if a small amount of it adversely affected nest success. Second, we would go where blue meanies were still abundant, the Far North. Had pesticides swept into their arctic wilderness, as in Finland?

It was 1965. In the eight years since the launch of Sputnik, the smoke had not yet cleared. The National Science Foundation was still flush with cash, the better to shore up American science. NSF, with money to give away, bought into our plans. We would set out to see if the abundant and accessible prairie falcon, as a test species, could put up with pesticides. Even more exciting, we would go north in honest-to-goodness exploration for peregrines and pesticides (Chapter VI).

As it turned out, our prairie falcon work proved little. We fed dieldrin-laced starlings to the wild falcons before they laid eggs, just as goats are tethered as bait for tigers. The prairies gobbled them down, and subsequent tests of a few of their eggs did verify the falcons carried substantial dieldrin. Unfortunately, there was a surprise. The tests showed the falcons also carried plenty of other pesticides, including the parent compound DDT, and of course the DDE that had formed from it.

Who would have guessed prairie falcons on the Wyoming plains, far from intensive crop cultivation, would carry a plethora of alien chemicals? Because of the mix in every falcon, there would be no way to tell which chemical was a villain. About all we could show was that mother falcons carrying the greater loads of the mixture had fewer youngsters in the end. The dieldrin-fed falcons could not be singled out as worse off. Our result was not the stuff of a Nobel Prize.

Derek Ratcliffe reviewed our first reports on the prairie falcon work. He wrote that "the experiment did not work" and that the case against dieldrin remains "entirely circumstantial." Ratcliffe had suffered bitter assault by his critics in Britain who searched for loopholes in the arguments against pesticides. He was hoping to save us from the same fate.

DRAGON SLAYERS   But despite battles lost, Ratcliffe, who bears a close resemblance to King George VI, persevered. A friend of Ratcliffe's, Desmond Nethersole-Thompson, was a collector of bird eggs. He noticed that peregrine eggshells found in the 1960s seemed more flexible and less handsome than those collected before. Nethersole-Thompson suggested to Ratcliffe that shell thickness should be measured. Curious, Ratcliffe weighed empty shells from both eras (before the advent of pesticides in the mid-1940s, and after). Egg collectors provided the samples. Nethersole-Thompson was able to convince the underworld of egg collectors that Ratcliffe was not a gumshoe. Not one illegal collector denied Ratcliffe access to his collection.

The importance of what Ratcliffe found cannot be overstated. In March of 1967, Hickey sent a memo to "Raptor field investigators." My copy is now barely legible because of the old blue mimeograph ink. Hickey wrote that Ratcliffe had found a "startlingly significant" decline in peregrine eggshell weight beginning after 1945. The decline became evident nationwide in Britain from 1947. Ratcliffe made his discovery available to us, even before it was set in concrete by publication.

It turned out that Ratcliffe measured shells in secret private collections dating back to 1900. Egg collecting dated from the eighteenth century. The goal of collectors was to gather unique and handsome eggshells. No doubt collectors engaged in rampant one-upmanship. In the 1930s collecting became unlawful, but second-story eggnapping persisted anyway. Hawk and falcon eggs were especially prized and were common in collections. While it can be said that the most important part of an egg is not its shell, the shell collectors provided a priceless service.

In his memo to us, Hickey outlined, in beautiful simplicity, what we must now do. We must see if Ratcliffe's revelation of bad eggshells in Britain also applied to North America. Further, we needed to find out if bad eggshells correlated with pesticides in the falcons that laid them, or with pesticides in the contents of the eggs themselves. Finally, could bad shells be induced in wild or captive raptors by feeding them a suspect pesticide?

In the four years following 1967, all of those things came to pass. Hickey sent his favorite student, Dan Anderson, to public and private eggshell collections from coast to coast. Sure enough, if you were a bird that ate fish or other birds after about 1947, your eggshells were thinner than before. Sometimes, depending on locality, they were as much as 25 percent thinner. This was the wildlife disaster of the century.

Berger and I immediately collected more prairie falcon eggs. Some of the shells were mighty thin. The ones with more pesticide inside were thinner. Even though there was a mix of pesticides, the amounts of DDE seemed to match the amount of observed shell thinning best. One of my students, Peter Wrege, confirmed this a few years later. Cade and his colleagues, including Jeff Lincer, Clayton White, and Jerry Swartz, found that Alaskan peregrines laid eggs with DDE in their contents and that the greater the DDE, the thinner the shells. These were major breakthroughs, paralleled by similar findings in Britain.

Then came the first conclusive evidence that DDE actually causes thin shells. Dee Porter and Stan Wiemeyer had a captive colony of kestrels at the FWS research lab at Patuxent, Maryland. They fed captive females small amounts of DDE before eggs were laid. Other kestrels were kept on clean food. Bingo! The DDE kestrels laid eggs with thin shells; the little falcons fed clean food laid normal eggs. Later, Lincer would be able to confirm these results in both captive and wild kestrels.

Why had the Stickels at Patuxent failed to show years before that DDT/DDE causes eggshell problems? They had fed DDT to hundreds of ducks and chickens by the time of the Madison meeting. They saw no problem, even with fairly stiff doses. Why not? It turns out not all kinds of birds are equally sensitive to DDE. Ducks and domestic fowl are really egg factories, and normally lay many eggs in their nests. Not so the raptors; their shell-producing machinery is much less capable, and a little bit of DDE upsets it.

THE NAYSAYERS   Quite naturally, as the case against these nasty chlorine-bearing chemicals erupted, a backlash grew, driven by the folks who made the stuff, and those who used it. Because materials like DDT, DDE, and dieldrin are very durable in the outdoors, and because they stick to the fat molecules of every creature that inadvertently eats them, they were gradually spread far and wide. Phrases like "global contamination" and "ubiquitous toxins" appeared in the popular press. Newspapers made famous the discovery of pesticides in penguins in Antarctica.

The companies that made the pesticides hired Don Spencer to keep an eye on the studies that might finger pesticides as culprits. I knew Spencer from the Madison conference. A few years later he bought my lunch. There are no free lunches. He probed for weaknesses in our results. Sure, prairie falcons produced thin shells if there were lots of DDE. But, he said, other chemicals were present; maybe one of these was the problem. He pointed out there were other chemicals that may have been mistakenly identified as DDE in the work with kestrels by Porter and Wiemeyer, so their findings proved nothing. He said even women's hairspray contained chemicals that could interfere with the substances normally regulating reproduction. He lost me on that one. What raptor has close contact with hairspray? Spencer was clearly a man with a mission.

By 1971, the case against DDE was very compelling, except to those who had ulterior reasons to deny the evidence. The skeptics rested their case on the notion that DDE could not possibly have spread so widely by 1948 as to affect so many raptors in so many places. After all, DDT was not put on the land at all until about 1946. Here the naysayers made their last real stand, and it was the hill they would die on.

LAST NAIL IN THE COFFIN   In the late 1960s, the late Dave Peakall was at Cornell University developing a large-scale national system to store records of nesting birds. Clay White and I were also there, sharing an office. Peakall, who was a Brit, studied in his spare time how DDE actually worked to cause thin eggshells. He was a wonderfully pleasant and soft-spoken man and often said hello as he passed our door, a test tube or a favorite ringdove in hand.

Peakall was seeing to the last nail in the DDT coffin. How early had DDT/ DDE become effective in causing thin shells? People with a vested interest in DDT argued that peregrines were in trouble by the late 1940s, too early for DDT to have become significant in the environment. They said DDT was not used widely until 1947, and it would have taken several years, into the 1950s, for the substance to pass up the food chain and reach toxic levels in birds of prey. In essence, "You can't have the effect before the cause."

With the help of Lloyd Kiff, overseer of the vast egg collection at the Western Foundation for Vertebrate Zoology in California, Peakall rounded up empty peregrine eggshells collected in the middle of the twentieth century. Some had been taken from eyries before DDT/DDE, and some in the crucial years, 1946–1951, when the falcons became stricken. Initially, Kiff was against lending the precious shells to anyone. Fortunately, Joe Hickey convinced Kiff the loan was critical. He shipped the carefully packed shells to Peakall. A note in the package warned Peakall to handle the shells like a "pregnant queen."

Peakall's plan was elegant and simple. It occurred to him that DDE passed on to the egg from the female was not only in the yolk and egg white, but also in the membrane lining of the shell. When egg collectors emptied the contents of the egg, a remnant of the DDE would be left behind. It would not be much, but modern testing equipment could find extremely tiny traces. Further, Peakall imagined that the amount left in the shell would be proportional to the original amount in the egg contents.

How does one get pesticide out of an unbroken but empty eggshell? It was simple. Egg collectors empty out the egg contents through a tiny hole they bore through the shell. Peakall used a syringe through the hole to fill the shell with ether, a solvent that dissolves DDE. He let it sit for a while. Then he drew out a sample. When the sample of ether was put in the detector, DDE was found.

Then came the clincher. Peakall also measured DDE from the shells of recently collected eggs whose egg white and yolk had also been tested. In that way, he could closely link the amount of DDE found in the shell with the amount found in the liquid egg contents. All that remained was to test shells collected in the 1940s and 1950s to see when the corresponding DDE in the egg contents had been sufficient to correlate with poor hatching. To his great satisfaction, those conditions occurred as early as 1948. Cause and effect coincided.

Peakall shipped the priceless eggshells back to Kiff immediately. A letter that followed bore a simple declaration: "The queen has delivered."

The timing was right after all. Peregrines were in trouble within a couple of years of heavy DDT use. There was a bizarre irony. The very property of DDT/DDE molecules that makes them so troublesome in the environment—their extreme durability—enabled Peakall to prove their presence in deadly amounts in shells laid almost twenty-five years earlier. He gets the gold for establishing, beyond doubt, the abundance of DDE in blue meanies at the time when the population in the United States was first stricken.

Peakall's paper appeared in the journal *Science* in 1974, a little over a year after DDT was banned for most uses in the United States. The ban was the result of an unpopular decision. Administrator William Ruckelshaus, first chief of the Environmental Protection Agency, bravely gave his verdict, contrary to the views of his advisors. By the time of the ban, many thousands of tons of DDT had been strewn across the land to kill insects in forests, swamps, and cultivated fields over the twenty-six years it was available. Peregrines to this day still show its effect.

REVIEW   Hickey's Madison meeting in 1965 exposed the worldwide plight of raptors. Not just peregrines were hit. The great scope and depth of the problem energized the participants, and fear of complete disaster became the engine driving a massive inquiry. The pattern of sickness centered on reproduction, and within five years the full significance of the DDE/shell-thinning syndrome had been dug clear from an array of false leads. The last milestone discovery in the pesticide debacle came with Peakall's brilliant demonstration that DDE was already causing havoc in peregrine eyries in the United States by 1948. Finally, DDT was outlawed in 1972. Although we did not know it at the time, a future for the stricken raptors was assured.

VI » BIG RIVER

ESCAPE FROM FORT RESOLUTION   Ten miles of choppy water separated the mouth of the Slave River on Great Slave Lake from Fort Resolution, Northwest Territories. It was late June 1966, and not the time or place to run out of gas. Wind and wave would surely wreck a floundering freight canoe on the boulder-strewn beach on the south shore of the huge lake.

The big red fuel drum in the middle of the canoe was nearly empty. Imagine our relief as the settlement of Resolution came into view. We rounded a curve in the shore and saw the little village set back in the black spruce. Beyond, to the west, was the vast entrance to Resolution Bay. Our relief was to be short-lived.

We tied to the big dock piled high with crates and oil barrels awaiting the supply barge. Berger and my student Skip Walker unloaded the empty gasoline drum and headed for the trading post a quarter of a mile off. I offloaded the tent and other gear, and looked about for a spot to camp near the boat.

Before long my unshaven crew returned with a wheelbarrow loaded with fuel. They bought extra gas because the transit of Great Slave Lake to the head of the Mackenzie was about 130 miles. There was no current to help us and the wind would be on the bow. The first 50 miles would be directly across Resolution Bay. The shoreline route would have been much longer. With any luck, the wind would drop and the waves would lessen by morning.

Two women, probably of Dogrib descent, had followed Walker and Berger from the store. They seemed very interested in us, but did not come close to the canoe. We busied ourselves with the job of setting out what we would need for the camp. It was about 10 P.M., the sun slicing though the spires of black spruce in a shallow dive for the horizon.

Before long, one of the girls called out from the dock and motioned for me to come to them. As I approached, both of the black-haired women stepped behind a stack of wooden crates. They waved me ahead, and I followed them to a secluded part of the dock. What was the problem? Suddenly, both girls came up very close, one removing my glasses, the other unzipping my jacket.

My first thought was that I was being mugged. If only Berger and Walker could save me. Then one lady reached for the buttons on my shirt and the other put her hand on my belt buckle. The lights came on. I was being sexu-

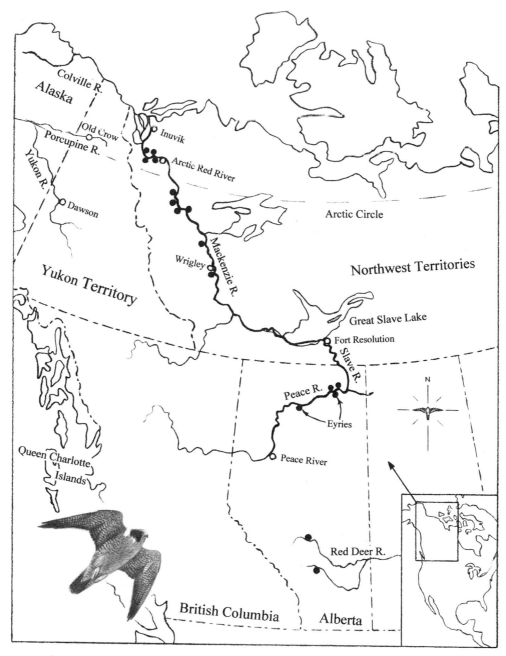

Map of northwestern North America including regions of peregrine searches referred to in the text.

ally assaulted. Me, Jimmy Enderson! Those girls were ladies of the night. They intended a ménage à trois right there in the mosquitoes. I grabbed my glasses, wheeled, and bolted for the canoe a hundred feet away.

Soon, two men appeared at our canoe, perhaps friends or relatives of the women. Apparently, the women did not like the rebuff at all, and their displeasure seemed to anger the men. Other people appeared on the road and had noticed the commotion. We needed to be gone from that place. In a most cowardly way, we threw our belongings into the canoe and struck out across Resolution Bay. The name was somehow appropriate.

Ahead were fifty miles of open water. No land was visible across the bay or to the north beyond the lake. Wind and waves were up; the sun was below the horizon. It was 11 P.M. Canoes, however big, are not good in heavy seas. The slender bow knifes too deeply into waves, and there is no means of diverting the spray. We ran diagonally to the swells. To run with them would bury both ends of the craft simultaneously when the middle was in a trough.

I admit now to great apprehension. If we had swamped, the chill of the water would surely have done us in. But we were committed. Even the risk of turning the canoe around was great. On we went, into the growing cold.

About halfway across the bay we discovered a small rocky island, an outcrop too small to appear on the chart. We motored into its lee, then ran directly northwest toward it in relatively smooth water. But there was no safe harbor. Only boulders jutted from the lake. Worse, a rain of bird guano fell on us from the hundreds of gulls we had excited. After a brief discussion of our predicament, we turned back to the open water and the deep cold.

By 4:30 A.M. we had traversed the bay and reached the south shore of Great Slave Lake. The beach was buried under drift logs and pack ice. Our condition was not good. Chill and fatigue now created desperation. The waves were still pretty high and menacing. No matter what, we had to get warm. I steered for the shore. As it turned out, the logs on the beach provided a surface on which the canoe could be landed without damage by rocks or ice. I picked out several smooth, straw-colored logs that seemed to lie at the right angle and drove the canoe upon them, killing the motor and tilting it up before it could be damaged.

We climbed onto the logs. I was shivering uncontrollably. Quickly we gathered two huge piles of driftwood about thirty feet apart, poured on gasoline, and set them ablaze. We sat midway between the fires, heated from both sides. The towering bright-orange flames, the warmth, the dark blue of Great Slave Lake, are as vivid now as they were that June morning in 1966.

BORROWED FUNDS AND STOLEN EGG   What had taken us to the prostitutes at Fort Resolution in the first place? In August 1965, the conference in Madison created the necessity of knowing the extent of the pesticide threat to blue meanies in the north. Berger and I had decided to float the Peace-Slave-Mackenzie river system to find out. The three rivers flow in an indirect path to the Arctic.

Our plan was simple. In Edmonton, Alberta, we would buy a boat, drive to the village of Peace River, put into the river, and float to the ocean. It would be the Arctic Ocean. Along the way we would collect spoiled blue meanie eggs, fat taken by biopsy from all the adult falcons we could catch, and birds that falcons eat. Later, all these things would be tested for pesticides.

We planned to sell the boat and motor at Inuvik at the mouth of the Mackenzie, fly back to Edmonton, and ride a bus back north to Peace River to pick up the station wagon. Navigation charts of the rivers confirmed what we had seen on a globe. The Peace flows into the Slave, which hooks up with the Mackenzie via Great Slave Lake. We greatly underestimated the scale. In some places, you can look down the Mackenzie and not see land.

In April 1966, the National Science Foundation said, "Go." I found that saying "go" and making "go" happen are very different. I committed the college to all sorts of indebtedness because NSF had sent no money. Government agencies are always tardy in payment of grants. I hoped NSF would honor its word. If it did not, my career might be at risk. I was a lowly assistant professor.

The borrowed funds were for field equipment, a tent, and surgical supplies. Rather than shoot peregrines, we knew we could trap them and take a bit of fat from under the skin (biopsy) for pesticide testing. Morgan Berthrong, pathologist and boyhood friend of the Craigheads, used a pigeon to show me how to tie sutures to close the small wound where a bit of fat had been removed.

Our list of items bought on credit included an outboard motor. We could not row the distance. The Peace-Slave-Mackenzie system is not as long as the Amazon, the Nile, or perhaps the Missouri/Mississippi, but is a match for any other. Johnson Motors shipped a new twenty-horsepower outboard, priced at an "educational discount." The cost to the college was twenty cents on the dollar. The motor would push us, without fail, more than two thousand miles.

By the end of May, not one NSF dollar had been sent to Colorado College. We were ready to go. We needed cash. The business manager of the college would advance no more money. The president's secretary called and said, "Come to his office." When I got there Lew Worner was in a meeting with the Board of Trustees. His secretary called him from the meeting. This was not a good thing to do. There I stood, hat in hand. He looked at the invoice for several thousand dollars in travel funds, pursed his lips, and signed the form. "I will have to look into procedures in matters like this," he said. We were on our way. And there was no going back. We had already spent a lot of other people's money.

Walker, who was my student, volunteered to join the expedition. We drove to Canada (it never crossed my mind that we would be foreigners, working in a foreign country). Our letter of transit was a "Scientist's and Explorer's Permit," printed on tan parchment with a crimson seal, signed by the commissioner of the Northwest Territories.

Whenever we needed authority, the permit was the silver bullet. I believe there is something of a Walter Mitty in all of us. Perry, Byrd, Amundsen, Shackleton—they had no document more powerful than ours. The decree with the red seal hangs before me, behind glass, as I write this.

What we did *not* have was authorization to collect falcon eggs in Alberta. The silver bullet would not work there. Alberta and the Northwest Territories are different. I called Joe Hickey from Edmonton. He in turn talked to the Alberta wildlife people. They had received our application weeks before, but would not budge. Apparently, word of our expedition had reached the university group that had been so protective in 1964 when I sought help for the first survey. We could not collect in Alberta.

Two days before we knew the permit had been denied, we found a spoiled egg in a nest on the Red Deer River. I had seen the site from the river in 1964 and noticed a nearby road. In 1966 we simply drove to the place; a boat was unnecessary. Now we had a stolen egg with no permit. We did not discard it; the egg was conveniently bootlegged in with those gathered later in the NWT. That egg was far too important to lose.

The Alberta wildlife officials did help in one vital respect. They found a boat for us. It was a canoe. "We cannot paddle all the way to the Arctic Ocean," I said. They laughed. The canoe was special. It was a freight canoe, twenty-two feet long and four feet wide. Resting on flat ground, the top of the bow reached my waist. The interior of the vessel was huge. It could easily carry two tons and had a V-stern for a motor. The craft had just been refinished dark green with gray inside. The price was $200 Canadian. We lashed it, upside down, on top of the Chevy station wagon and struck out for the Peace.

TWO-THOUSAND-MILE TRIAL RUN   In central Alberta, the Peace flows at a brisk eight miles an hour or so, about the speed of our loaded canoe under medium throttle. Once we launched from the Alberta Wildlife Department dock in Peace River, there would be no going back. The only way was downstream. The motor greatly increased the pace and provided a way to maneuver. We pushed off on June 3 and were immediately impressed with the power of the current.

The Peace was too muddy to see more than a foot into its murk. We had not motored more than a mile when the propeller struck a rock. How could this be? We were well out from the nearest bank. Damn. Fortunately the motor was okay and we had a spare prop. But that was a wake-up call. "Read the river or run aground" was the message. It was simple. Big wide eddies, and big waves, meant deep water. Beware when the water was smooth with a surface rippled by small eddies less than three feet wide.

Because the canoe was completely open, it was not a lot of fun in the rain, or when the wind whipped spray from waves. We fiddled incessantly with the tarp covering our gear. Sleeping bags and food had to be kept dry. On the plus side, a bit of water improved the texture of Marvin's Biscuits. Crafted commercially from hardtack (mainly a baked mixture of flour and water), the dry, cookie-sized discs barely amounted to "a food-like substance." But they were durable.

Of most concern was our floating menagerie. On board were a dozen or so pigeons and starlings. They were needed as lures to attract blue meanies into our net. A stuffed owl was also there, in case the falcons were not hungry. We knew peregrines were especially aggressive in the case of owls. Our owl, placed near their eggs or young, might draw the parent into the net.

The first human settlement downriver from Peace River was Fort Vermillion. Fuel for the motor was carried in a thirty-five-gallon drum, plus the usual red six-gallon tank. In all, over forty gallons were available. We thought this would be enough for long stretches of river with sluggish flow. We learned otherwise.

At Fort Vermillion, on the Indian Reservation, the Royal Canadian Mounted Police officer arranged a portage around Vermillion Chutes, the only serious fast water on the lower Peace. While awaiting confirmation by radio that a freight wagon would be sent to carry us around the Chutes, we discovered Berger's binoculars were missing, apparently stolen. They disappeared while we were in the Hudson Bay Company store. "Don't worry," the Mountie said, "they never take things to keep." We headed on downstream, thinking the binos were gone forever. A couple of days later we stopped at a village called Peace Point for fuel. The binoculars were there, sent downriver on the mail plane.

On June 6, we camped at the Upper Chutes landing, marked by a small log shed. We spent the night in the tent with the mosquitoes. Ordinarily, we chose campsites on sandbars in the river, the less vegetation the better. Out on the river, breezes kept the pests away.

The next morning, with horses and wagon, a full-blooded Cree named Ben Nosgay emerged from the bush. He spoke no English, we no Cree. Everything we had was put on his wagon. The motor was mounted on the back, and the canoe lashed upside down on top. Then we all climbed aboard and rode through the forest like four on an elephant.

We had been told mosquitoes do not bother the Cree. This would be the test of the hypothesis. The insects were extremely numerous and aggressive. We wore head nets. I watched Nosgay, reins in his hands. Presently, he

Dan Berger and Ben Nosgay prepare for the portage on the Peace River, 1966.

reached into his pocket and produced a can of repellent. He sprayed his hands and the back of his neck. We learned later that historically, Cree did not often travel on foot in the bush in summer, relying on the smoke of permanent campfires to put down the insects. When they did move, they traveled at a brisk pace and quickly built a fire whenever they stopped.

The trail to the lower landing was a few miles long. On arrival we unloaded the wagon and had lunch. Nosgay was tickled about something, a wide grin shown on his dark red face. He pointed to the peanut-butter jar and laughed. We learned latter the Cree are supplied peanut butter only in tins, not glass jars.

Once loaded, we paid Nosgay and shook hands. He had earned the five-dollar tip and was a happy man. Once out on the river, we peered upstream and saw the obstacle he had helped us avoid. The rapid was more than just serious whitewater—it was *vertical* water. The river simply fell twelve feet from a ledge spanning the entire channel. In the eighteen hundred miles below us there was but one more portage.

PEACE PEREGRINES   Not far below the rapid was a small island. It had steep sides of the same black shale that lay beneath the rapid. On the top of the island a peregrine incubated four eggs. She fell for the stuffed-owl trick and was caught. We later found that the tiny sample of fat we took from her was loaded with DDT/DDE.

A black Labrador retriever named Bud rode the last miles of the Peace with us. We picked up the big steady dog in Wood Buffalo Park and agreed to deliver him to his owner a hundred miles downstream. Bud loved us. He seemed to think it was his expedition too. We became much attached to him in the three days he was with us. When he had to leave he did not want to go, and ran along the riverbank after the canoe. Perhaps he was drawn to us only by the smell of starlings and pigeons. But black labs have been special to me ever since.

The pigeons and starlings in the large cage on the canoe were of course types not found in the bush country of northern Canada. Children at the settlements along the river flocked to the canoe wherever we landed. They were awestruck by the birds. Whenever we left the canoe to buy supplies, Berger would say to them in a deep Darth Vader tone, "If you touch those birds I will squash you like a bug." This impressed the little boys and girls. The cage was never bothered.

Boyer Rapids on the Peace is not really rapid, but just a stretch of pretty fast water. Blue meanies nest there. At one site a female felt so secure in a small deep cave that she did not reveal herself until we dislodged rubble at the opening. We collected a few prey birds typical of falcon food in the area. Many of these also contained plenty of pesticides, no doubt acquired in winter far to the south. The small birds brought the chemicals with them to the Peace and to the peregrines.

People along the river seemed to know of our presence before we arrived. One can only guess what they said about the characters in the canoe bound for the ocean. The ranger at Peace Point, on the river bordering Wood Buffalo Park, asked if we would like to see a woodland buffalo. The last bison types to inhabit North America (there were several Ice Age forms) were separated in two regions, the northern forests and, of course, the temperate grasslands. The woodland variant had a limited distribution and probably never reached the enormous numbers of the plains bison.

Berger, Walker, and I crowded into the battered pickup. Behind the seat, lying beside the jack and lug-nut wrench, was a beat-up rifle, once Winchester's finest. The caliber, inscribed on the barrel, was .375 Holland and Holland Magnum. The ranger said, "We have to match the power of the buffalo when they go bad." Bison sometimes become dangerous rogues, and sometimes they get sick. On the Slave River, we were to pass huge fires. Park people were destroying old barns that once held anthrax-stricken bison.

Suddenly, ahead of the truck, in a tunnel of vegetation over the trail in the spruce thicket, was a black wall. The wall was a magnificent bull bison. We felt dwarfed. Then he was gone.

FALCON HIATUS   Eleven days would separate the peregrines at Boyer Rapids and the next ones we would see, five hundred miles to the north. The hiatus was due mainly to the low relief of the country. We motored the meandering Peace, then the gentle Slave. Gentle, except for a section not passable by ordinary boats. The Canadian Wildlife Service carried us around the turbulence in a truck, and then they drove us to Fort Smith, just inside the Northwest Territories.

A federal biologist at Fort Smith by the name of Ernie Kuyt had a passion for wolves. The passion was clearly contagious, because so many people have it today. In a huge wire enclosure Kuyt kept a pair of white tundra wolves from the Thelon River country west of Hudson Bay. In the center of the pen was a pallet made of planks nailed together. Under the pallet was a litter of five wolf pups, eyes still closed. Kuyt reached down and lifted a pup. The mother crowded in, tail wagging. Clearly, Kuyt was the central member of her pack. Needless to say, we stayed out of the wolf enclosure. None of us had proper social status.

Kuyt knew peregrines from the Thelon country. He told us a youngster he banded there in summer was found dead in Argentina the following winter. Arctic meanies hold a different itinerary than did the original, but now-extinct, sedentary duck hawks of Appalachia. No duck hawk was ever recovered south of central Georgia.

The Athabasca and the Peace join to form the Slave, creating a really large river. Above Fort Smith, one section is mighty rough. Below it, the Slave meanders gently for a couple of hundred miles through flat monotonous spruce forest populated with bald eagles. It is as if the river took one last fling with whitewater, and then settled down to a snail's pace.

No chance for blue meanies nesting along the lower river. The banks were low and the gradient slight. Our motor was put to heavy work. Somewhere in that stretch, the term *outboard motor* changed to the parochial *kicker*. We had a brand new twenty-horsepower kicker, the envy of Indian boys from there on north.

A dilemma arose the first "night" down from Smith. Should we press on after ten hours on the river, possibly finding an island with a proper sandbar? Or should we camp in the willows on some low, muddy bank? We elected the first option, but were finally forced to the second by growing exhaustion. "This looks okay" was Walker's very hopeful appraisal. Berger muttered something about quicksand. His was the better assessment.

Finally the tent was set on a mattress made from willow branches, and dinner was on the Coleman. The fare was fried chicken. Who knows how long the wretched thing had been frozen in Fort Smith. We feared the taste might be tainted by too much time in the freezer with beaver skins or the like. Not to worry. The flavor of the chicken would not be its own in any case. Vast hoards of mosquitoes flew too close to the Coleman, were cremated in flight, and fell into the frying pan. The sauce appeared as if it had been very heavily peppered, a sauté of mosquito.

The Slave is very tortuous, the banks on the outside of the curves caved away by the relentless cutting of the river. Great lenses of ice, called permafrost, were exposed where the banks collapsed. And with the collapse, spruce and birch were tossed down, forming logjams clinging to the banks.

The second day out, the river became even less resolute. The meanderings grew into a sluggish maze of islands and oxbows. We lost track of our position on the map, but surely the great lake was not far off. Finally, in the evening of the second day, fuel nearly gone, we motored around a bend, and the horizon of black spruce vanished. Before us was Great Slave Lake. It could easily have passed for the ocean.

This was not to be a clean union of river with lake. We held to the west as soon as the current vanished. The canoe immediately ran aground. Of course, silt carried by the Slave formed a great muddy delta just below the surface. We felt our way, Walker in the bow using a paddle to test the depth. It was exhausting work, backing, turning, then going ahead. Finally we gained the deeper, clearer water of the lake and new hazards—big waves and the women at Fort Resolution, described above.

THE MACKENZIE   After the escape from the women at Fort Resolution and the crossing of Resolution Bay, the heat from the twin fires on the south shore and Marvin's Biscuits restored our energy. We pushed off. Had we stayed longer, the canoe might have been battered to pieces by the waves as it rolled about on the logs. Finally, at 10 A.M. and far to the west, we nosed out of the lake into the mouth of the Hay River. The water there was wonderfully smooth. The most hazardous segment of the voyage, Great Slave Lake, was behind us. We set up the tent and slept for fifteen hours.

The Hay dumps into the far west end of the lake. The lake is only twenty miles wide at that point, and although there is no perceptible current, the water there is committed to the Mackenzie. We motored west. The river refused to present itself. The wind died and the surface was smooth. Cakes of ice, remnants from the recent breakup, were few and far between.

Gradually we motored into what had to be the river; a subtle swirling of the surface grew. We passed an isolated eddy. Then we saw another. We passed several islands. The surface was more disturbed between them. This was the beginning of a mighty river. We could see down perhaps twenty feet, but could not see the bottom.

A thousand miles ahead lay Inuvik. The settlements along the way had names like Fort Providence, Fort Simpson, Wrigley, Fort Good Hope, and

Arctic Red River. At Fort Providence, the Royal Canadian Mounted Police learned of my encounter with the girls on the dock at Resolution. The Mounties were amused. The two women, Peaches and Smokey, were infamous in those parts of the Northwest Territories. Allegedly, men who had unprotected encounters with them were long-suffering, always in need of a certain type of medical attention.

A hundred miles down the Mackenzie we began to find cliffs or high banks, but only one was in use by blue meanies. We wondered why so many seemingly suitable places were vacant. No doubt we missed pairs because the river was too wide to always check bluffs on both sides in the same section. Also, some eyries may have been on banks we dismissed as too poor. We dragged up to have lunch under a high sandy bank with almost no vertical surface. Halfway through lunch, the long wailing cry of a peregrine led us to investigate. Behind a pillar of sand, on a platform hardly more than a foot in diameter, were two eggs. We had only to walk up the slope and reach down to touch them.

Boats have been lost in the Sans Sault rapids of the Mackenzie, but by using navigation targets and noting warning buoys, we went through in deep water. In late summer, when the river is lower, the rapids might be exciting.

Targets were huge signs, placed in pairs, each with a vertical black line. One target was set well in front of the other, but lower on the bank. As the signs were approached from far upriver the task was to keep the line on the upper target exactly above the line on the lower target. This was done by motoring to the left or right, ensuring our canoe was on a course passing through deep water—if the river bottom had stayed put, which it never did. As we approached the pair of targets, we kept on the lookout for the next set farther downstream, and when those two new lines were lined up, we abandoned the old targets and headed directly for the new ones.

There were very few other craft on the river. The *Hugh A. Young*, a forty-foot tug, carried the Territories' boiler inspector. We tied alongside and chatted. It seemed the boilers used to heat schools tended to blow up. So boiler inspectors were important and traveled in a proper tugboat. The black iron vessel seemed out of place in our wilderness.

Even more out of place was a fiberglass runabout loaded with Indians. It labored against the current near the bank opposite our camp on a midriver sandbar. Its kicker was wholly inadequate for the task. The boat was on a collision course with a moose cow and her calf that had crossed the nose of our island and made for the far side of the river. As the cow climbed out of the water, there was a volley of rifle fire. The cow fell back into the river, but the calf made it to the safety of the shielding spruce. The calf was a yearling and surely able to fend for itself.

The Indians were soon to learn that a twelve-hundred-pound moose is a big animal. Cutting up the animal on dry land is one thing. In the river was another. In no time at all, the plastic runabout, the Indians, and the barely floating dead moose were swept away by the massive Mackenzie.

WRIGLEY   "Inuvik, eh?" said the man across the table. He and his wife had invited us to dinner. The place was Wrigley, Northwest Territories, deep in the heartland of the northern Canadian wilderness. The other whites in the village were three nuns and a teenage boy. He kept the Hudson Bay Company store, the only enterprise in a hundred miles. In 1966, very few outsiders came to town; access was by boat or bush plane. The plane came once a week with mail. Almost no boats came, except the monthly supply barge.

I had just told the teacher our aim was to continue on down the river to Inuvik on the delta of one of the mightiest rivers on the planet. His face reflected great skepticism. Clearly he had heard of Inuvik. He was having a problem with the distance. Our destination was almost seven hundred miles downriver.

The river was the Mackenzie and the man was the schoolmaster. The Hudson Bay Company store was small with a high false front like those on the set of an old western. It sat sixty feet above the river on the high bank, out of reach of ten-ton chunks of river ice when breakup came in May. Next door to the store was a small white frame house where the teacher and his wife lived. A low white picket fence, with a gate in front, surrounded the yard. The fence contained two noisy terriers.

Wrigley was once a fur station. It, and a handful of others like it, was established soon after the expedition of Sir Alexander Mackenzie in 1879. This was western Canada's last fur frontier. Of course, in 1966, the fur trade had long since disappeared. The duty of the storekeeper now was simply to provision the fifteen or twenty Cree Indian families in the village, and the few others in the bush nearby. He also handled the mail.

Besides his teaching, the schoolteacher arranged for medical attention from the "outside" when the Indians needed it, and performed a peacekeeping role. There was no Royal Canadian Mounted Police station at Wrigley. Life there could only have been incredibly challenging owing to boredom.

"Have some more spaghetti," his wife offered. She was a fairly tall and pretty woman in her mid-thirties. When we first climbed up the steep riverbank four hours before, she was tending her flowers wearing baggy slacks and a denim jacket, both protections from the never-absent mosquitoes. Now she wore a crisp, clean white blouse and very short shorts. I had the feeling she did not wear the shorts often. The mosquitoes would have had a field day.

Suddenly there was a pounding at the door. We heard unintelligible shouting punctuated by mumbling. Then came more pounding. We peered out. A seemingly drunk Cree, in his middle age, was teetering on the stoop, cussing as best he could at the schoolmaster. None of us could understand the nature of his grievance. The confrontation was cut short by the two terriers, one hanging from each cuff of the poor drunken man. He fled, shaking his fists and uttering oaths as he went. The schoolteacher was clearly the authority figure in the village.

He told us alcohol is not sold by the Bay Company store. However, home brew was not unlawful. Two days before, the villagers had received monthly support checks from the Bureau of Northern Affairs. Much of the money was spent on raisins, sugar, and yeast at the little store. The mixture was allowed to ferment. Most of it was drunk before its time, and intoxication was mostly imagined. We guessed the Cree at the door had taken a snootful of a fully fermented batch.

Wrigley lies on the "left limit" of the Mackenzie, the term referring to the left-hand bank when facing downstream. At the town, the river is about a quarter-mile wide and at least forty feet deep. The water on the east side of the river, opposite the town, was clear; water on the village side was muddy.

More than two hundred miles upstream, the cold, clear Mackenzie flows out of Great Slave Lake, which acts like a giant settling basin. But a hundred miles downstream, the muddy Liard, laden with silt from runoff in the Canadian Rockies to the west, joins the big river. Almost unbelievably, the two masses of water, flowing in the same channel, remain distinct. Drinking water for the village was obtained by boat from the clear east side. The west side looked like hot chocolate.

By the time we reached Wrigley we had been on the river more that two weeks and were, arguably, seasoned boatmen. When we arrived the wind from the north was increasing and blowing upstream. The current there is about eight miles per hour, and because it flows into the wind the waves seem to move very little relative to the banks. The harder the wind blows, the taller these stationary, standing walls of water. The waves were pretty tall; this was no time to get back in the canoe.

We camped in the yard of the schoolmaster and planned to leave in the morning. The wind howled all night. Once I got up to check the river in the bright glow of the sun just below the horizon. The water was impassable.

We spent the next day at the village. The three nuns showed us photos taken after they arrived in the previous winter. Most impressive were those of the breakup. Huge cakes of ice, bigger than trucks, were jammed in the river channel almost to the level of the store. The village owed its existence to the sixty-foot bank.

The next day the surf was down and we moved on. I remember clearly we obtained from the store a new supply of Marvin's Biscuits. They must have a half-life longer than sloth dung in an Arizona cave. Marvin's creation would not have been edible without generous applications of peanut butter and jelly. Things like this seemed to take on special meaning in the wilderness. Simple things enriched the experience. This is one reason why wilderness is important.

THE LOWER RIVER   Two-thirds of the way to the ocean, the Mackenzie squeezes between limestone walls called the Ramparts. It is a spectacular place compared to the endless stretches of uneventful forest typical of the upper river. In places the river is only two hundred yards wide. With so much unyielding rock on either side, imagine the comfort in knowing the water flowed more than one hundred feet deep.

We spotted a nest of young ravens high up on the wall. One raven was about to make its first flight, which in that setting would be fly, swim, or sink. We shouted encouragement. "You can make it." "You can make it!" The raven launched into the air, but was unable to reach the top of the rock wall. Down it came, flapping in vain. We fished the drowning raven from the water. He was so grateful. He stayed with us for the remainder of the voyage, finally becoming the beneficiary of the Canadian Wildlife Service at Inuvik. We used the jet-black bird as a decoy to entice defensive peregrines into the net. His name was Malcolm, after the civil rights leader of the time.

We spent the night of 21 June in jail. We were guests, not inmates. When we arrived at Fort Good Hope at the lower end of the Ramparts it was raining mighty hard. The Mountie was attending to matters elsewhere in the district. His wife took pity on us and offered bunks in the log jail. It was very comfortable, actually, but somehow strange to sleep under a roof.

Fifty miles above Arctic Red River, the last settlement above Inuvik, we crossed the Arctic Circle. It was 26 June, only a few days after the summer solstice. The sun only just failed to disappear completely below the horizon at midnight. Farther north, the sun would remain higher in the sky at midnight. Actually, we had not been in the dark for nearly a month. Continual light is wearisome at first. This was because of our tendency to keep on traveling, hopeful of finding blue meanies around the next bend. Exhaustion soon forced a more sensible schedule.

We found several pairs of peregrines near Arctic Red River and spent a day catching falcons for fat samples. We shot a dozen prey birds, including a spotted sandpiper. "Spotties" were constant companions from Peace River onward. The falcon youngsters were just hatching, about six weeks later than those in Colorado. The difference underscored how far from home we were.

A newly hatched chick was accidentally kicked by the parent from its ledge on a low dirt bank and was killed in the fall. In the end we sent it off for chemical analysis with the prey birds, just to see how the pesticides com-

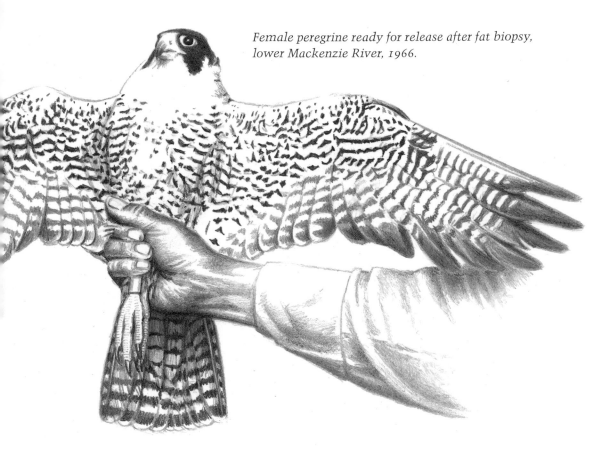

Female peregrine ready for release after fat biopsy, lower Mackenzie River, 1966.

pared. It turned out the day-old falcon carried more DDE from the egg than we found in any of the prey birds we collected. Its mother had passed on the contamination to the chick when she made the yolk that nourished it in the egg.

Now the river became slower and wider, and islands became more numerous. Close attention was required to follow our course on the chart. We found the outlet from Campbell Lake and motored upstream to its source. The lake was a few miles long and was bordered by several good cliffs. We had been told two or three pairs of peregrines nested there. Curiously, no meanies were found. We were especially observant because of the chance that gyrfalcons might nest there. These arctic birds like open tundra, and Campbell Lake was the first place where we saw the forest yielding to treeless tundra.

The water in the lake was clear and warm to the touch. It was bath time. I jumped off the freight canoe into the deep water. Surprise! The top six inches were tepid, but the rest of the lake was literally near freezing. My bath was brief.

We had topped off the fuel at Arctic Red River, confident the supply would see us to Inuvik. It did not. Eight miles above Inuvik the kicker kicked its last, the fuel supply drained to exhaustion by the slow current and the side trip to Campbell Lake. We resigned ourselves to an ignoble finale for the journey. We would simply drift into town, hoping no one would see us.

But before long there came an Indian with a huge flotilla of freshly cut spruce logs tied to his small boat. The little kicker strained against the load. Not much could be ascertained about the motor's make or size. Like most we saw in that country, it had long since lost its paint and cowling. The Indian sold us one gallon of gasoline. He was richly rewarded, mainly because of the indignity from which we were spared. Soon, under full power, we motored into the settlement. A month had passed since we began at Peace River.

In all, we found about a dozen pairs of peregrines, no doubt missing at least as many more. In 1995, about ninety pairs were known to nest on the Mackenzie, and the number was increasing. We could not have realized in 1966 that the population we saw was so drastically depressed. The samples of prey and biopsied fat we collected, in retrospect, bore evidence, in the form of DDE, of a population of falcons in peril. We had shown DDE prevalent a thousand miles from anywhere it had been used in significant amounts. It had come to the Arctic on the wings of birds: the migrant falcons and their migrant prey.

Our canoe and kicker brought $500 at the trading post, as much as we had paid. That evening we relaxed in the Legion Hall, musing at the roof over our heads. An hour before we had cut short our dinner in the hotel because the butter used in the cooking had been stored all winter with hundreds of fox pelts. The odor of musk at each bite was overwhelming.

Two days later, we climbed a stairway into a four-engine, propeller-driven DC-6. As we taxied to the runway I noticed a fuel cap on the right wing was rolling about, held to the airplane by its chain. There was no flight attendant, so I walked to the cockpit and described the obvious irregularity. The copilot came back and peered out my window. "Better fix that," he said. Finally, cap in place, we flew south to Edmonton and the comfort of darkness.

VII » NORTHERN PEREGRINES

THE YUKON BEAR   "What the . . . ?" Stan Temple sat straight up in his sleeping bag, his hand on his face. Moments before, I had been awakened by the sound of tearing canvas. I rolled in my bag to see bewilderment on Temple's face. I struggled to grasp what had happened. There, in clear view, were four long parallel marks on the wall of the tent.

We were camped in the twilight of the northern night, sixty miles upstream from the Alaskan border on the north bank of the Yukon River. Our tent was pitched in a cool aspen grove. A hundred feet in front of the tent was a gravel bar, and beyond was the fast flat surface of the river. On the far shore a vertical yellow cliff, the Old Woman, rose from the water's edge. High up, the rock had fallen away in a grotesque pattern, resulting in the crude likeness of an ugly face. In scale, the face matched those on Mount Rushmore. Peregrines nested on the upstream side in full view of the profile.

The lines on the tent wall were claw marks! I blurted out the obvious: "Stan, this just happened." The marks on the tent were brand new. In what seemed like a long time, we put it together. The claw marks had to have been made by an animal heavy enough to push the canvas into Temple's face. It must have been a *bear*. If the marks had just been made, the bear must still be here. Damn.

I climbed out of the sack and stuck my head through the tent door, heart pounding. There was no sign of anything to the left or right. I settled back and sat down on the bag. Temple was not hurt. Wait a second, this was still happening. I slipped the little 1892 Winchester carbine from its case and stepped outside. Temple, resplendent in his shorts, joined me. "It must still be here," I said. No sooner said than done. A huge black bear stepped from behind the tent and lumbered up to us.

We yelled like baboons under leopard attack. He kept coming. "Should I shoot?" "Yes!" At a distance of two feet, the bear died in its tracks. Then the valley was silent. We were pretty shaken by the encounter, and of course I regretted having to shoot the poor critter. We finished off the port wine and tried to sleep, the dead bear heaped beside the tent. I vividly remember the recoil of the .44, the hollow report, and its echo from the Old Woman.

In the morning, inspection revealed an ancient bear. There was not a whole tooth in its head. One canine was broken off below the gum line. Other teeth, not broken, were worn to the gums and decaying. We guessed the bear was at least twenty years old, and reasoned we had had no other course of action (nor, probably, did the bear). Medical help, had it become necessary, was a day away downriver. Later we learned five firefighters had been mauled in their sleeping bags by a black bear on the Yukon River the previous year. One was seriously hurt. That bear was soon found by helicopter and destroyed.

A few days after the aspen grove incident, we came down from a high cliff to discover a bear sitting in our boat. This bruin was small and tan colored. It was busy biting holes in soda pop cans. We interrupted by rolling rocks down the slope to the boat. The bear took a quick glance our way and then bolted down the shoreline. That was the kind of behavior I admired in a bear.

SEARCH FOR MISBEHAVIOR   The North Country has a curious effect on most people. After a few weeks in the north, it was always good to get back to the comforts of civilization. But I always soon found myself plotting ways to go north again. Perhaps it was the lure of the blue meanies, given that so few were to be found nesting south of the spruce forests in North America.

The bear confrontation on the Yukon was four years after the 1966 Mackenzie journey. I had been on northern rivers almost every summer in the interim. When we encountered the bear, Temple, Jerry Swartz, and I were following up the suggestion, raised at the Madison conference, that nesting failures were caused by abnormal adult behavior. Perhaps pesticides adversely affected behavior in addition to causing thin eggshells.

Promising to be very frugal, we convinced Roland Clement of the National Audubon Society to back the operation on the Yukon River. Swartz said he could round up a boat and motor. There was a hint in the discussion that the rig would be swiped from the fisheries people at the University of Alaska in Fairbanks, where Swartz taught parasitology. As a full professor, he was in a position to guarantee the boat. In any case, our low-budget expedition would use automatic cameras, set near peregrine nests, to record what the adults did while incubating eggs or rearing their young.

Inexpensive motion picture cameras were modified with a timer to take one picture every minute. A roll of film was long enough to last four days. The Yukon River was the perfect place for the work because pairs were close enough to be reached by boat, two per day. In all, we could hope to photograph eight pairs, renewing the film in each camera just in time to provide a seamless record.

Two of us always worked as a team. We knew the river well. The most upstream eyrie was at the mouth of the Forty Mile River in the Yukon Territory. The others were strewn downstream to the splendid cliffs called the Woodchopper Volcanics in Alaska. Our flat-bottomed riverboat was fast enough to make high speed against the current.

The cameras were in place, each set a few feet from the clutches of eggs. Our task was to replace each film cartridge every few days. The difficulty was that the Yukon flows in a scenic valley cut deep in the mountains. The peregrine cliffs were often several hundred feet above the river. We were soon forced into excellent physical condition.

The photographic work was almost too successful. Over seventy-eight thousand photos were gathered. I examined them, one at a time, through a microscope. We found no pattern of bad behavior. The adults all seemed to be steadfast parents. Recorded on film was the death of a newly hatched youngster in a brood of four. Its tiny body, covered with white down, lay beside the rest, but just out from under the mother as she covered the survivors to keep them warm. Suddenly, from one minute to the next, the dead chick disappeared on its first and last flight, apparently carried away by a parent falcon.

The cameras recorded lots of normal activities and a few strange events. A female drowsed off while incubating four eggs. In her slumber she continued to shift position, inadvertently shuffling off the eggs. There she was, six inches from the eggs, asleep. A few moments later she apparently saw her error. The next photo showed her back where she belonged.

At another eyrie the female was photographed standing over her eggs with a fully feathered pine grosbeak in her beak. The dead grosbeak, a medium-sized songbird, was seemingly intended as food for the eggs. The parent must have been impatient for the hatching.

Encouraging was evidence of peregrines willing to put up with great stress for the sake of their eggs. A female, panting heavily, stood with wings slightly spread, shading her new chicks from the scorching sun at Forty-Mile bluff (at the mouth of the river of the same name). Without the precious shade, the tiny young could not have lasted long. At another eyrie, the photos showed a small adult male braving the onslaught of his two grown daughters. They were clearly bigger than he, and each was bent on stealing the prey he brought to them. In the end the images showed the two youngsters standing before their dad, reaching in turn for each tidbit of food he offered. Even in the world of blue meanies there is discipline.

THE PORCUPINE   In June 1967, Bob Berry, John Campbell, Dave Glaister, and I set out from Dawson, on the Yukon, bound for the mouth of the Porcupine River, four hundred miles downstream. Few rivers in the North match the Porcupine for simple, quiet beauty. The watercourse meanders from its headwaters in the northern Yukon Territory to intercept the Yukon in central Alaska. Even though the drainage is north of the Arctic Circle, where tundra might be expected, the valley is covered with a deep spruce forest called taiga. Most of the valley showed no evidence of human impact. This was uncut primary forest, except where scattered areas had burned.

Dawson was a historic mining settlement, harking back to the days of the Klondike gold frenzy. An old Yukon River paddle-wheel steamer sat on the gravel, high and dry, safe from river ice at breakup. Gold nuggets the size of pecan clusters gleamed from locked cases in the local curio shop. The old tin-covered hotel, the Flora Dora, still offered rooms with a full view of the river for ten dollars a night. We imagined the guest list from 1903 was full of colorful characters. The cabin where Robert Service wrote *The Cremation of Sam Magee* was a few blocks away, at the edge of the bush.

Only five miles below the town we found the first peregrines, eight hundred feet up from the valley floor. We discovered pair after pair, far more than I had seen on the Mackenzie the year before. We could not have known then that even this population was in decline. It would be another decade before real improvement would begin.

Below Circle, Alaska, the Yukon grew sluggish as it approached the mouth of the Porcupine. This was the Yukon Flats. There were many braided channels, and close attention to navigation was required to keep on course. We topped the fuel at Fort Yukon, and then pointed the slender nose of the Peterborough freight canoe into the tea-colored water of the Porcupine. Our destination was Old Crow, three hundred miles upstream in the Yukon Territory.

Howling Dog Canyon, with its palisades of yellow rock, was home to four pairs of blue meanies. The canyon lived up to its name. Wolves howled at night, and we caught a glimpse of one as it flushed from its bed on a gravel bar. Wolves sought the windswept gravel for relief from mosquitoes. Even more vicious than mosquitoes were the "white knees," a kind of tiny black fly.

The current against our sleek green canoe quickened as we motored upstream. A hundred miles short of Old Crow the fuel reserve was clearly critical. We could not make our destination. A party of geologists, exploring for gas and oil just inside the Alaska-Yukon border, saved the day. They radioed Circle, the nearest village with an air charter service, and requested extra fuel be put on board their supply plane. Next morning, a floatplane arrived with three precious five-gallon tins of fuel.

Old Crow was a community whose economy was based on muskrats. The people plied the swampy Old Crow river flats, trapping the rodents by the canoe-load for their rich meat and valuable fur. The Old Crow people were handsome. They had high cheeks and round faces, reminiscent of coastal Eskimos farther north. Most unusual was that they all looked pretty much alike. These people, fairly isolated in the northern Yukon Territory, apparently had not mixed greatly with outsiders.

I quickly came to admire those folks. At an all-night square dance in the meeting hall, a little old man, seemingly blind, served up tune after tune with his fiddle. His music was pretty rough, but the spirit was there and the performance priceless. We were comfortable among the people because of their open hospitality.

There is no runway at Old Crow, but in summer the gravel bar across the river was long and smooth. Unfortunately, it was not straight. Berry and I loaded into a 1940s Twin Beech, along with four Indians headed for the outside. The takeoff run was curved, following the shoreline. The big oversize tires were partially deflated to smooth the ride. At last the pilot eased back on the wheel and the noise of the tires on the gravel bar was gone. My view of the takeoff was exceptional. That was the first and last time I flew as copilot on a commercial flight.

We quickly published the results of our survey and the pesticide levels found in fat biopsied from adult peregrines. A more exciting goal was to obtain young peregrines in the hopes of breeding them in captivity. Up to that time, 1967, only a few peregrines had been hatched from pairs belonging to falconers. We talked of breeding falcons, and dreamed about how wonderful it would be to ensure peregrines for falconry. The notion that enough peregrines could be bred in captivity to restore wild populations had not yet crossed our minds. But it would.

We captured six young. Berry and Campbell each kept a pair. A male went to Richard Fyfe, and I kept a male. These friends soon made great progress in captive breeding. Campbell produced young from captive northern birds in 1973. Berry would breed goshawks, peregrines, and many gyrfalcons, eventually establishing the North American Raptor Breeders Association. Fyfe would direct the Canadian Wildlife Service breeding-and-release program at Fort Wainwright, Alberta.

THE COLVILLE   The Yukon and Porcupine valleys are walled off from northern Alaska by a cordillera of mountains, including the Brooks Range. It is part of the Continental Divide. North of the mountains the world is arctic tundra, and the big river there is the Colville. It flows eastward along the north side of the Brooks Range, fed by streams draining the flanks of the mountains to the south. Finally the river swings north and dumps into the Arctic Ocean not far from Prudhoe Bay.

One of the Colville tributaries is the Etivluk. I first saw the mouth of the Etivluk in 1968 from the front seat of a Cessna 206. It was a truck of an airplane made to haul big loads, then filled with provisions, rubber raft, motor, and all, enough for two weeks on the Colville.

As we descended to land, I asked the pilot where the runway was, a bit of concern in my tone. "There," he said. There where? On the rocky beach ahead was a path, only a few feet wide, where willows had been trimmed from a gravel bar. He set the loaded machine right down at the threshold, chin up to avoid tripping on the nose wheel. We hit, and then bounced along in a rivet-loosening clatter. Finally, all was quiet.

We had arrived from the Naval Arctic Research Laboratory at Point Barrow. Tom Cade, who had kept track of the Colville peregrines since the 1950s, had asked for my help. I was to remain at the mouth of the Etivluk while the pilot flew downstream to fetch Clay White, my partner on this trip. I unloaded the airplane. The pilot climbed aboard and was gone. Suddenly, I was utterly alone. As far as I knew, there was no other human on the ground within two hundred miles.

I took stock of the supplies and equipment. The laboratory always sent people into the wilderness with food double the anticipated need, in case bad weather prevented a scheduled pickup. I found twenty-five pounds of frozen ribeye steaks. They would soon thaw in the warm arctic summer, and every meal from then on would include steaks until the flavor changed for the worse. Overall, I had enough food to last the entire summer.

There I was, sitting beside a huge pile of great-smelling food in a world of barren-ground grizzlies. It was no small comfort to discover in the gear a heavy rifle and a supply of huge cartridges. The plane would not return with White for several hours, so I walked a mile to the low bluff where the Etivluk dumps into the Colville, rifle in hand. *Cack, cack, cack*—an adult blue meanie gave the alarm. I scurried up the slope. There on a small ledge in the dirt were three dark brown eggs.

Tundra peregrines are of a different sort. They are willing to nest on dirt river bluffs or on hummocks near water in that prey-rich tundra. They play the odds. If a wolf, lynx, or grizzly finds the nest, there is no defense. Even arctic foxes can wreck a nest if the adults are inattentive. The only hope is to gamble on not being discovered. The gamble pays because the tundra is relatively predator-poor. This is partly because the severe winter limits creatures that cannot migrate or hibernate. Perhaps less than two in three nests succeed. Those that succeed produce a supply of young each year, and they sustain the population in the long run.

Finally, I heard the faint sound of a plane. When Clay and the pilot stepped from the craft, I concealed my great relief. After a few hours' sleep in the midnight sun, we had steak for breakfast. I was anxious to trap the female on the bluff because she clearly wore an aluminum band on her leg. Who had banded her, and where had it happened?

We set up a stuffed horned owl and put a noose-covered halo on its head. Fortunately, she had learned to hate owls. Perhaps her hatred was innate, written somehow on the genes that code for peregrine. She dove at the owl, struck it in the head, ran her toes through the heavy nylon nooses of the halo, and was caught. We recorded the band number and set her free. Undaunted, she resumed her attack until we retreated some two hundred yards. Then she settled back down on her eggs.

Eventually, we learned that Cade had banded her there at the mouth of the Etivluk a year earlier, almost to the day. We then realized the biological marvel. After she had finished the nesting season, she migrated south, surely a minimum of three thousand miles to the Gulf of Mexico or the Baja California region. Possibly, she went on to Brazil or Argentina. There she spent the winter. Then, in the spring, she flew north again, somehow homing to that little dirt bluff at the mouth of the Etivluk. The round-trip was at least six thousand miles. The distance alone seems overwhelming, even when allowing for the speed and endurance of peregrines. But the true feat was one of navigation, so featureless were the tundra and the tens of thousands of square miles of spruce forest to the south.

Clay and I found peregrines, gyrfalcons, and rough-legged hawks in good numbers all the way down the Colville to Umiat. The young gyrs were old enough to fly the first week of July, but the peregrines were just hatching. The gyrs nested in protected places under rock ledges, because the weather was stormy when they laid their eggs in April.

Rough-legged hawks, which spend winter throughout the contiguous United States, nest about the same time as peregrines. Sometimes they nest close to blue meanies. Oddly, we found two hawk eggs in an eyrie with one peregrine egg. We speculated the falcons decided they wanted the exact spot already chosen by the hawks. Living up to their name, the blue meanies drove the hawks away. The falcon simply laid her egg among the hawk eggs, having no other way to deal with them.

Umiat, our point of debarkation, was deserted. It had been a busy base in World War II, an outpost against the threat of Japanese action. A few years after our visit, it came to life again as a hub for the development of the Prudhoe Bay oil fields and the Alaska pipeline. That probably meant the wolverines were forced to leave the Quonset hut by the runway, and that the old hangars once again became off-limits to roosting ravens in the long arctic winters.

GREENLAND   The only way to get to Greenland was to ride for a very long time in something like a cold, dark, and very noisy subway tunnel. Whether a C-130 turboprop or a C-141 jet, these military cargo planes were not designed for human conveyance. Earplugs were mandatory. A box lunch, probably assembled a month in advance, provided a way to pass the time in the darkness. We few civilians joined enlisted personnel stationed in Greenland on the flights. Both going up and coming back, the enlisted folks slept all the way.

Bill Mattox, pioneer peregrine researcher, emerging from his beer cellar in the permafrost, western Greenland, 1995.

The excitement of going to falcon paradise always offset the discomfort of the five-hour trip. On the first voyage up, in 1976, I stood at a tiny frost-streaked window the size of a saucer, nose pressed to the glass, waiting for the first glimpse of the ice cap. On the west side of Greenland the ice sheet lies inland from the sea. The ice-free tundra, transected by rivers arising at the melting ice, and pockmarked with ponds and lakes, is the bastion of Greenland peregrines.

This tundra area is almost seventy miles east to west at the widest, and extends north-south a few hundred miles along the west side of the ice cap. Gyrfalcons are also present, but the mild inland regions to the west and south of the ice seem to favor blue meanies. The gyrs experience annual ups and downs because of the fortunes of their prey, such as ptarmigan and arctic hares. In some years, gyr cliffs are mostly occupied; in others they are mainly vacant.

Greenland gyrs were the objects of raids by falconers from the United States after World War II. Dozens of gyrs were caught and brought south. But husbandry then was not up to the challenge. Most died in captivity of diseases to which the falcons had no resistance. Most devastating was a lung fungus called *Aspergillus*. Unlike peregrines that migrate in fall to temperate and tropical North America, most Greenland gyrfalcons probably spend their entire lives on the island, in adjacent Canada, or eastward to Spitsbergen (north of Iceland) and beyond, and do not normally experience southern pathogens.

Bill Mattox, with Bill Burnham, was responsible for early serious inquiry into the population biology of peregrines in western Greenland. They first walked the tundra there in 1972. Not much later, Scott Ward of the Army research center at Aberdeen, Maryland, provided long-term funding for the work in the region of Sondre Stromfjord.

FORCED MARCH ON THE TUNDRA   "Anybody like a potato for a snack?" I said. The potatoes were raw, but I was desperate to lighten my load. Two days before, we had shuffled out of Sondrestrom Air Base loaded with food and gear sufficient for a weeklong walkabout. Some of the falcon eyries we needed to check were as far as twelve miles out. We had plenty of fruit and vegetables, but most of it was in my pack. Thirty pounds of potatoes and oranges, plus my gear, was in my Kelty. It did not matter to me that Burnham had four canned hams, or that Bob Martin had half a case of canned beans. The produce on my back was about to finish me off.

The year was 1976. Clay White and Tom Cade were with us. We were the second team to take to the field that season. Our job was to check as many of the 20 known nest-cliffs as possible. Each year Mattox arranged for expanded searches and more thorough observations. By the end of the 1990s, the number of cliffs known to be used for nesting by blue meanies increased from about 20 to about 120.

After a few days of hiking with the heavy loads on the mattress-like tundra, we were fairly crippled. Tendons began to fail, blisters bled, and feet were bruised. For excitement, I made the foolish mistake of approaching a herd of musk oxen to see if they would live up to their reputation for encircling their calves for protection. I clapped and shouted at a distance of fifty yards. At first, all went well. They formed a circle, calves inside, according to legend. Then, to my dismay, four of them broke away and charged in my direction. No longer crippled, I raced among several huge boulders, slipped away, and meekly returned to the expedition. Obviously, I had not amounted to the menace of a wolf pack or a polar bear.

Mattox and his friends were able to amass a huge body of information on Greenland peregrines over the years, partly because of his marvelous field-workers. Many volunteered year after year. Among them were Tom Maechtle, Mike Yates, Ralph Rogers, Bob Rosenfield, and Jack Oar. Surely they were spared the task of hauling potatoes and oranges.

SIMPLE FAUNA   West Greenland began to lose its load of ice over ten thousand years ago. The terrain along the coast cleared first and began to rise, owing to the loss of the massive ice burden. The land is actually lower in elevation near the ice cap. In the center of Greenland, the weight of the great ice sheet depresses the land far below sea level. The ice cap is roughly ten thousand feet thick near the center of the island. We hiked to eyries near the western edge of the cap. Imagine looking to the east to see a steeply sloping white horizon against a cold blue sky. The ice dominated the entire panorama.

Slowly, the ice continues to retreat. Behind it, the tundra slowly expands. It must do so without the expected complement of certain tundra animals, given its isolation from northern Canada. West Greenland has no mammals smaller than arctic hares. It is tundra without lemmings. There are no snowy owls or rough-legged hawks. Arctic foxes abound, foraging on birds and young hares in summer, and carrion in winter.

Winter is the test for caribou (reindeer). There are no wolves with which to contend. It is difficult to imagine caribou without wolves. Wolves are generally the major predator of caribou. But Greenland caribou have another nemesis. Bot flies lay eggs beneath the skin of otherwise healthy caribou. The developing larvae weaken heavily infested animals. The eggs develop into thumb-sized maggots under the skin, and several dozen at once amount to a serious burden. Winter sorts out the winners and losers.

Of course birds migrate annually to Greenland to harvest the summer bounty. White-fronted geese and mallards are too big for peregrines, as are ravens, loons, and gulls. Northern phalaropes, which are small insectivorous shorebirds, are sometimes eaten by peregrines. But the base that sustains the falcon includes five abundant little songbirds: redpolls, longspurs, snow buntings, pipits, and wheatears (see Chapter I). This last species leaves Greenland in late summer and makes perhaps the longest direct over-water nonstop flight of any small land bird, to reach southern Europe.

Add a few more kinds of gulls and ducks along the coast, and the rock ptarmigan inland, and you have the great bulk of the birds seen. But like ptarmigan elsewhere in the Arctic, and in the Rocky Mountains farther south, their numbers fluctuate widely every few years. Unlike gyrfalcons, the smaller and more agile peregrines are versatile enough to rely on small birds as a more reliable food base.

There are no trees in this region. Only dwarf birch and dwarf willow prevail, both less than knee-high. On steep slopes, these grow in a curious pattern of lines on the contour. The repeated freezing and thawing of the thin soil causes it to expand and contract, each cycle loosening the peat-like mat a tiny bit, which causes it to slowly sag, like the surface of fudge in a pan, tilted before it is hardened. Caribou and musk oxen make regular use of the little horizontal ridges, and their trails exaggerate the pattern.

By mid-August the exodus of migrant birds begins. Mattox and his coworkers have found some peregrine youngsters are not able to fly before early September. The pressure is very great on these fledglings. They must migrate immediately, joining what is left of their prey, or starve. Migrate they do. Falcons banded by Mattox ordinarily showed up in the United States and the West Indies by late September, and in South America a month later.

NORTHERN GREENLAND   Five hundred miles up the west coast of Greenland from Sondre Stromfjord, glacial tongues from the ice cap shear off into Baffin Bay. The slowly flowing ice is like a conveyor belt creating a flotilla of icebergs each summer. Northward, the bay narrows to a hundred miles or so, which separates Canada (Ellesmere Island) and Greenland. In summer, the thin sea ice, called pack ice, breaks up, freeing the embedded icebergs. The two kinds of floating ice sometimes move about at a lively speed, depending on the wind.

Before the beginnings of European settlement, the natural harbor at Thule was the site of a native Greenlander village called Dundas. In the early 1900s, whalers plied the waters of Baffin Strait. European settlers only trickled in, unlike the case in southern Greenland.

After World War II, Thule became one of two powerful United States radar stations from which to watch the Russians across the North Pole. Today, the radar station remains at Thule. Another is in Alaska. The native village near the present site of the air base was moved sixty miles farther north a few decades ago. The hope was to buffer the Greenlanders from the inevitable unfortunate influences of the military base.

Overlooking the harbor at Thule is a prominent bluff with sheer faces on the seaward sides. Peregrines nest there, at latitude seventy-six degrees north. Until a few years ago, this was thought to be the northern nesting limit of the species. The problem there is surely not food; snow buntings and small sea birds are abundant. Instead, I believe it is here that the hardy blue meanies meet their match with climate.

The weather pattern at Thule causes two major problems. One is the permanent high pressure over the ice cap. At the edge of the cap, fierce winds are generated by great pressure differences. They blow at any time of year at speeds sufficient to buckle the sides of all the huge fuel storage tanks at the air base. Second, polar storms circle the planet, even in summer, on a repetitive basis. A major storm may hit Thule, move to the east, passing north of Scandinavia, skirt northern Asia and North America, and revisit Thule a week or so later. Rapid-fire weather like this must be a hardship during incubation and when the chicks are small.

Peregrines could probably handle the cold, were it the only adversity, but high wind and snow in the summer surely work against the survival of eggs and tiny chicks. In a kind of lottery, a few young are probably produced in some years, but hardly any in other years. Perhaps immigration of individuals from the more productive population to the south keeps the Thule population alive.

"Looks like falcon whitewash here," I said excitedly. Bill Burnham and his son Kurt, Tim Gallagher, and I were sitting fifty yards offshore in two big inflatable boats. Gallagher is a falconer who flies a peregrine and edits the journal *Living Bird*, published by the Cornell Laboratory of Ornithology. We had motored north from Thule across the twenty-mile expanse of Wolstenholme Fjord and turned northwest toward Cape Peary. We were at about seventy-seven degrees north latitude.

Wham! A rifle bullet slammed into the cliff. Then, as if in slow motion, an adult peregrine launched from the cliff high above and gave an alarm call. It was tempting to call it the most northern peregrine nesting on the planet. We were seventy miles north of the pair at Thule.

Maybe the real northern limit of this falcon will someday be known. Perhaps Kurt Burnham and his coworkers will soon find the northernmost eyrie. But one day, at the onset of the next ice age, the falcons will again abandon this outpost and gradually retreat southward.

DOVEKIES   The North Atlantic Ocean is a vast place. In winter it is home to the dovekie, a quail-sized seabird resembling a tiny black-and-white penguin. A better comparison is that of a small puffin with a short, slender black beak. Unlike penguins, dovekies can fly. In summer, most fly from the open Atlantic Ocean to the Greenland shores of Baffin Bay to raise their young.

When the ice breaks in June, the waters off Thule are teeming with small shrimp-like crustacea called krill, the major food of dovekies. Onshore, the coastal headlands rising several hundred feet above the sea are littered with boulder fields. It is in the crevices beneath the boulders that dovekies find the security they need to rear their chicks. When the single chick of each pair is ready, it makes the most crucial flight of its life, to the safety of the ocean, where it too forages for krill.

The adults must forage offshore every day. They transport food to the chick in an enlarged throat pouch. Each adult pair has its own nest beneath the boulders. Somehow, they must find the burrow trip after trip each day. The Burnhams have banded lots of dovekies and then trapped among the same boulders the next year. Sure enough, many of the dovekies had faithfully returned to nest among the same boulders after so long a time so far away.

By the way, dovekies are trapped Greenlander-style. A person with a long-handled net sits in the scree, waiting for a big flock to pass within reach. The wait is usually brief. In a kind of badminton using a living bird, scores are caught in the bright light of the midnight sun. Modern mist nets are more efficient.

It is not enough to just read about dovekie natural history in Greenland. Everything is in being there. The experience is beyond belief. Southward,

Dovekies near Thule, Greenland,
gather to breed in vast hordes.

thirty miles down the coast, is a wonderful little sheltered inlet at the mouth of a creek. Burnham had already set up camp. Immediately to the north was an immense calico cliff of banded black-and-white metamorphic rock, the bands offset and folded from the immense pressures of changing ice loads in the glacial periods. On either side of the valley of the creek, and farther south at the next creek, were expansive boulder fields, dappled in bright orange by crust-like lichens. Mixed in with the lichen orange was a filigree, almost like lace, of black-and-white specks. They were dovekies, in countless millions, fully reflecting the vastness of the North Atlantic that sustains them.

A glaucous gull flew over the boulder field. The speckled lace near the gull, really thousands of the little seabirds, drifted up. Then it drew into a mist-like flock and flew in a broad orbit over the colony. The combined calls of the anxious parents created a buzzing roar. The gull, a fully capable predator of dovekies, flew on down the coast.

The gulls and the arctic foxes can have dovekies whenever they wish. But the odds of any one dovekie being caught are vanishingly tiny. In these enormous colonies the little vulnerable birds simply swamp their predators. When dovekies flood the breeding grounds in spring they are suddenly present in such numbers that no population of carnivore can become numerous enough to be ready for them.

So it was when the Inuit killed dovekies. In summer, the natives stuffed sealskins full of the little bodies. Placed in the ground and stored for several months, the larder kept cool and slowly fermented. Nevertheless, they were a prized delicacy in winter, when life depended on the bounty stored the previous summer.

HIGH ARCTIC ADVENTURES   Anyone the least bit interested in serious adventure must read, in the safety of one's home, *Arctic Adventure: My Life in the Frozen North*, by Peter Freuchen. His account is of life among the Inuit in the early 1900s and the hazards they faced. Northern Greenland then was not for amateurs.

I ventured from the base camp under the big calico cliff. My kayak was a modern Klepper. I paddled out into the bay, finding passage among the cakes of pack ice. Oddly, the open channels were ephemeral. I paddled on not far from shore, but soon found that what had seemed like an open lead had disappeared.

A white speck materialized on a boulder high on the headland. Gyrfalcon! Suddenly the bird bolted off, flashing down the scree, and pitched up, a dovekie in its grasp. The flying gyr reached down and killed the prey with a quick bite. Out of nowhere a glaucous gull appeared, bent on theft. Glaucous gulls are nearly the largest of their kind, and weigh about the same as gyrfalcons (roughly three pounds).

But gulls are noted for their graceful, languid flight. This gull wanted the dovekie. It made for the falcon and the falcon stormed off up the coast. I watched the chase with binoculars for at least a mile. The gull was able to keep up with the "fastest bird in level flight." Perhaps the gyrfalcon could have pulled away were it not carrying the dovekie, but such a small load could hardly have slowed the falcon much. The gull and falcon, neck and neck, finally flew around a point of rocks and were lost from view. The big gull earned my respect as a speedster and pirate.

The pack ice had shifted during the gull encounter, so I lost passage ahead. I climbed out on the ice, dragging the kayak behind me. The great merit of such a lightweight vessel in the ice of the north is that it can be hauled out when larger boats risk being crushed. No doubt native hunters often saved themselves by haul-out.

When the sea ice surged against the bluffs, we could explore more on foot than by kayak. Derek Craighead (John's son) and I headed inland, up the stream from base camp. We had gone no more than two miles, hiking on grass in twenty shades of brilliant green. This vegetation was growing on peat that had accumulated in the draw over the centuries. Organic material had been synthesized faster than it had decayed. This latter process, decay, had been impaired relative to the former by the constant cold a few inches below the insulating surface. Plant material, which normally would have rotted at warmer latitudes, persisted and accumulated. Musk oxen are attracted to the lush grass. But some animals are crippled when they develop greatly over-grown hooves because of inadequate wear on the soft plants.

"Jim, look overhead with your binos," Craighead said. "Do you see them?" I shook my head. Above us were two flightways, one toward the coast, the other inland. From below we were seeing the dovekie routine of life. Most were beyond view of the naked eye. We lay down, binoculars trained upward. Flock after flock of dovekies, each hundreds strong, moved in opposite directions. Those flying west were bound for the sea and the rich krill supply. Going the other way, from sea to land, were intent parents, throat pouches stuffed, bringing home the day's catch. We had been unaware of this vast inland colony, so far removed from the obvious coastal hordes.

The sea was sometimes choked with the curious mix of icebergs and pack ice. The view was best from the top of the headland. Here and there a seal rested on a cake of pack ice. No doubt early peoples worked the high ground as well. Ruins of ancient stone hides (blinds) were common, their antiquity proven by undisturbed lichens covering them. Most curious were low stone fences that must have been used by early Greenlanders to direct caribou or musk oxen to waiting hunters. The fences seemed too low to have been a real barrier.

We walked the edge of the sea bluff looking for gyrfalcon eyries. Never were we out of sight of dovekies, which were either flying to and from off-shore feeding places or milling around a colony below us. In this dovekie cornucopia, why were gyrfalcon eyries uncommon? We found only two sites in use along a thirty-mile stretch of coast south of Thule. There were a few other places where gyrs once nested, but no evidence of recent use.

We settled on a trial explanation. Dovekies arrive to nest only after expanses of open water appear in May. They must have open water for feeding. But the gyrs nest in April and must rely on other prey before the dove-kies arrive. Only ptarmigan and perhaps arctic hares could be important food sources, and in some years they might be scarce. Of course there are a few other larger seabirds, and songbirds begin to show up in late April.

We guessed that in bad years, when ptarmigan and hares are low, gyrs are short of the food they need to nest. It would be better for them to delay nesting a year, or go where food is more abundant. Perhaps future biologists will be able to piece together the factors that are critical where the big falcon types live close to the edge.

Several rugged islands lie off Thule. One is a couple of miles or so in diameter and has spectacular cliffs towering five hundred feet over the sea. We motored ten miles to its shores and found a gyrfalcon and countless thick-billed murres in a massive colony.

Farther south was a tiny island, barely rising above the sea. It was a mix of boulders and grassy tundra meadows. We tied to a boulder and went ashore. The place was famous for the hundreds of common eiders that nest there. This duck is truly marine, and is rarely far from salt water. I carried a very big-bore rifle, in case we should find an egg-eating polar bear that did not wish to share the bounty.

We found no bear, and no eider. Plenty of empty nests of eiderdown, enough for several comforters, littered the grassy nooks and crannies. Perhaps Eskimos had already carried out an egg raid. In the old days the loot from such raids was stored, all eggs intact, in little waist-high huts made of heavy rocks. These could be visited easily when the sea froze in fall. Overall, the eiders persisted because travel to eider islands by native peoples was difficult without powerboats.

In recent years, a more destructive exploitation of eider eggs has sprung up. Sled dogs, useless in summer and burdens to feed, are taken by their masters to eider islands and marooned. The dogs eat all they can find until their masters return for them in the fall. All nests, eider and otherwise, are plundered by the Crusoe dogs.

While we were on a sortie to a far island in search of falcons, a fog formed low over the water. The cold sea lowered the temperature of the moist air to the dew point. The fog was not thick; plenty of light penetrated from overhead. But horizontal visual range dropped to a few yards.

Bill Burnham slowed the boat, fearing we might overrun a piece of ice, or get too close to a large iceberg. The latter is risky because icebergs melt below the surface, become top-heavy, then capsize in a very impressive display of raw power. The sound of it carries for miles.

We were very far from any land. We had skirted several huge slabs of ice and a few small icebergs. Icebergs are fresh water and, unlike frozen seawater, are pale blue. But ice is ice, and I feared we were badly lost, many miles from the big calico cliff above camp. If we went the wrong way we might run out of fuel, lost in Baffin Bay. Compasses were useless this close to the magnetic pole. Compass error was about seventy degrees.

"Not to worry." Burnham reached into the map drawer on the wheel console and produced a small battery-powered radio receiver. It was a global positioning system radio, GPS for short. He had stored the coordinates of the calico cliff, and now the unit pointed the way home using repeated fixes on satellites in stationary Earth orbits. More than an hour passed as we snaked among the bergs and pack ice. Finally, looming before us, above the fog and in full sunlight, stood the black-and-white banded cliff. One must wonder how many Inuit, after they colonized Greenland a few thousand years ago, were permanently lost for want of a GPS, adrift with the ice in Baffin Bay.

SYNOPSIS   No one knows how many pairs of blue meanies nest on banks and bluffs in the world's northern forests and tundras. Some people argue that any estimate is only a gloriously wild guess; others claim ballpark accuracy. All agree that migrant northern peregrines are the most abundant of their kind. I venture to say the total exceeds four thousand pairs in North America alone, and no doubt northern Eurasia has a similar number.

For the peregrine falcon, the strategy of following the great masses of migrant prey birds northward to their summer homes has paid off handsomely. The energy costs and risks of long-distance migration by peregrines are somehow offset by the gains. It is tempting to think these wandering falcons also gain a reward in winter when they join other migrant birds on warm prey-ridden beaches and coastal wash flats far to the south. That is the topic of the next chapter.

VIII » FALCONS ON THE BEACH

TEXAS GULF COAST   In 1964, Luff Meredith wrote me describing the conspicuous fall flights of peregrines migrating along the Gulf Coast in Texas. Blue meanies make their way to Mexico and points south along the barrier beaches and the Inland Waterway. That year in October, Clay White and I traveled to Matagorda Island (between Galveston and Corpus Christi) for the first time. How many meanies were there, and could they be banded in large numbers?

The commanding officer, Colonel Sharpless, indulged us with permission to travel the beaches adjacent to the Air Force bombing range. He insisted on supplying the jeep and a driver. He saw this as a perfect way to punish a career sergeant who had wrecked the launch used to reach the mainland. What could be worse than to have to baby-sit two bird-watchers, driving them up and down the monotonous beach for four days?

Early that first morning we careened onto the beach from the access road, surly sergeant at the wheel. In a matter of minutes, we found a young peregrine sitting on the sand. I shouted "Step on it," and off we went. The bewildered boatman did as we asked.

By the end of the day we had caught, banded, and released four peregrines. They were the first beach peregrines White and I had trapped. We were very pleased with ourselves. So was our driver. Despite himself, the sarge was completely converted. Now a born-again falcon trapper, he bought us dinner that night at the noncommissioned officers' club, overjoyed to spend his four days of punishment with us.

In 1975, I was back on Matagorda Island with other friends. We were testing the newly available radio transmitters attached to the falcons. With luck, the radio beacons might tell us how these arctic falcons use the coast, and where they go. It also seemed possible to estimate the well-being of the vast arctic peregrine population by inventing a scheme to count the migrants each year.

Radios small enough for a falcon to carry easily had been developed only a few years before, using electronic parts originally intended for hearing aids. We tied our little transmitter to the two center tail feathers of the falcon so it would not get in the falcon's way. Our hope was to follow the signal with a directional antenna attached to an airplane.

The surly sergeant and Clay White on Matagorda Island, Texas, 1964. The black mark on the chest of the falcon enabled identification from a distance.

"Hang on, y'all!" We were in trouble. The steering gear box and the linkage to the front wheels on the little dark blue Air Force jeep had parted company. "Hang on, y'all," repeated John Smith, the sound of utmost urgency in his voice. Smith was a biologist for the Texas Game and Fish Department. He had been driving our open jeep along the beach on the Matagorda Island bombing range.

Now the jeep was driving itself. We plunged from the narrow ranch road, flew through a ditch filled with water, and finally lurched to a halt in a herd of Santa Gertrudis cattle. A light tan cow with big horns and a hump on her back stood twenty feet away. A calf stood nearby. She regarded us carefully, and then bolted off in the cloud of gnats that had befriended her.

Despite a pretty severe bounce, we were okay. Jerry Swartz and Jerry Craig had come with Smith to help trap falcons and track radio signals. We had been hurrying to the mess hall that humid October evening. The road, from which we had so suddenly departed, ran along the interior of the island and was to have made our trip back to the base faster after the day's work on the beach. Smith repaired the steering with a couple of pieces of barbed wire and we crept in the broken vehicle to the motor pool.

The next morning Smith, our official link to the military, talked the Air Force out of another jeep. Down the beach we went. We were speeding at water's edge when Smith shouted, "There's a peregrine." Craig reached into a box and pulled out a pigeon, and fitted a small leather vest to the hapless bird. The vest was covered with a couple of dozen nooses made of nylon fishing line. The nooses were securely fastened. Also tied to the vest was a long cord with a lead weight secured to the end. The cord and the weight would prevent the pigeon from flying away.

There she was, a dark brown juvenile. She was on the beach about a football field's length away, facing into a wicked wind blowing onshore. Smith was a man on a mission. He plunged the throttle down and we hurtled toward the bird. We had schooled Smith in such matters, and he now endeavored to get close to the falcon. When the falcon flew, our pigeon would be in full view. Smith deftly avoided driftwood and other debris scattered on the beach. As if it were Daytona, we raced to the brown meanie. The broken steering of the previous evening was totally forgotten.

The big dark falcon was off. Craig heaved the pigeon, dragline and all, as high as he could. "Keep going," I ordered over the roar of the wind. Smith obeyed. The peregrine wheeled around from her course into the wind and swooped in behind the climbing pigeon. Just as the pigeon came to the end of the dragline the falcon was there, sharp talons open. The pigeon gave a burst of power, but was caught from behind.

Instead of settling to the sand with her prey, the peregrine poured on the power. She caught the full lift of the gale. In an instant, she noticed we were only a few yards away. She released the pigeon, the better to escape. The pigeon, no worse for wear, did not fall free, but dangled five inches below the falcon, the length of a drawn-up noose. The peregrine was caught by a toe. In the shock of being caught, the falcon poured on more power and climbed away.

The weight of our dragline was too little. The big falcon was fresh from the Arctic, where there are no pigeons. She gained fifty feet altitude and was pitched by the wind back over the dunes inland from the beach. She was gone. We learned then to always use a very long, stout dragline with a weight no falcon could carry.

Damn! Smith instantly saw the gravity of the matter. If the falcon, which was securely attached to the pigeon, were to fly far inland she might go down in the tall grass and be lost. Impaired by the pigeon, she would be easy prey for a coyote or she might starve to death. Smith wheeled the vehicle between two dunes and we shot out onto the wash flats on the leeward side of the island.

Just as we gained full view of the island behind the dunes, Craig saw the flash of a wing as the falcon was finally dragged down. "She's off to the right three hundred yards," he shouted over the rattle of the jeep. In moments we were there. Now, imagine the surface of a pond. Near its center was a floundering falcon attached to a pigeon. Smith slammed on the brakes. He leaped from the jeep and ran into the water, intent on saving the drowning falcon.

The pond proved unexpectedly deep. In an instant, all that was visible on the rippled surface of the stagnant water was a struggling falcon and Smith's baseball cap. Now up from below came Smith. Without so much as a glance in our direction, he freestyled to the sinking bird, swept it over his head, and dog-paddled one-handed to shore. Soon the soaking biologist was on dry land, amid cheering admirers. He examined his wallet to see what valuable contents had been ruined. Little cash was damaged, given the meager salary of a state biologist.

Smith soon had his turn at laughing. The next day we steadily worked the beaches until midday. Then we drove up the interior road, heading for lunch at the Wynn Ranch on the island's south end. Presently a peregrine flew overhead as we sped along in the jeep. I grabbed a pigeon and gave it a mighty heave. It flew beautifully, trailing the dragline far out into the pasture. But meanies are not always mean. The peregrine gave no indication of even the slightest interest, and soon disappeared over the distant dunes.

Smith stopped the jeep, backed up along the road, and stopped again. "I'll get the pigeon," I said. The pasture was too muddy for the vehicle. I jumped out the back of the open vehicle and jogged to the lucky pigeon. It was hiding, stone still, some two hundred feet from the road. I reached down to pick up the bird and paid no attention to the cattle grazing nearby. Things took a turn for the worse.

I looked up and discovered a charging Brahma bull in a vignette of airborne mud flung skyward by his hooves. Only fifty feet separated us, and the distance would soon be negligible. In absolute terror, I turned and ran as never before. What do clowns do in rodeos? There was no hope of finding a barrel. It was like a running of the bulls in a dead-end alley. I knew I would soon be gored. Fortunately, having made his point, the bull called off his attack midway in my sprint. I crawled into the jeep to a concert of laughter.

Over lunch at the ranch house, the story of the tawny bull with a wrinkled brow and manure all over his rump was retold. The ranch foreman thought it was funny. "That's the same bull that ran three cowboys out of the pasture last week," he said. There was consolation in knowing that cowboys also flee.

The work of trapping falcons was of course great fun. Swartz and Craig were experienced with falcons, but this was all new to Smith. He was fresh out of college with a degree in wildlife management. He had loads of enthusiasm, not yet dampened by the realities of his job. Unlike college teachers, state biologists usually do not choose which species they prefer to study. Smith was a budding peregrine biologist, but was soon transferred to work on alligators in eastern Texas, never to work on blue meanies again.

MIGRANT FALCONS   Not all peregrines migrate. In some parts of the world they are nearly sedentary. For example, many have been banded at eyries on the British Isles, but only two have been recovered off those islands (in nearby Europe). The narrow English Channel is hardly a barrier; the UK falcons simply lack wanderlust. Peregrines nesting in many temperate regions show little tendency toward annual migration. For example, those living in Spain and Australia move hardly at all. The race of peregrine that nests in Africa south of the Sahara is not known to be migratory. Before DDT wiped them out, no duck hawk banded in the eastern United States was found later south of that region in winter.

The northern parts of continents in the Northern Hemisphere are too severe for blue meanies in winter. The same can be said for their prey. All must escape southward at the onset of the energy-draining cold. Peregrines fly with their food to warmer places.

A simple question emerges. Why didn't peregrines simply *remain* south, where it was always warm and prey was sufficient all year long? Why did some bother going north to nest in spring, only to retreat in fall? They did so because of the marvelous opportunity. Species make their way through time by seizing opportunities when they appear. In this case, the prize was the hoard of prey birds that moved northward to the edge of the ice to feed on insects flourishing in the brief arctic summers.

In one possible scenario, the migratory habit began when some of those ancient peregrines followed the gradual northward retreat of the continental ice sheet beginning thirteen thousand years ago. Down through the subsequent millennia, the ice receded farther. The glacier followers kept to the tundra at the edge of the ice each summer, retreating southward each winter. They eventually became more and more separated from the sedentary temperate falcons, and the fall migration grew longer. Perhaps a growing barrier between the two types of falcon was a vast band of featureless spruce forest. The northern migratory falcons and the southern sedentary falcons, although not completely isolated and physically similar in most ways, took increasingly separate paths to different lifestyles.

The migrants seized on behaviors best enabling them to cope with long-distance navigation and unpredictable cold weather in the northern summers. Just as challenging was the problem of avoiding the nonmigratory temperate peregrines to the south when the arctic summer was over. The southern permanent residents, sedentary on their home territories, probably did not take kindly to the flood of northern meanies in the fall.

There is perhaps a better scenario for the presence of both nonmigrants and northern migrant peregrines in North America. Northeastern Asia and present-day northern Alaska (Beringia) were mainly ice-free at the height of the last ice period. When the ice sheets began to recede thirteen or more millennia ago, the peregrines in mid-latitude North America may have only slowly spread northward, gradually adjusting to the moderating climate of their world. Adjacent to the receding ice, the tundra slowly widened, ripe for the picking. Peregrines from northern Eurasia and Beringia, already accomplished high-latitude migrants, dispersed eastward across North America along the lip of the ice to nest. Each fall, these immigrants followed ancient migratory instincts southward, and eventually to milder latitudes in the New World.

Southbound northern falcons found it easier, we can imagine, to avoid the home territories belonging to resident blue meanies and to go instead where southern residents were scarce and food plentiful. In North America, vast tracks of flatlands south of the Appalachians and the coastal plains and barrier islands west to Baja California attracted northern peregrines and their prey.

The disappearing ice sheet laid bare the vast Canadian and Alaskan Arctic tundra. Immigrants from the west struck it rich, their numbers expanding to the limit of the huge new land. In winter, they ventured farther south to tropical marshes in Central and South America and the West Indies, compelling because of rich hunting opportunities. Their migrant counterparts in Eurasia were similar. Scandinavian peregrines sought the balmy Mediterranean and North Africa in winter, while those nesting farther east in Siberia wander now to the Middle East, India, and Southeast Asia.

OCEAN VOYAGERS   The layout of every continent is different, and the challenges faced by migrants are varied. North America is broad in the far north and narrows to a peninsula (Florida) and an isthmus (Panama) to the south. Acting like a giant funnel, the land tends to concentrate southbound peregrines in the fall from Greenland, the huge arctic islands, and the vast northern mainland.

At middle latitudes, prevailing winds from the northwest may create a southeast drift of migrants, causing them to encounter the eastern seaboard in the United States and the Gulf Coast of Texas. It is tempting to think meanies are numerous in migration at barrier islands like Assateague Island in Maryland and Padre and Matagorda islands in Texas because the falcons are afraid to cross expanses of ocean and instead cling to the shoreline as they move south.

Several observations tend to discredit that notion. Blue meanies are not landlubbers. Tom Smylie banded migrating peregrines in the fall for several years in the Dry Tortugas. These small islands lie sixty-five miles west of Key West, Florida, in the middle of nowhere. The falcons are numerous there in passage to the West Indies and South America. The little islands provide a place to rest and catch migrant songbirds also crossing the Gulf.

Islands are few in the Gulf south of Louisiana and eastern Texas. But offshore oil rigs far out in the ocean offer hundreds of peregrines places to ambush prey birds also in ocean transit.

Blue meanies sometimes accomplish really long over-water flight, as seen in the many records of peregrines coming aboard ships in the open ocean. Recently peregrines have been observed hitchhiking on the superstructures of mammoth tankers sailing southward along the Atlantic seaboard bound for the Panama Canal. The falcons were seen to dine on smaller feathered passengers that otherwise would have shared the cruise to the wintering grounds.

Occasional sightings occur in the Hawaiian Islands, an archipelago with no resident falcons at all. My guess was that the birds seen in Hawaii were from arctic North America, but Clay White tells me the museum specimens he has seen from Hawaii may also include very weathered peregrines from the Aleutians and Japan. It seems unlikely that peregrines seen in Hawaii island-hopped from breeding populations in the southwest Pacific. Such falcons would probably be capable breeders in the Hawaiian setting and probably would have founded a population there.

Peregrines certainly do catch migrating land birds over the ocean, sometimes snatching them from the surface after a forced ditching. They pluck and eat their prey with ease while in a soar. Plenty of water is available in their food, so there is no need to drink. We can imagine that peregrines even sleep, dozing briefly in their own way, while soaring lazy circles a couple of thousand feet above open ocean.

THE GREAT CULIACÁN MARSH   One hundred miles up the Pacific coast from Mazatlán, Mexico, and due east of the southern tip of Baja California sprawls the Great Culiacán Marsh. Supplied by the Culiacán River, the sixty square miles of freshwater and brackish wetland is winter home to tens of thousands of waterfowl and uncountable hordes of shorebirds, doves, blackbirds, and other songbirds. Many are migrants from breeding grounds far to the north. Adjacent to the marsh, the coastal plain is intensely farmed in grain, sugarcane, and produce. Together, marsh and plain create a world-class supply of bird food. The food attracts utterly countless hordes of birds. Best of all, many of the species present are the right size to fit the feet of blue meanies.

The marsh is in the perfect location for different kinds of peregrines. It is far enough southward to meet the standard of a far migration destination preferred by arctic peregrines. Further, the marsh is only a few hundred miles south of the mouth of the Colorado River. Falcons nesting in the interior of western temperate North America, which are less migratory compared to arctic peregrines, find the marsh close enough to reach in a week or two of leisurely drifting. Add to these falcons a few vagrants from the coast of British Columbia with extraordinary wanderlust, and possibly a handful of Mexican locals from mountain eyries east of the Culiacán plain and Baja California.

Perhaps another reason the Culiacán Marsh is so popular among falcons is that it is easy to find. Simply fly down the Pacific coast, or the Colorado River, take a turn toward the mainland at the tip of Baja, and presto! The stage is set for a melee of meanies in a world of limitless food. There are, no doubt, other places in the world that are hugely bountiful, perfect for peregrines in winter. But surely none matches Culiacán.

For years, Pete Widener hunted ducks on the marsh and recognized the wonderful opportunity to study wintering peregrines there. In 1989, Widener convinced the owner of a gun club on the marsh, Tony Pico, to cooperate in such a study. With help from Bill Burnham, I rounded up a few able field-workers and headed off to Mexico to put radio transmitters on peregrines.

Finding meanies on the marsh is ridiculously easy. You climb into an airboat and roar out to open water. Before long the boat has flushed several thousand waterfowl and the sky is filled with wings. The trick is to sort out the peregrines from the masses of ducks. This is no small task, since the size and wingbeat of many ducks are similar to those of the falcons. Sometimes we saw what seemed to be a collision of two ducks, only to discover a falcon had simply caught its meal.

We watched carefully to see how falcons attack. Usually the ducks were in flocks, some with hundreds of birds, but ranging down to just a few. From the perspective of a duck, we saw little to support the notion of safety in numbers. A blue meanie seemed to decide on a duck and dash at it, regardless of the size of the flock. Large duck or small, all seemed to be caught with ease if the falcon was intent. Some were simply released when the falcon found itself too far from a dry place to land with its catch. Most catches were more than a hundred feet above the water and were usually spectacular.

We saw two other styles of hunting involving prey other than ducks. Frequently huge flocks of blackbirds, hundreds of feet in the air, would draw up tight in fluid, viscous masses ever changing in shape. At a distance the flocks appeared as turbulent clouds of black smoke. This bizarre response resulted from the attack of an aerial predator.

I saw peregrines attack four or five flocks. The strategy was the same each time: rush the flock and grab the first blackbird that passes within reach. Imagine the plight of each blackbird in the confusion. Because of so many compatriots wheeling nearby, the chore is to keep the falcon in sight, so easily could the view be blocked. Add to that the need to avoid collision with other flock members. One must admire how well members of such flocks retain their presence of mind in such dire circumstances.

The other distinct type of hunt at Culiacán began when sitting falcons saw the prey at a good distance and rushed at it, attempting to gain height that would facilitate a stoop. I saw a peregrine we were trying to trap attack a small group of shorebirds on a sand flat. She left a piece of driftwood in a fast, shallow, full-power *climb*. After covering perhaps four hundred yards, she went over into a shallow full-power *dive* from a height of about a hundred feet. The shorebirds were apparently on, or very near, the sand. With the abrupt arrival of the high-speed falcon the shorebirds scattered, every man for himself. We saw similar attacks on prey birds high above the ground.

TETON CONNECTION   The first peregrine we caught at Culiacán was very significant. We first saw her, a big dark-headed adult, sitting on driftwood in easy view of the two-track trail leading to beach on the seaward side of the marsh. I threw a pigeon with a noose harness out of the speeding truck. No response. We drove off a safe distance, turned around, and roared back down the trail in the battered old white Suburban. Pete Jenny tossed up a pigeon without a harness, secured only to a long line with a weight. Sometimes the extra action of a pigeon unhampered by a leather vest is more interesting to a falcon.

Sure enough, the peregrine watched intently as the pigeon landed. Through the spotting scope we could see she was interested, bobbing her head, as falcons do, to gain a better feel for the distance. We figured she would soon attack because often she looked straight at the pigeon with both eyes at once, gazing forward over her beak, rather than with one eye at a time, as they do when interest is more casual.

While Craig Flatten and I peered through spotting scopes, Jenny readied a kind of trap I had not seen before. It consisted of a chicken-wire sleeve, flattened a bit, but big enough to hold a dead pigeon. One side of the sleeve was covered with nylon nooses and was attached to a long dragline. The scheme was to draw on the strong tendency of falcons to return to a kill when they have been forced to leave it.

All went as planned. The big blue meanie finally stood up, bobbed her head a few more times to stimulate our anxiety, muted (defecated), as falcons usually do before flight, and launched herself at the pigeon. Her flight seemed less than full power, and she stayed within a foot or two of the sand. She quickly dispatched the prey and proceeded to pluck. "We'll let her break into it," said Jenny. "Yes," I said, concurring even though the technique was new to me. Before long the plucking falcon created a steam of feathers trailing downwind across the sand. Now and then she glared directly at us.

Finally, as the suspense was becoming unbearable, Jenny climbed out of the truck, noose sleeve in hand. Out on the sand flat, there was no way to be inconspicuous. So he strolled directly toward the feeding meanie, wonderfully Ivy League in his pressed pale blue shirt, tan dockers, and white canvas deck shoes. The peregrine watched his approach. Finally, when Jenny was only fifty yards away, she lifted off, prey in her feet, and turned downwind. The dragline tightened, slowing her. In order to stay aloft, she dropped the pigeon. In the excitement, I lost sight of her.

Jenny walked quickly to the pigeon carcass, plucked a handful of feathers, and spread them on the sand. He slipped the bird in the sleeve of nooses, placed it noose side up in the middle of the feathers on the sand, and jogged back to the truck. "Let's give her some room," he said, wiping pigeon blood from his hand onto his trousers. We drove off a quarter-mile, turned broadside, and stuck a scope out the window. I focused the glass on the pigeon while Flatten and Jenny scanned for the falcon with binoculars. She had tasted pigeon, and she would likely be back for the rest.

I wondered to myself if she could find the pigeon on all that expanse of sand. What a silly notion. Peregrines can navigate precisely over the entire expanse of North America. This sand flat should be no problem. Jenny found her sitting a few hundred yards from the pigeon, staring in its direction. Ten minutes passed. She was still watching the spot. "Come on bird, you can do it," I said. The mental tension of falcon trapping is powerfully addictive.

And then she came. She landed six feet from the pigeon, walked to it, and stepped on. She was not hesitant about feeding, but the wire mesh prevented progress. She shuffled on the sleeve, looking for a part of the pigeon she could reach. One could almost sense the frustration. Then she paused, glanced at the sand a few inches to the side, and lifted a foot to step to the spot. But a closed noose held her foot. She tripped. The tripping is telltale. Experienced trappers quickly learn to recognize the subtle movement.

We shot down the trail and out on the flat as far as the soft sand would support the truck. Jenny jumped out and ran to the snared peregrine. As he arrived, she turned from her frantic flapping to face him, to make a last stand. Slowly, with the deliberate style of someone who has caught a lot of falcons, Jenny eased his fingers around her legs from below and lifted her up. Peregrines seldom struggle once held gently.

"She's banded," he exclaimed. Unbelievable. What are the odds of trapping a banded falcon on the wintering grounds so far from where anyone bands falcons? We copied down the band number, and checked it twice again to be sure there was no mistake. Flatten repeated the number aloud as I read it. Then we attached a tiny transmitter to the top of her tail and set her free.

We called Bill Heinrich in Boise. Heinrich had access to most of the recently used peregrine band numbers. He called back with startling news. This female had been one of four youngsters released early in the recovery program in Wyoming. The release site was at Death Canyon in the Teton Range near Yellowstone. I like to think she had nested in that region the spring before we caught her, and then made her way in fall down the ridges of the Rockies to the Colorado River, and onward to the Sea of Cortez and the coast of Sinaloa and the Great Culiacán Marsh.

We returned to the marsh in late fall of 1990 to put more radios on wintering peregrines. We expected never to hear from the falcons we radio-tagged once we left for home just before Christmas. We were wrong. A few score miles downstream from Eagle, Alaska, on the Yukon River is a majestic bluff on Kathul Mountain. The bluff provides the peregrines that nest there with a commanding view of the lazy meanders and vast gravel bars of the river. In July 1991, FWS employees checked Kathul to see if a pair was present. They noticed an antenna trailing the tail of the female and realized she had a transmitter. Because she was attending her young, and very defensive, the biologists read her band numbers from a distance, with binoculars. She was one of our Culiacán birds.

TEXAS FALCONS IN WINTER   In the course of the radio study of peregrines at Culiacán we learned each bird seemed to hang out in an area of a few square miles, rather than roaming all over the marsh. Further, individuals seemed to hold those places separate from other meanies, each protecting its domain. The notion that the beaches and wash flats are more than just a migration corridor began to intrigue us. We wondered if many peregrines stop in migration and stake out winter territories in these prey-laden places, calling off an extended flight southward.

Almost no information existed on falcons at the Texas beaches in winter because people watching the migration went home when the counts waned in late October. Years before I had read most of the Audubon Christmas count records for peregrines in the United States, and found a pattern of numerous sightings of blue meanies on the Gulf Coast in midwinter. These could not have been migrants, because the migration was surely over by December.

Further, back in 1975, our first work with John Smith and the little transmitters showed that not all of the falcons headed on down the coast after we released them. Some of the peregrines moved inland a short way and hung around.

A final bit of evidence supported the idea of falcons wintering on the Texas coast. Dan Slowe, the falconer from Corpus Christi, complained that in the 1960s wild peregrines often harassed his trained birds when he took them out to Padre Island to hunt ducks.

By the early 1990s, Tom Maechtle and Bill Seegar had taken up the work of counting peregrines in migration at South Padre Island. They were enthusiastic about helping with a winter search. In 1993, several students and I went to South Padre Island to see what we could find. Instantly reassuring was the presence of a big haggard (adult) peregrine on a tall hotel on the island at the end of the Port Isabel causeway.

Bill Heinrich and Brian Mutch, both practiced falcon trappers, showed up to help. We found plenty of blue meanies. Perhaps twenty or more lived on South Padre and the adjacent mainland. In the two years of the study, we followed eight falcons with radios, including two adult females. These two old birds knew the drill.

Peregrines see it like this. Once you get to Padre Island, find a quiet lagoon with a few pieces of driftwood or maybe a channel marker offering a good view. Next, chase away all other peregrines and keep them out. The rest is easy and makes for a pleasant winter until time to return north in the spring. Sit a few hours in the best snags; when hungry, flash out and score a tern, willet, or duck foolish enough to cross the tidal flats. The only real discomfort will be the odd cold front pushing down from the Great Plains, the kind of front that freezes the palm trees in Houston every few years.

Other than those two haggards, most of the falcons we tagged were less than a year old. The youngsters, called passage falcons, were spending their first winter on the sand. You could tell they were new at the game. They moved more, and they moved farther. We were compelled to climb to the top of more dunes with directional antenna and receiver to get a fix on their positions. In a way this was more fun. It meant plying the sand flats on an all-terrain vehicle with big soft tires.

Perhaps the youngsters moved more because they continually blundered into the territories of old birds and were chased away. We saw several such encounters. It seemed to us the intruders were treated pretty roughly. But they managed to save themselves by flipping over and showing their talons to the attacker. Usually the falcon being attacked shrieked in protest, perhaps a lifesaving signal of submission.

One young female seemed to be absent a lot. The signal from her radio was elusive: one day we could find it, the next we could not. By and by, we discovered the signal could often be found by pointing the directional antenna toward the open water of the Gulf. Just visible on the horizon was an oil-drilling platform, a "Texas tower." The female had taken to perching on it, coming onshore to make a run for groceries. I like to think she had found the rig a good way to avoid the drifting sands of the wash flats. Recently, Paul Dickson, a former student, spent a week in winter watching birds on a platform. Peregrines were regular boarders.

IMPATIENT VULTURE   In the course of trapping hundreds of falcons over the years, I have had great opportunities to watch how feeding peregrines respond to other birds of prey. Some are potential thieves. Most of the trapping employed pigeons wearing a leather vest covered with nylon nooses. Often the falcon was not immediately caught and undertook the business of plucking and dining.

The sprawling Laguna Atascosa Wildlife Refuge and adjacent Cullen Ranch are on the west side of the waterway separating South Padre Island from the mainland. The wash flats, named for flooding by seawater during hurricanes, have virtually no vegetation except for occasional mats of algae. The flats are sometimes a thousand yards or more across and are favorite places for peregrines to sit, the better to avoid mosquitoes.

In our study of movements of peregrines on the coast in winter, we attempted to trap every falcon we saw. I found a young female sitting on a piece of driftwood in a large flat on the Cullen Ranch. I drove at high speed toward her at an angle, in hopes she would not flush before the pigeon and its dragline were readied for release. My four-wheel ATV passed within fifty yards. The pigeon flew strongly and made for the trees at the edge of the flat a quarter of a mile away.

Predictably, the pigeon landed well short of the trees, held back by the dragline. The dark brown meanie finally decided to attack the pigeon. It easily caught the tethered bait, killed it with a bite to the base of the skull, plucked half the bird, and began to eat. Every beakful was punctuated by careful glances in all directions. Feeding peregrines are vulnerable and always remain on red alert.

Turkey vulture edges in for a meal, eventually displacing the young female peregrine feeding on a pigeon, Cullen Ranch, Texas.

I had moved off three hundred yards and was now hiding behind my ATV. I studied the falcon through the spotting scope, waiting for the first indication it had stepped into a noose and entangled a toe. As I watched, a shadow swept across the sand, passed over the falcon, and vanished out of the field in my scope. Then the shadow appeared from another direction, passed by the peregrine on its prey, and disappeared again. It was a big shadow, but the falcon showed little concern.

Soon the shadow appeared again, this time followed by its source, a turkey vulture. The scavenger landed a few yards from the meanie, which stared at it for a few moments. The peregrine soon resumed its meal, and I forgot about the big gray-black vulture. Only once have I seen peregrines pay attention to vultures, and that incident was an attack by falcons that had young in their eyrie.

The peregrine looked at the vulture again, and so did I. How odd—the big black scavenger now seemed closer to the falcon and its food. Again the peregrine glared at the vulture, and again the big bird seemed nearer. Unfolding before me was a case of vulture aggression. The bird was ever so slowly shuffling, by imperceptibly small steps, toward a meal it hoped to pirate.

Within five minutes, the vulture was standing beside the peregrine on its pigeon, the vulture's shadow darkening the falcon. Although the latter was not seemingly frightened by the nearness of the much larger bird, it was now too nervous to eat. Then, in one more shuffle, the vulture actually nudged the peregrine with its shoulder.

The poor peregrine looked up at the ugly head of the vulture, and then stepped off the pigeon. The vulture stepped onto the dead bird, and in a few moments the brown falcon flew away. It has often been said that vultures are a kind of predator that has the patience to let its prey die on its own. That vulture seemed short on patience.

I raced to the spot. A smelly vulture caught on a pigeon harness would be very undesirable. My luck held and the big bird labored into the air.

ASSATEAGUE   If North America is indeed a huge funnel for migrant peregrines pouring out of the far north each autumn, then the seaboard of Maryland, Virginia, and the Carolinas is where the funnel narrows. Blue meanies should appear in good numbers as they slide along the Atlantic Coast bound for the tropics. And so it is.

Falconers discovered the peregrine migration at Assateague, a barrier island shared by Maryland and Virginia, in the 1930s. The island soon became a mecca. Early visitors to the sandy strand included Jim Rice, Al Nye, Brian MacDonald, Heinz Meng, and Halter Cunningham, falconers all. Several hundred falcons were no doubt trapped for falconry over the following three decades.

*Scott Ward and Betty Enderson counting and banding peregrines
on Assateague Island, Virginia, 1984.*

The birds most sought were passage females because they were larger
than the males. Most of the birds trapped were given to falconers in the eastern United States, a region generally unsuited for hunting with peregrines.
The difficulties were brush, woodlots, and forests. Quarry under attack
often make good an escape into cover. Further, those northern falcons often
resumed their migrations at the first opportunity, much to the dismay of the
falconer. If the bird flew beyond nearby trees it was difficult to retrieve.

"Good morning, ma'am." Scott Ward climbed out of our jeep and walked
toward a woman sitting in a lawn chair thirty yards from the surf. Her husband, waist deep in the rollers on the Assateague coast, cast his bait far out
to a sandbar beyond. He was too far away to hear the small talk. "I see the
fishing is good." Scott gestured to a big plastic bucket with an assortment of
pretty nice fish.

Scott changed the subject, but I knew he would return to the fish. "My
name is Dr. Ward, and we are here doing research on peregrine falcons." Her

expression revealed she had no idea what he was talking about. But she was impressed and watched him intently, barely noticing me as I peered into the fish bucket. Scott, who reminds one of a handsome Ernie Kovacs, has a wonderful charm that people find irresistible. The talk went on, touching lightly on where these birds nested, where they were going, why people band them, and how poorly they had fared because of pesticides. It was the usual stuff.

"Those fish are sure impressive," he said, returning to the topic of fish. "I don't suppose you might have one or two more than you need." She looked at the bucket and then smiled warmly at Scott. I could tell right then how this was going to go. "We surely do," she said, "Y'all just help yourself." Out in the surf, the poor fellow who caught the fish watched helplessly as Scott lifted up a couple of nice redfish and thanked the lady for her kindness. Scott climbed into the jeep, throwing the fish into the bucket he had brought for this predictable contingency. By day's end the bucket held enough fish to feed the whole lot of us falcon trappers camped at the old Coast Guard Station. And all the way back along the coast to Ocean City the beach was littered with disgruntled fishermen whose wives gave away their best fish.

COUNTS OF MIGRANT MEANIES   Ward and Bill Seegar saw the potential for banding large numbers of peregrines at Assateague to find out where they go. Maybe they could even detect an upward trend in counts, now that DDT had been outlawed. With the help of Bob Berry and Lou Woyce, they standardized counts of blue meanies on the island from 1970 onward. In the 1980s Mike Yates took a central role in the fieldwork, similar to that of his counterpart, Tom Maechtle, on South Padre Island.

It is no trick at all to drive down the beach at Assateague or Padre Island in early October and count lots of peregrines. At the end of your effort you can produce a nice hard number. You might say, for example, "I saw sixteen juvenile females today." But a total count of falcons seen in a day, or a week, or even the entire fall means little by itself. So you resolve to *repeat* the count over more days, or, better, throughout the same period in several years.

But here's the rub. Duplicate counts are nearly impossible. Lots of things inevitably change, and you can't tell if the change is for better or for worse. For example, one day the wind is light, the next it blows hard. You see fewer meanies the second day; is it because there are actually fewer, or because they seek shelter in the lee of the dunes, where they are hidden?

Further, in no two years is the weather the same north of Assateague in October. The cold fronts and the winds that seem to cause the falcons to fly near the coastline are inevitably different year to year. For these reasons, people who count migrant meanies on the sand must count as much as they can, day after day, week after week, and year after year. Only with lots of counts do the vagaries begin to cancel out and the real patterns emerge.

The folks have done pretty well at Assateague over the years. Serious counts started there in 1970. Of course the observers weren't just counting; they were trying to trap and band every bird they saw. That remained a goal over all those years. By 1994, after the field-workers had driven the beach and wash flats in twenty-five migrations, we could put some confidence in what they report. Don't confuse confidence and precision. No one claims the counts they obtained precisely disclosed the actual numbers of peregrines that flew down the Assateague beaches each year. Most of us feel that the counts were really samples that generally revealed population trends.

The number of migrating meanies counted on the beaches over the last two decades increased about threefold, comparing the early years with the last few. It is tempting to attribute the higher counts to an actual increase in per-egrines in the far north, owing perhaps to the reduced use of DDT. But biologists must be skeptical by nature. There is no place for conclusion-jumping if we are really to understand.

Fortunately, others were counting migrant falcons in other places. Dan Berger and Helmut Mueller counted on the western shore of Lake Michigan. Also, many kinds of hawks and falcons were counted over the years at Hawk Mountain in Pennsylvania. The numbers from those places were also up about threefold.

What's more, surveyors of nesting falcons here and there in the far north claim the number of breeding pairs has increased. For example, Gordon Court found nesting peregrines increased from about ten to about thirty pairs between 1980 and 1994 far north on Hudson Bay at Rankin Inlet, Northwest Territories.

HOW MANY NORTHERN FALCONS? Something in human nature drives us to count. How many are there of this or that? Bean counters are everywhere. National censuses of humans are institutionalized in many countries, but apparently accuracy even for our own species is not always good. Our concern is the total number of pairs of peregrines now breeding each year at high latitudes in North America.

A very rough estimate is possible because Yates and Maechtle and their helpers counted peregrines in migration. In 1993 Yates's people saw about 175 first-year *female* meanies on Assateague, and the Maechtle people on Padre Island, Texas, saw about 1,200; call it 1,400 in all. Maybe a few of the Yates birds flew by the Maechtle folks and were counted twice. The opposite is not likely, for the birds would have needed to backtrack (it is also likely both teams counted at least a few falcons twice).

If 1,400 new young females were seen in 1993, then there were probably at least 1,400 new young *males* migrating also, because males and females are fledged in the north in equal numbers. The males and females add up to 2,800 peregrines hatched in 1993.

Now, you ask, how many pairs of adults in 1993 produced those 2,800 young? Well, if each pair produced only one young, on average, then 2,800 adult pairs would have been needed to get the job done. Northern peregrines actually do better than one fledged youngster on average, but perhaps an average of one per pair survives long enough to be counted in the fall.

But now, you wonder, did Yates and Macchtle actually count all the migrating young females? Surely not. If twice as many migrated down North America as they actually saw and counted, then our estimate of the northern adult pairs would have to be doubled. If only one in three were seen, the estimate would need to be tripled, amounting to 8,400 pairs. What proportion did they actually see? There is no easy way to know. Future peregrine biologists may someday be able to judge by tracking migrants with radios to find out just how likely it is that a migrating falcon will be seen on the beaches. In the meantime, we can rest assured there are lots of peregrines in the north each summer. But of course the people who study nesting peregrines up there have already told us that.

This brings us to a major mystery concerning the passage of thousands of arctic peregrines southward each fall. Where are all the adult males? In order of abundance, the sexes and age groups show up in this order: juvenile females (most common), adult and yearling females, juvenile males, and adult males. This last type is seldom seen, and only a few are banded each year on Assateague and Padre islands. Adult males, which must be about as numerous as adult females, simply do not migrate much along the coasts.

My field notes for October 1964, when Clay White and I first counted peregrines on Padre and Matagorda, show that we saw forty-nine peregrines in all. Only one was an adult male and seventeen were adult females. The rest were immature birds, mostly females.

Either adult males use the coasts, but just don't often come down so they can be seen, or they pay no heed to land or ocean at all. Perhaps they are such effective hunters by the time they reach adulthood that food can be caught anywhere without the advantage of the open flats or beaches seemingly required by females and young males. I like that idea. If true, it helps to define the role of adult males as super-hunters. In spring and summer, when they alone provide for their mates and up to four hungry young, adult males are indeed killers par excellence. At other times of the year, the sky almost everywhere has enough small birds to supply wandering adult males.

SUMMARY   No other falcon or hawk routinely mounts an annual southward migration over such great distances compared to the northern peregrine. It is in this performance that peregrines fully earn the German name for their species, *Wanderfalke*. In the late summer they leave the Arctic and subarctic wilderness in North America and Eurasia, fly southward at the rate of a few hundred miles a day, and find a place where the living is easy in regions totally unlike those of the breeding grounds.

One might be tempted to equate the treeless tundra and braided gravel bars of northern rivers on the breeding grounds with the beaches and sand flats of Padre Island, and conclude the birds seek similar environments, summer and winter. This comparison is difficult. The bluffs north of Thule, Greenland, overlooking the fickle ice pack of Baffin Strait, do not match the view from a high-rise building in Rio de Janeiro. The meeting place of big rivers, the Forty Mile and the Yukon, is unlike the wintering haunts in the Everglades. And how can one compare the sea cliffs east of Nome, Alaska, with the Culiacán Marsh? Peregrines are superb habitat generalists. Wherever prey can be found and caught in the open, blue meanies thrive.

Best of all, the migration brings these birds to us. In their fall and spring migrations, and in winter, they are accessible for study or bird-watching. Further, their appearance on the beaches is a powerful presence, enough so as to cause a permanent following of bird people who thrill at the sight. Finally, the falcon's spectacular attraction to beaches, wash flats, and marshes in winter reminds us to permanently conserve these relatively scarce environments.

IX » EARLY FALCONRY IN NORTH AMERICA

Falconry was conceived more than three millennia ago in Eurasia. An ancient manuscript from the third century B.C. leaves little doubt that the Hittites, in what is now Turkey, hunted with raptors. The practice had surely spread to India, Persia, eastern Asia, and North Africa by the Middle Ages, and not much later to Europe. By the seventeenth century, hunting with trained birds of prey was a major pastime in Europe, predating widespread use of firearms. Although a few early colonists in the 1600s were falconers, the practice did not reach North America in significant measure until the fourth decade of the twentieth century.

The art of falconry failed to gain a toehold in North America until just before World War II. Perhaps the advent of firearms worked against its popularity everywhere. Even more surprising is that falconry (hawking) never really flourished in Australia and is actually illegal there. Only in the last few decades did it catch on to any extent in Africa south of the Sahara, and in South America.

The delay in the arrival of falconry in North America from Europe owes to several factors. There were excellent falconers in Britain before 1850, often among the aristocracy. One can guess they were not attracted to the rough frontier that was America. Further, the frontier placed great demands on its people. Little free time was available; merely surviving was task enough. What is more, the dispersal of hawking was hindered because different parts of the world often require different kinds of hawking. Finally, literature on falconry was surely limited to a few large libraries.

FALCONRY: THE ART   A major problem with falconry is that it is difficult to become proficient before one feels like giving up. This is especially true when help is not at hand. Falconry is not especially demanding, but it has its subtle intricacies. A successful falconer, if he or she is to hunt with a wild raptor, must see to it that several fairly simple conditions fall in place at the right times. The bird must fly to the falconer's lure or respond to a call for a food reward. The bird must be hungry, but not too hungry; otherwise, the raptor might be weakened. And the type of falcon or hawk must be suited to the landscape as well as to the quarry.

Dutch and Indian falcon hoods, swivel used to connect leash and jesses, and bells. Both hoods are modified from the historical types.

The aspiring falconer must see to the routine care and keeping of his or her charge. For the beginner, the temptation is to reinvent the wheel, to ignore the experiences of others. Basic equipment such as food, housing, perches, hoods, leashes, and jesses (leg straps) have been tested in a long, uncertain evolution. Nevertheless, unworkable versions of these necessities seem to reappear. For example, very few of the several kinds of perches, to which the raptor is tethered, are truly safe. The others portend ill for the falcon. The bird may become entangled, or hang, with disastrous consequences.

FALCONRY MENTORS   The essence of falconry is technique, not equipment. In the fall of 1962 I tried repeatedly to encourage Lil, the peregrine from Wyoming, to catch ducks. Peregrines are famous for their great fondness for ducks; hence their old name, duck hawk.

Lil was not interested in waterfowl. Bob Dandrea, a practiced Colorado Springs falconer, took an interest in my problem. He verified her weight and agreed she was indeed hungry. But evening after evening, we hooded her (to keep her calm), placed her on the backseat of the car, and drove the twenty miles to the duck ponds. On arrival, I removed her hood and set her free. When she flew in full view of the pond, we flushed the ducks. My big fierce blue meanie ignored them.

My frustration grew. How could I call myself a falconer if my falcon never caught anything wild? I would be regarded as a mere pet keeper. True falconers held in disdain people who kept falcons as pets. What would Beebe and Hunter think of me?

Then one evening Dandrea saw the problem. "Lil is carsick," he muttered. "Let's take her out tomorrow evening without her hood." Off we went, Lil tethered to the backseat of the station wagon, watching the passing countryside intently. Once at the pond, she left my glove. When she came around upwind of the ducks, a mere fifty feet from the ground, we flushed them.

Lil was transformed. She doubled her wingbeat, streaked for the flock, overtook the rear duck, and dragged it from the sky. Then and there, I became a falconer. Today, forty years later, I can take you to the very spot on the grassland where duck and meanie came to earth.

Lil and Black Shane from the Charlotte Islands became proficient at catching ducks. Their success was partly due to careful advice I received from Ken Riddle, an enlisted airman at the Air Force Academy. He was assigned to the veterinary clinic as a technician, cleaning cages.

Riddle was a master at setting ducks to flight from big ponds. When it was time for the ducks to go, Riddle would come up over the dike and crack his long bullwhip. The snapper on the tip would then exceed the speed of sound. A mini sonic boom resulted. The report resembled gunfire.

Riddle had not finished high school at the time. The big blue falcons profoundly marked him. They changed his life. As soon as possible he left the Air Force and finished high school, and eventually veterinary school. For many years he directed a large hospital in the Middle East that cared for hundreds of Arab falcons.

Obviously, a would-be falconer should find a successful falconer and become his journeyman. "Monkey see, monkey do" may seem demeaning, but it is the best way to win when giving up seems the only option. There are two other requisites for the neophyte. The first is free time. An hour or two a day must be arranged on a more or less steady basis, depending on the season and intended quarry. Unlike most other kinds of hunting, the falcon cannot be put on the shelf between seasons, but must be cared for all year. Another critical component is attitude. You must have empathy for your bird besides simple admiration. Last, falconers must be pragmatic, willing to discard what seems not to work, and eager to seek a better way. These things come easiest to people who are careful observers.

HOW FALCONRY WORKS   Birds in general, including hawks and falcons, emerge from the egg with an internal behavior program. This set of stereotyped responses is inherent to the species; it is action "written on genes." Certain things a bird sees or hears trigger particular responses. Every species has a different program. Every program has a part that allows for a bit of learning.

Brand new brown meanies instinctively pursue; they really can't help themselves. In what appears to us as a sky-wide game of tag between wild siblings newly on the wing, youngsters actually hone the business of aerial encounter. This skill is needed if they are to avoid starvation or being eaten.

Let's return to the falconer, new brown falcon on the glove. Whether his bird is a youngster, which only yesterday finished growing its first set of feathers and can barely fly, or a bird trapped in the fall in its first migration, the task is to make use of what the bird knows inherently, and to modify what it may have already learned.

Peregrines are usually tractable and have no built-in behaviors that work against the falconer (female Peale's falcons are ornery by reputation). In the best of worlds, a peregrine would make an ideal bird for the beginner. This assumes a willing mentor who carefully guides the training of both falconer and falcon. A male falcon (often called a tiercel) might be the better choice because his eagerness is a match for the zeal of the student.

The following is not a guide to falconry, but simply a thumbnail sketch of what must be done when one trains a falcon. Hawks are a bit different but require similar techniques. Anyone interested in falconry must find a competent falconer for guidance. It is important to study a few of the better books, and then remember to test what the monkey sees.

Obtain a good hood made to fit the sex and species of falcon. The most popular are those fashioned after historical Dutch hoods, with braces (straps) that close the back and secure it to the falcon. A welcome modification was a wide opening for the beak so that it can protrude fully. Too big a hood is better than too small. There are little tricks to make hoods fit. The beak opening can be made comfortable by wetting the edges and rolling them outward so they do not press on the sensitive tissue at the base of the beak.

The open hood is placed on the falcon's head with a deliberate, steady movement lasting a second or two. Once the motion begins it is best to persist, or the falcon will teach *you* to hesitate. On the other hand, do not be too quick. If the falcon avoids the hood, more speed on your part will not help. When the hood is on the falcon, draw the braces only partway at first, so the bird becomes familiar with the weight and feel of the hood. In the moments after the falcon accepts the hood, remove it, and then replace it in a sort of drill. Each time the braces may be drawn a bit farther. This procedure gives the handler an opportunity to judge the fit progressively. Most peregrines are easy to hood if the hood fits, and seldom are bothered by it except to scratch once in a while with a talon.

The falcon is taught to step to the fist for a tidbit of food in the same manner that a dog is trained to come to a whistle. The hungry bird, whose total weight should be down about 10 percent from what it was when fat, is encouraged to step, then jump to the glove. In trial after trial indoors, the distance is increased. Move outdoors with a longer line, anticipating more distractions. Weight control is everything in this. Be sure the bird does not gain weight undetected. Conversely, no falconer can win with a starving bird. Weigh the falcon daily so as to prevent too much weight loss.

The falcon must know what to catch. If ducks are to be hunted, the new bird is fed from a lure to which a few dry duck wings are tied, along with half of the day's ration of food. The body of the lure is a leather pillow, sized to match the biggest duck to be sought.

Each day, increase the distance the falcon must come to the lure. In just a few days you should require the falcon to fly up to a hanging lure, rather than allowing the bird to land on it. Initially, stick to two trials each day so that each involves a good amount of food as a reward. As soon as the falcon attacks instantly at the sight of the lure, over a distance of a couple of hundred feet or more, it can be flown free. You now have a means of recovery. I use the lure for recovery only. Whenever a lure is produced from the lure bag and swung around on its eight-foot line, the falcon should come to it and be allowed to feed. However great the distance, the lure means food. The falcon has learned the lure is a reward, no matter what.

Review your progress to this point. The falcon can now be easily hooded. It jumps to the glove expecting to be fed. It flies to you at the sight of the swinging lure. The lure looks like a duck. The peregrine is ready to hunt. Sometimes it is good to let the falcon eat part of a dead duck, just to reinforce the idea. Some falcons catch on because of the duck wings on the lure. In all, a fresh falcon can usually be trained for release in two or three weeks.

Go to a small pond, in the open, where only a few medium-sized ducks dabble about. Teal often refuse to leave the safety of a pond with a falcon overhead. And they are exceedingly shifty, avoiding the rush of the falcon at the last moment. Mallards are too big and strong (for now). Cast off the falcon; wait until it circles a time or two, looking for the lure. When it has gained a bit of altitude and is facing the pond, show yourself to the ducks. Ensure that they flush.

This first attempt may fail because the falcon got a late start or was not in a good position. Or you failed to ensure a flush. Get it right. If no duck is caught, retrieve the falcon with the lure before it is too tired to fly. Reward its return to you with food. Then try again the next day, and the next. With each flight the bird gains stamina, and each day the playing field becomes more level.

There are, of course, pitfalls in training a peregrine. The more serious involve food. Never take food from a falcon, or do anything resembling food theft. For example, if a hungry bird on your glove has trouble swallowing a piece of food, resist the temptation to reach up and help; the bird might see that as attempted theft. Let the falcon swallow the piece, or cast it out.

Another problem with food is that the falcon might hit and run. Be sure to prevent the meanie from grabbing all the food on the lure or at the glove. If the bird manages to free the food and hold it in its foot, it may bolt away and learn that such tactics are rewarding. The falconer must anticipate the potential lessons, for better or worse, that he might unwittingly teach the trainee.

It is a mistake to fly a falcon free without attaching a small radio transmitter. Know *beforehand* how to use the receiver to find a distant transmitter. At stake is the future of the bird and your success. If the bird is lost, it will be necessary to begin all over again. The telemetry equipment must be tested each day it is taken into the field.

FALCONRY BEGINNINGS IN NORTH AMERICA   In 1920 there appeared in the *National Geographic* a forty-page article by the famous bird artist and naturalist, Louis Agassiz Fuertes, titled "Falconry, the Sport of Kings." It was the first account of falconry widely available in North America. The article described falcons, hawks, equipment, and methods of falconry, and included scores of graphic paintings and photographs. It seemed enough to ignite a passion for falconry in the heart of many a youth. Apparently it did not.

The 1920s were a kind of falconry vacuum, aside from a small group of interested folks that did gather briefly in the middle of the decade on Long Island. Finally, in 1936, a group called the Peregrine Club was formed in Philadelphia under the leadership of Bob Stabler. Its members were involved, at least, in banding local nestling falcons. My records show that Stabler kept a peregrine named Tommy in 1935. The club was remarkable in that blue meanies were its main interest.

In the mid-1930s, the old Fuertes article inspired Frank and John Craighead of Washington, D.C. They acquired several birds of prey, read all they could, took hundreds of remarkable photos, and, in 1937, published "Adventures with Birds of Prey" in the *Geographic*. The seeds of falconry on this continent had been sown. Morgan Berthrong, who now lives near me, was one of the few in the Craighead group to persist in falconry.

The following year, 1938, the Peregrine Club hosted the first falconry meet for regional aficionados in the country near Philadelphia. It was there that the concept of a national organization was discussed. The Falconers' Association of North America was soon formed. Stabler edited FANA's first journal, the *American Falconer*, in 1942. Unfortunately, only a few issues went to press.

At about the same time, a reporter for the *Brooklyn Eagle* by the name of Ed Reid organized a small group of raptor buffs and held a falconry meet in 1941. The group was known as the American Falconer's Association. At least one journal was printed, in 1941. The war effort would then interrupt falconry for several years.

The author's tiercel peregrine Spike with transmitter, ready for the hunt.

In the meantime, the Craigheads enjoyed the opportunity of their lives. They spent five months in India, the guests of an Indian prince who was an ardent falconer. His Majesty had seen the 1937 *National Geographic* "Birds of Prey" article. When the twins returned, they wrote of their experiences with falconry in India, again in the *Geographic*, in 1942. In 2001, the Archives of American Falconry, Boise, Idaho, published the full, richly illustrated record of their experiences. The treatise is of historic merit because it describes an Indian royalty that no longer exists.

The old Fuertes article of 1920 became an important stimulus for would-be falconers two decades later. The peregrine falcon was the centerpiece of the article. Illustrations of that falcon appear four times as often as those of the goshawk, Fuertes's second favorite raptor. Little wonder the peregrine became the icon of falconry in its beginnings on the continent.

In 1938, a phenomenal new source of peregrines was discovered. Bill Turner learned from his father that birds like those taken from local eyries could be found on the beach at Assateague Island, Virginia, in the fall. Turner's father produced a pair of peregrine feet to prove it. As it turned out, his hunting cronies found falcon shooting adequately challenging when the ducks weren't flying.

Al Nye, a friend of Turner's, trapped several of these pale-colored migrating falcons from the far north. My friend Halter Cunningham soon helped Nye discover ways to trap blue meanies. Perhaps a few dozen passage peregrines (immature birds in their first southward migration) were sent to falconers across the continent in the next five years. Early falconers could hardly have realized these migrants were but the tip of the iceberg that was the vast arctic and subarctic population in North America.

News of the Assateague bonanza was kept as quiet as possible. In 1942 Joe Hickey completed his benchmark study of the duck hawk in the eastern United States, published in the *Auk*. Soon afterward, he reflected on the study in the *American Falconer* and suggested the reason so few northern peregrines were seen was that they stayed out to sea or flew very high. How odd that he had not yet understood the magnitude of the Assateague migration. Surely falconers knew of the migration by that time. How could birds have been shipped off to falconers without their wondering where they came from? The secret was no better kept than that of gold at Sutter's Mill.

It would be another five years or so before Luff Meredith, stationed just after the war in Harlingen, Texas, would discover for falconers the Padre Island phenomenon. It was a falcon migration exceeding that at Assateague. In the 1950s, migration concentrations at Duluth, Minnesota, and on the western shore of Lake Michigan became popular. Migrant juvenile peregrines from the Far North were now available to those who knew the trappers, or had the time and skills to trap their own. Despite these discoveries, I doubt if more than a hundred or so northern peregrines were caught and kept in any year in that decade.

THE DUCK HAWK MEN   By the time World War II was over in 1945, both nestling and passage peregrines had become broadly available. It is safe to say that anyone who had established himself with the core of falconers in the eastern states could obtain a duck hawk. Nestlings may have been harder to get because eyrie raiding was pretty intense at the better-known cliffs.

The eyrie at Harper's Ferry, the village that was attacked just before the Civil War by John Brown, was especially popular. Further, egg collectors still prized sets of the big mottled mahogany-colored eggs. The easy supply of blue meanies might have set the stage for first-rate falconry, but it did not.

Falconry with peregrines in North America floundered in the postwar era. Plenty of duck hawks were collected from cliffs in Pennsylvania, New York, and Vermont, or caught on the strands of coastal sand in the fall. Very few ever caught wild quarry at the hands of their masters.

The difficulties were threefold. First, people who had access to nestlings or migrant peregrines in the eastern states faced the problem of catching game in forested regions where falcons were at a great disadvantage. Cover for quarry was never far away. Captive pigeons were often substituted for wild game. Unfortunately, pigeons had a bewildering tendency to out-fly the falcons, leading them miles over the forests. Neither pigeon nor falcon might be seen again. Second, falconers who trapped passage peregrines faced an additional problem. Passage falcons had an annoying tendency to continue migrating when they were flown free. Either way, the peregrine man either lost his bird or ended up with one he could not hope to fly properly at game in the open. Finally, there were few mentors. Early falconry in North America was mainly self-taught.

GETTING IT RIGHT   Among the earliest North American falconers to systematically use duck hawks to catch wild game was Al Nye. His unorthodox technique in the late 1930s was to put the falcon in the sky, then to run through the fields, hoping for some unseen bird to flush to its doom. Nye was a runner, both in the fields and on the football gridiron at Penn.

Other falconers with peregrines began to get it right. After the war, Morley Nelson settled in Boise. His skill on skis with the Tenth Mountain Division in Italy landed him a job measuring alpine snow depth for the Soil Conservation Service. Nelson obtained a female duck hawk named Blackie that made a strong impression on ducks on the numerous ponds around Boise. Nowhere else on the continent did ducks hear, day after day, the harmonic sound of the lightweight bells placed on falcons to help the falconer keep track of his hunter.

Kent Carnie, curator of the magnificent collection of falconry books and memorabilia at the World Center for Birds of Prey in Boise, told me the story of how Nelson acquired Blackie. Boy Scouts held a camporee on the Appalachian Trail. They discovered a peregrine eyrie, accessible without rope, at a place called Rip Rap. Of course scouts are nothing if not resourceful; they ate two of the three nestlings. The third was taken as a pet but soon proved too much of a chore for the Scout. Eventually the bird was given to a falconer by the name of Fox, who shipped it to Nelson in Boise.

Blackie was imprinted on humans because of her early upbringing. In that way she became the first blue meanie to lay eggs in captivity in North America. Not only did she lay eggs under her perch, thinking Nelson was her mate, but she reared downy prairie falcon chicks supplied by Nelson.

About 1940, a pigeon racer named Pete Asborno, of Denver, met Bill Russell, who had spent several years in England with C. W. R. Knight, known for his public lectures on eagles. Knight's golden eagle, Mr. Ramshaw, was often released in an auditorium to fly over the heads of thrilled spectators. Dr. Russell had learned the rudiments of falconry during his several years in Britain with Knight, and wrote a handbook on falconry, one of the earliest published in the United States.

Under Russell's guidance, Asborno flew prairie falcons for several years, learning the skills needed to catch ducks. In the early 1950s, Fred Cassler, a World War II P-38 pilot from Oklahoma, learned of the Padre Island peregrines and sent several to Asborno over the years. By 1954, Asborno hawked daily, and surely was one of the few very early falconers to systematically catch large numbers of quarry with peregrines in North America.

Asborno was a master machinist. He designed machines that made machines. His legacy in falconry was the invention, about 1960, of modern falcon bells. Unlike inferior handmade bells available from Pakistan and other places in the Middle East, Asborno bells were assembled from two swagged cups, one overlapping the other. The most durable alloys were used to withstand wear and tear and the constant hits by the striker inside. A falcon wearing a pair of tuned Asborno bells produced a wonderful resonating sound as it flew overhead. Asborno was also a falconry mentor. Another veteran of World War II, Larry Zuk, had been stationed in San Diego. Zuk moved to Denver after the war and fell in with Asborno. He followed his teacher deep into gamehawking with beach peregrines from Cassler.

Between 1946 and 1960, perhaps forty falconers in North America had kept a peregrine. Only a handful had the opportunity, or the vision, to develop their falconry to the level seen in nineteenth-century Europe. Otherwise, wild quarry was rarely caught. In a single season in Europe the old falconers were able to catch scores of ducks and grouse with a single falcon. Gamehawking was yet to evolve on this side of the Atlantic.

In 1955 or 1956, a musician and schoolteacher named Bob Klimes formed the Southern California Falconers Association. Other members of the group included Tom Cade and Yvon Chouinard. The latter eventually founded a company once famous for fine rock-climbing gear, which is now known as the Patagonia Sportswear Company. Klimes obtained a local nestling duck hawk, named Masai, and for a few years systematically hunted crows, doves, and a variety of other birds. He was surely a peregrine pioneer.

Early in the spring of 1962 Dan Cover showed up at my house in Laramie. Cover had brought along two peregrines from his home in southern Missouri. Both were wild-trapped birds in adult plumage; the male was the only meanie I have ever seen that was not handsome. His name was Ugly George. His head was angular, rather than smoothly rounded, and his eyes seemed ill-fitted to the front of his skull.

The female, trapped in North Africa, was remarkable. She was huge, noticeably bigger than a prairie falcon. We found a flock of sage grouse near Bosler, Wyoming. I watched dumbfounded as the big falcon chased down a grouse in a flight covering a half-mile. Only good work with binoculars prevented her loss. By the time we hiked to the spot, Rouge had scattered grouse feathers through the sagebrush and was busy filling her crop. That sage grouse may well have been the first of its kind caught by any falconer. It was certainly the first quarry I had seen taken by a trained raptor.

I was hooked. We flew Rouge at a pond with ducks, but she went for an avocet, a large shorebird, and was left in a stall as the intended quarry climbed like a rocket. Late in the day, Ugly George stooped vertically to the ground, hitting a horned lark just in time to avoid a collision with the prairie surface. Cover had been flying these falcons since 1959.

Cover and Erich Awender later hunted smaller grouse in Saskatchewan with Tom Ennenga. Sometimes Bob Widmeier, a Minnesota falconer who trapped peregrines near Lake Superior in the fall, joined them. But Cover's real claim to fame was to be quail and dove hawking in Missouri. He used two male peregrines, flown together (as a "cast"). It is a chore to keep track of one bird at a time, let alone two. Two are a handful. Further, Cover hunted in cleared areas near woodlands on his farm. He managed the vegetation, cutting back the weedy forest and planting seed-bearing ground cover for dove and quail food. Tiger and Speedy together sometimes caught two or three birds in a single flight. No one else, before or since, has achieved Cover's mastery of a blue meanie team.

Recently, in a magnificent act of generosity, Cover and his wife, Maureen, gave his huge farm to the people of Missouri as a prairie conservation area. Etched in a granite monument overlooking the flying field are these words: "Look high in the sky, no they are gone now, Tiger and Speedy, they gave me their best repeatedly, no falconer can ask for more."

Two other falconers reached the status of "gamehawker" with peregrines in the late 1950s. Bob McCallum began with a male California duck hawk. He commonly hunted the ponds in central California and quickly set the stage for things to come. McCallum still flies peregrines over the same ponds he knew in 1958. This is very unusual. Most of the early peregrine people have passed away, given up falconry, or moved to other kinds of birds of prey. The other falconer, Bob Winslow, often flew peregrines with McCallum but was also proficient with goshawks.

THE SECOND GENERATION   The peregrine people, and falconers using other raptors, were widely scattered and in poor communication in the late 1950s. "Monkey see, monkey do" was not possible for many of those who kept birds of prey. Most could go no further than just plain pet keeping. What was worse, the supply of duck hawks in temperate North America had dried up. DDT was on the ground. The supply of passage birds from the beaches continued to the end of the 1960s, but seldom did people keep from losing them.

Despite the few success stories from earlier years, most falconers simply could not see how to proceed from falcon caretaking to serious gamehawking. About 1960, Bill Shinners, who worked for the Nevada Gaming Commission, and Jim Weaver of Rockford, Illinois, learned to catch ducks and pheasants with peregrines. Weaver first flew a falcon he took from a nest on the Canadian tundra. He would eventually be prominent in the national restoration of blue meanies and would persist in falconry. Both Shinners and Weaver were mainly self-taught.

In 1961, Ken Riddle lived in Texas. So did Dan Slowe, a falconer and peregrine trapper on Padre Island. They mastered duck hawking. Other names come to mind from about that time, including Dennis Grisco of California, and, somewhat later, Madison Haley of New Mexico. Both were catching ducks with great regularity.

Haley lived in Roswell, New Mexico. Just of age in the early 1970s, he earned his keep as a bartender at the Roswell Country Club. His uniform was a formal jacket, bow tie, and cummerbund. The scores of tiny irrigation reservoirs that dot the otherwise dry landscape at Roswell were just right for winter duck hawking. At lunchtime, Haley, in formal attire, would run to his car and waiting peregrine, race to the ponds, and fly the falcon with such efficiency that he was seldom overdue at the bar. More than once, waitresses at the Country Club wondered about the blood on his hands and the duck feathers in his hair. Literally hundreds of ducks saw Haley's tundra falcon. He is a strong contender for the gold medal rewarding grand-scale early duck hawking in North America.

Bob Martin and Mike Arnold were serious hawkers by 1964, and Martin remained in falconry for many years. He worked several summers on peregrines in Greenland. Martin is a great chap, largely because of his warmth and sense of humor. His renditions of John Wayne are better than the Duke himself.

In Washington state in the early 1960s, a fellow by the name of Richard Fitzsimmons was a friend of Les Boyd's who had a prairie falcon at the time. Fitzsimmons visited Frank Beebe in British Columbia. Beebe, fresh from the Queen Charlotte Islands, had more blue meanies than he required, and gave Fitzsimmons a female. She was to catch many pheasants in the rich farmlands of western Washington.

In the mid-1960s, Mike Brewer of Oklahoma, a protégé of Cassler and Riddle, caught many ducks with blue meanies. Tom Smylie, one of my oldest falconer cronies, began important hawking with peregrines at that time. Eventually, he was to refine crow hawking in New Mexico, to the extent the wily crow allows.

At about the same time, the preeminent duck hawker, Mike Connolly, now a retired construction contractor, caught ducks daily in southern California with a peregrine called Witch. The story of his falconry career with blue meanies and ducks is written in an outstanding chapter in *Gamehawking*, published by Harold Webster. The beauty of the account is that Connolly not only understood the falcon he flew, but was a student of the many types of ducks he sought. Pintails were held in great esteem because of their intelligence, often letting other ducks flush first to draw off the overhead falcon before making their exodus from the pond. Connolly called the fish-eating mergansers "alligators with wings," to be left alone for the sake of falcon and falconer. Urban sprawl in the San Diego area eventually put an end to his hawking.

In 1963 I met Bob Berry at a gathering of falconers at Don Hunter's farm in South Dakota (the first meet had been held the preceding year in Reno). Berry was from Pennsylvania and faced the same problem of too much cover that had deterred so many of the early folks with duck hawks. Despite the problem, Berry used dogs to mark down the hidden pheasants so that they could be flushed when the falcon was high overhead. By 1966 his method yielded clear success. He had actually succeeded in country where many had given up.

THE MEETS   In 1943 the old Falconers' Association of North America disappeared. Its demise related to a waning interest in the sport caused by the war effort. Further, Bob Stabler alone managed the organization, and the membership was small and select. These conditions were not conducive to club survival in troubled times.

A new organization, the Falconry Club of America, was formed in 1953. Its members published a newsletter, *Falconry News and Notes*, that October.

Luff Meredith and Stabler also led the new FCA. Unfortunately, the group was mainly inactive after 1958, and published its last newsletter in 1961. The old gentleman, Meredith, was in poor health at that time and passed away in 1965. He was buried at West Point Military Academy with his peregrine tiercel.

In 1961, the North American Falconers Association (NAFA) was formed at a conclave outside of Denver. Perhaps because of little previous opportunity for people interested in raptors to get together for several years, there was great enthusiasm. NAFA still thrives. Its longevity is due in part to bylaws that distribute the elected leadership over the country. And from the beginning, members got their money's worth, including an annual journal and a quarterly newsletter.

In the next few years, national NAFA meets were held in the fall in Nevada, South Dakota, Illinois, and Colorado. Foreign guests were invited, and falconers traveled from the corners of the country and from Canada. They brought their birds and exchanged tall tales and new ideas too. The effect was catalytic. The attendance increased to a few hundred, and the hawks and falcons were set out on so many perches that huge fenced yards were needed.

The first NAFA meet, held in Reno, Nevada, in the fall of 1962, was momentous. A new level of falconry was then to be seen. The people who raised the bar were young and talented. Louis Davis showed up from California with a female peregrine that he had caught pheasants with the previous year. Word got around that Davis had a wonderful gamehawk. When he drove off to fly her, a parade of cars followed. Presently a covey of quail ran across the road. Davis stopped and put up his peregrine; when she had good height, he flushed the quarry, followed by a crowd of onlookers flowing into the field. The meanie hit two quail. One was picked up; the falcon held the other. Suddenly Davis's dog Golf went on point. The peregrine was off again. She went too high, but Davis waited, walking way off and then returning. When the bird had the right height overhead, the quail was flushed and caught. The crowd of would-be falconers had seen three quail taken in a single flight. Many of us then knew what was possible and what we might expect to achieve.

At Reno, I shared a bedroom with Tom Smylie at the home of Bill Shinners. Our bedroom was separated from another by only a drape. Smylie and I retired in the wee hours after a night on the town. To our disgust, we were soon awakened. The drape flew open and there stood a tall, slender character with uncombed hair. In a slow Texas drawl the young man said, "Well, let's go hawkin'." Grainger Hunt, who eventually earned a Ph.D. in genetics at the University of Texas, has been my close friend ever since. At the time of the Reno meet, Hunt was very successful as a singer with his small rock-and-roll band. Concurrently, he achieved near perfection with a peregrine over the duck ponds of west Texas.

The formation of NAFA erased a major impediment to the establishment of really good gamehawking on the continent. Formerly, a novice could mature in the sport only by the great good fortune of living near a mentor in the art. The early falconry clubs simply had not catalyzed the thinly spread interest. NAFA led to wide communication. Hundreds attended the annual meets, always held the week before Thanksgiving. The gatherings created experiences worth a dozen books. Falconry was on the verge of transformation. Unfortunately, the peregrine could not be a part of it until the great decline of its population, under way at the time, was reversed. Falconry is now a legal form of hunting in all states except Hawaii, and in several Canadian provinces.

PERSPECTIVES   It is difficult to understate the meager beginnings of the Sport of Kings in North America. The practice had long since become almost ritualized in parts of the Old World, but those practitioners were of little help in the New World. Many early falcon keepers in the United States were perhaps more stimulated by the several magazine articles that appeared before the end of World War II than by the falconry treatises already available in the larger libraries. Most of the people who kept peregrines in the decade after the war did not progress and remained simple custodians of their birds, never catching game systematically. But to their credit, many were deeply enthusiastic in support of falconry and wrote many popular articles. Some remain advocates to this day.

I have pointed to the few who, early on, became serious gamehawkers with blue meanies. Their achievements with peregrines easily equaled those of the European falconers of the nineteenth century. The North Americans flew both migrant peregrines and local birds taken from eyries. Either way, the falcons became deadly in the hands of those self-taught masters. Not surprisingly, most lived in parts of the country where open expanses allowed the peregrines to realize their potential.

The advent of a new national falconry club in 1961, NAFA, and the introduction of an annual national field meet in 1962 created a pivotal environment for rapid informal information exchange. The two NAFA publications accelerated learning and reduced the risk of failure. Help was but a phone call away. Falconry with peregrines became less significant in the 1970s because of the bird's decline and increases in protective regulations. Many falconers' birds had been sent to breeding projects. A new kind of husbandry, captive breeding, would finally secure the place of blue meanies in the future of falconry. The next chapter explores the beginnings of the domestication of the peregrine.

X »   THE TIMELY INVENTION OF PEREGRINE HUSBANDRY

UNDER THE HAT   It is as if it happened only yesterday. Cal Sandfort of the Peregrine Fund was my coach. "Walk slowly to the middle of the loft, crouch just a bit, divert your eyes to the side, and then call to him." Sandfort slipped a canvas aviator's helmet on my head, the sort used by navy fliers. A foam-rubber ring had been glued to the top of the helmet with Goop, the stuff used to repair worn-out tennis shoes.

Sandfort slowly opened the door. I took a deep breath and stepped inside the small room. Standing on the shelf perch on the far wall was my old blue meanie BC, long since lent to the breeding project. I slowly crouched just a bit, stared straight ahead at the wall, and uttered sounds that were music to the ears of male peregrines in the breeding season. *Ee-chup, ee-chup, eee-chup*. I froze, and then glanced at the falcon. He glared at me. I lowered the tone just a bit, and turned down the volume: *ee-chup*. It was almost a seductive murmur. What more could I do?

Apparently, my signal tripped a switch. BC launched from his shelf, flew directly to my head, landed on the hat, lowered his tail down to the rubber ring, and ejaculated. Despite the motion of his flapping wings, the better to maintain his balance, I could feel a few weak shudders. The whole thing lasted but a few moments, and he flew back to his shelf.

Inside the rubber ring were four or five drops of viscous, cloudy semen. Sandfort touched each with a glass capillary tube. The semen was drawn inside. "It's a good sample," Sandfort said, and then he rushed off to divide it between two gravid females who were about to lay.

I went "under the hat" just once. It wasn't half bad. Whenever I explain the details, especially to students, they usually snicker and mutter something like "Oh, gross," or "Kinky." The hat trick reveals the extent of our determination to make more peregrines from the ones we already had.

ARTIFICIAL INSEMINATION   Through the mid-1970s we obtained semen for artificial insemination by forcefully stripping the fluid from unwilling participants. Stripping meant precise handiwork. The sperm ducts, located along the top of the body cavity under the tail, had to be milked properly. We learned the technique by trial and error in 1971. Stan Temple, my partner on the Yukon and in the bear incident the previous year, flew out to Colorado Springs from Cornell. We trapped an adult male prairie falcon in the peak of the breeding season at a local eyrie. High on the top of the cliff, we taught ourselves how to milk semen from falcons.

There was a big problem with getting semen by force. The falcons did not like it at all. After a few sessions, they loathed the sight of the stripper. Poor semen was another problem. More often than not, squeezing the ducts unfortunately resulted in the release of undesirable white excrement along with the fluid containing the sperm. Nevertheless, people intent on breeding peregrines needed the semen. Female peregrines were dropping eggs left and right, and many were infertile. Most falcons in captivity at the time would not mate naturally. By the mid-1970s, I had mastered forcing semen from peregrines.

Apparently my skills became known internationally. The Canadian Wildlife Service beckoned me to its new peregrine breeding facility at Wainwright, Alberta. Using their captive males, I showed Phil Trefrey and Richard Fyfe all that I knew. After that, I became widely known as Magic Fingers Enderson.

But my days in the limelight were numbered. In 1972 Les Boyd and Fred Dobler learned how to induce male falcons to mate with people. The birds were reared by hand, and hence thought they were people. What could be simpler? The only real problem was that of catching the semen before it dribbled away. Enter the helmet with a foam-rubber ring.

The hat trick requires only a male peregrine that thinks he is a human. BC was taken from a Colorado cliff, in 1971, at the age of two days. He rode home in my climbing helmet, kept warm by shredded paper towel. He grew up with the family, the kids rolling empty aluminum cans across the floor for him to catch. As a house pet, BC hated other peregrines.

Before the invention of the hat trick, BC was wasted in captivity; better to have left him in the stricken wild population. Fortunately, I sent the bird to Dan Konkel in Fort Collins, Colorado, who had learned of the Boyd/Dobler Hat. In the end BC became a sperm donor par excellence, and hundreds of his offspring were used to restock the country. His descendents now litter temperate North America.

Female meanies imprinted on people also interacted with their keepers. When provided with a gravel-covered ledge, such birds usually laid eggs in the normal way. Some stood voluntarily for insemination from a short glass tube. Others had to be held and forcefully inseminated. For some reason, Magic Fingers Enderson was never very good with the females.

THE FORCES WERE WITH US   Two incentives drove the invention of breeding blue meanies in captivity. Above all else, falconers feared they would lose the bird for the glove. I was among them. Without peregrines,

Dan Konkel collecting semen from BC, ca. 1978. Photo by Jeanne Konkel.

falconry would somehow be reduced, not to mention the tragedy of quiet cliffs in the spring and empty beaches in the fall. By 1968, the ominous threat of DDT was clear. It all boiled down to "breed 'em or lose 'em." There was really no option. The other force was the possibility that the big black-headed falcon could be restored to the wild. In 1970 Walter Spofford and I went to Lake Willoughby, Vermont, on a tip from local birders. We found the last duck hawk to be seen on a cliff in the eastern United States. None had been seen since the late 1960s. Spoff and I talked about how very late it was for the peregrine.

In 1967, the year of the canoe trip on the Yukon and Porcupine rivers, a large envelope arrived at my office from Richard Fyfe. Not many years before, he had become interested in peregrines and falconry while teaching school in the Canadian Arctic. Fyfe wrote about a pair of arctic peregrines he had in a loft. He was already testing the use of artificial light on captive falcons. He realized change in day-length in the spring caused birds to nest. He anticipated that falcons migrating from the far south to the Arctic must encounter, and perhaps require, a far different daylight pattern than they would find as captives in his loft near Edmonton.

Fyfe also enclosed a proposal he had sent to the Canadian Wildlife Service. The proposal was for a "peregrine breeding project." The first goal was to develop a captive-bred reserve of these falcons "to eliminate any possibility of extinction." The second goal was to test ways to release peregrines in places where they had disappeared. Fyfe offered to run the project. In a few years his offer was accepted.

Only falconers were really in a position to attempt captive breeding. Only falconers had tame captive blue meanies. The United States Fish and Wildlife Service (FWS) tried using wild migrants and failed to get an egg. We knew fully that our selfish interest alone would not draw the public funding or foundation money that would be needed. So for several reasons, including the prevention of extinction and the (wild) dream of restocking decimated populations, we set out to make peregrine falcons in captivity.

PIONEER BREEDERS   Even though large falcons had been bred in captivity at least three times before 1970, I figured it would be nearly impossible to breed blue meanies in quantity. Proof that I was wrong is now found in the many dozens of successful breeding projects in a score of countries worldwide. The few historical successes were noteworthy because they were simple: no special lofts, no special food, and no artificial insemination. In 1942–1943 Renz Waller produced two young peregrines in Düsseldorf, Germany, with Allied bombers a constant threat. Waller was a wildlife artist and the falconry mentor of Erich Awender, an Illinois surgeon and early falconer friend of Dan Cover's.

In 1967 Frank Beebe's pair of Peale's falcons (the common name of blue meanies from the Pacific Northwest) hatched two chicks in a barn, but both chicks soon disappeared, and Beebe did not persist in his effort. A year later Larry Schram of Portland, Oregon, raised at least two fully grown young, but he also failed to carry on. In another first, Henry Kendall of St. Louis bred prairie falcons in a garage in 1967, and then quit. Incidentally, Kendall's prairie falcons were not the first of their kind to lay eggs in captivity. About two years before, Art Dodge, a veterinarian, kept three or four prairies in the attic of an old house in Buena Vista, Colorado. Dodge urged me to peek at his birds. I pushed up the hatch and poked my head up to floor level. Close enough to touch were five or six falcon eggs, and a very defensive mother falcon. The eggs never hatched: infertile, I think.

Why did the early "backyard" projects wash out? Waller's world was changed dramatically by war. For the others, perhaps the incentive wasn't there. Beebe was not convinced peregrines were in serious trouble, since those in the Charlottes seemed fine; he could go there and obtain more of them. Schram simply liked having a few falcons around. Kendall's prairies were apart from the peregrine crash and the need for captive breeding. Nevertheless, those of us who were not yet successful envied what they had done and fully recognized the new ground they had broken.

RAIDERS AT THE EYRIE   In the late 1960s, peregrines in the hands of falconers were a mixed lot of trapped migrants and hand-reared nestlings. The former were usually too wild to lay eggs in captivity, and the latter seldom mated with other peregrines. Pairs were often made up with borrowed birds.

At the end of 1966, I had only one peregrine. Lil, caught in Wyoming in 1962, was now alone. Her potential mate, Shane, was lost while hunting ducks in the fall. No telemetry was available in those days. I then entered the darkest period of my life. I began stealing peregrines for captive breeding at a time when public sentiment, and wildlife regulations, were turning against further human meddling with wild raptors.

The first raid was nearly my undoing. Wolf Creek, one of the few eyries in Colorado to remain active in the depths of the decline, contained three nestlings. Seen through a spotting scope, the ledge was clearly sheltered by a large overhang. But access seemed possible from the side after a descent down a rope over a series of step-like ridges in a big crevice. The rock was less than a mile from the road, and appeared to be about three hundred feet high. My rope was two hundred feet long, "easily long enough to reach the ledge." Those were famous last words.

A member of the local mountain-climbing club offered to help me rob the nest. He was lean and tough. Those attributes would come in handy at Wolf Creek. Very handy indeed. We reached the cliff before noon, but the hike to the top turned out to be a lot farther than expected. This theme would repeat itself.

We crawled down through a narrow cleft in the volcanic rock. The books call the rock type "breccia." The whole of the San Juan Mountains is volcanic. Some of it consists of pebbles embedded in once-molten lava. Today, such rocks and the cliffs they form are very rough and pockmarked because they did not erode smoothly. We found a boulder to anchor the rope. Now it was midafternoon. Big cumulonimbus clouds were gathering. Sometime in the preceding hours, the quest for a new male peregrine to pair with Lil had been transformed from goal to compulsion. I threw a forty-foot coil of the long rope down the chute. When it had fallen full length, its momentum whipped the remaining rope from a snarl at our feet. In an instant the whole two-hundred-foot length was dragged down. No matter how far we leaned out, the end of the rope was not in view.

Rule number one: "Never descend to the end of a rope unless it reaches the bottom; otherwise you must climb back up." Had I been thinking clearly, instead of being blindly driven to reach a falcon on the ledge, I might have wondered why the monster Douglas firs and ponderosa pines under the cliff seemed so tiny. My helper shrugged, his puny 120-foot rope coiled over his shoulder should we need it. This cliff was a *monster*.

It was too late to reconsider. I backed off the cliff with the rope playing through steel rings attached to my seat sling of hand-sewn nylon webbing. Eighty feet down, my predicament was obvious. The end of my rope was dangling in thin air twenty feet above the nest ledge. Worse, a glance above revealed that the "steps" I had seen from the road were actually overhanging ledges twenty feet apart. I had descended over three of them, and each loomed as an obstacle for the return to the top.

Then came the rain. The sky darkened, the better to display flashes of lightning. I hung there, spinning slowly in the gloom, knowing I could not reach the eyrie. The countryside, horizontal from my vertical wall, was gray with rain. The big groove now channeled a small stream of rainwater, and the overhangs created waterfalls. My plan had been to ascend hand over hand on the rope, given the presumed mild slope. There was no way I could climb the vertical rope.

Today, in the quiet of my home, thirty-five years removed from that moment, the events unfold. Suddenly the end of another rope appeared from above. My man had lowered his short line. He shouted, but wind, rain, and waterfalls made hearing impossible. He was out of view above the top ledge. He wanted me to do something, but what?

There was only one solution, other than waiting for a search-and-rescue team. I descended to the next ledge and crawled aside on a narrow ledge where I could stand. Then I relocated my rope through a single ring on the sling and tied the second rope to its end.

"Pull!" I yelled as loud as I could. In a kind of pulley system, the end of my rope went up. So did I, helping to lessen the burden of my weight by lifting myself hand over hand. I remember little else of the ordeal, other than my reluctance to leave the safety of the house for the next two days.

A week later I took a nestling female called Little Bird from an eyrie on land where access was forbidden. No other climbable eyrie was known. I hiked through brush undetected and snatched the chick from a ledge only ten feet from the cliff-top. The parents screamed loudly as if to give me, "both poacher and game warden," away. I like to think that, in certain cases, the means are justified by the end. Scores of Little Bird's descendants were later released to restock peregrines in the western United States.

I obtained mates for the two females in 1969. No eyrie in Colorado with young was accessible, so we went north. One nestling was obtained vicariously. A friend in California gave me the phone number of a bird-watcher in Montana. Monte Kirven said his old friend knew of an active peregrine eyrie. I called from a Billings pay phone one Sunday morning.

"The falcons are no longer nesting there," said the elderly man. Nonetheless he seemed eager to show me the cliff anyway. We met at a parking lot in Billings. He must have wondered about us. There we were, my wife, Dayle, and our two children, a travel trailer, a canoe on the station wagon, and a dog called Moppus. We did not seem like a raiding party with a mission.

The old gentleman pointed to the canyon where the pair had nested for years. He believed they too had gone the way of the species in Wyoming, Colorado, and elsewhere. In a way, his fears were soon realized. Montana would lose virtually all of its known pairs in the next decade.

We stood chatting beside the busy highway. I set up the tripod and scope, and carelessly scanned the cave-riddled sandstone cliff. There was a bit of whitewash here and a bit there. Very interesting. Then, as if in slow motion, a big blue meanie, carrying a blackbird, pitched up and landed in a cave. Three snow-white downy chicks rushed out of the shadows to be fed. I said nothing. In my silence, I suppressed the guilt of my dishonesty. After a while, we drove the bird-watcher to his car.

Two of the three young fledged from that eyrie in 1969. Nothing is known of their fate. The third youngster has left a genetic legacy up and down the Rocky Mountains. His name was Blue.

WE STRIKE IT RICH   Imagine our frenzy in the early 1970s. In the wild, peregrines were going down fast. Only five or six pairs were known to persist in Colorado, a dozen or so in California, and practically none in between. Fortunately, the people driven to breed meanies in captivity had the stock they needed. It was none too soon. By 1973, peregrines were protected everywhere, and scientific permits to take more were almost impossible to obtain.

The Canadian Wildlife Service endorsed Richard Fyfe's proposal to attempt breeding of peregrines. The CWS built a facility at the old army base at Fort Wainwright in the aspen parklands of central Alberta. In 1970–1972, Fyfe gathered up several nestling peregrines from northern Canada. In 1972, before the breeding facility was completed, Fyfe had dozens of falcons on his small farm near Edmonton. Make no mistake, Fyfe and his helpers were heroes.

My breakthrough in breeding falcons came in the spring of 1970. "They're still alive," I whispered, placing the last of the three prairie falcon eggs back in the incubator. Seen through the shells, in the bright light of an egg candler, the chicks seemed ready to hatch at any moment. But there was a big problem. We were leaving Cornell University by car in two days, heading back to Colorado. I quickly made a brooder from a Styrofoam box rigged with a thermostat and a couple of brake-light bulbs for heat. The makeshift contraption plugged into the car's cigarette lighter.

The parent prairies had bred in a barn on a farm near Ithaca, New York. I loaded them into the station wagon, along with two pairs of peregrines. All sat quietly in their hoods. The portable brooder rested in the middle of the front seat. Inside was a newly hatched prairie falcon, bedraggled but alive. The other two eggs were "pipped," the shell pushed outward from a small fracture.

The chicks wanted out. In a sort of cross-country hatchery, one emerged as we passed Buckeye, Ohio, and the other at Joliet, Illinois. Dayle kept them alive. No one knew what the proper temperature should be. When they sprawled flat they were too hot and when they huddled in a ball they were too cold. The new prairie falcons were eventually given to my friend the late Ed Freienmuth, a professor and falconer in southwest Colorado. He bred them with other prairies, and within the decade, the descendents of Buckeye and Joliet were given to falconers across the country.

In 1971 Heinz Meng, a falconer and biology professor in New Paltz, New York, hatched a peregrine chick in an incubator. His peregrine from the Queen Charlotte Islands had laid the egg. Meng produced seven more the next year. He knew that when egg collectors took a set of eggs, the falcons often produced a second set. Meng's pair obviously knew what to do.

Captive breeding of blue meanies came of age in 1973. Meng lent his two peregrines to Tom Cade and Jim Weaver at Cornell University. Weaver hatched twenty young from that pair and others borrowed from Jack Oar, Clayton White, and Grainger Hunt. The same year, John Campbell and

Wayne Nelson hatched three in Alberta. I hatched four (one soon died of herpesvirus) in Colorado. Within a year or two, Fyfe and Phil Trefry were routinely producing blue meanies in Canada. Willard Heck joined the crew at Cornell and soon became the number one peregrine midwife there. Captive breeding was no longer a stunt; the domestication of peregrines had begun.

SLOW START   Plenty of duck hawks could be made. All it would require was money. Like any other business, the cost per unit goes down as the number of units goes up. "Cheaper by the dozen" also applies to peregrines.

In 1971 my students and I built a six-chambered building to house several pairs at our country place near Colorado Springs. Each chamber was fourteen feet tall and was fitted with a nest ledge and one-way glass for observation. The birds could sense my presence behind the glass, so I kept a radio playing to cover my sounds. Each chamber had a large open panel in the roof covered with mesh to let in the elements.

Although we lived in the country, a permit by the regional building department was required for construction of the breeding barn. The big openings in the roof threw the engineer in charge of permits. "We will have to tighten the rules on things like this," he grumbled. But he issued the permit anyway.

In 1972, the New York Zoological Society (Bronx Zoo) gave me a grant of $2,700. No doubt Roland Clement of the National Audubon Society greased the skids under that gold. The cash bought incubators, brooders, and falcon food. At the time, no fewer than eighteen falcons lived in our backyard. They included my five peregrines and eight meanies on loan. There were five prairie falcons, including a nasty old female from my Wyoming days that served as door guard. Woe befell the stranger who walked in the door unescorted. She was meaner than a junkyard rottweiler.

In 1973 the first grant ran out. The Colorado Division of Wildlife (CDW) came through with $3,000, now that young had been produced. In all, we raised thirteen meanies at a cost of about $500 each, not counting labor and anxiety.

The chicks were reared in their own company. They were fed by hand. In 1973, we made a hand puppet in the likeness of a mother peregrine. We used it from behind a screen to feed the small young. They accepted the puppet and did not imprint (develop a permanent orientation) on us.

All but one of the captive-bred birds survived and made more meanies. Eventually, they accounted for a part of the enormous production of peregrines achieved by the Peregrine Fund and the CDW at Fort Collins.

RETURN TO THE WILD   Just like humans, young peregrines are dependent on their parents for support for a time after they leave the nest. In

Left to right: Jerry Craig, Recovery Team Leader; Bill Heinrich, manager of peregrine releases for the Peregrine Fund; Morley Nelson, falconer and conservationist; and Bill Burnham, now president of the Peregrine Fund, at a Colorado eyrie in 1976.

Jim Weaver places two peregrines in the Royal Gorge, 1974, the first successful fostering of captive-bred peregrines to wild parents.

falcons, dependency lasts about four weeks. Human parents know it is usually much longer in the case of our own species, sometimes several decades. Naïve young falcons cannot be simply turned loose. They would surely perish. We used two techniques to put the youngsters safely in the wild: fostering and hacking, the latter an old falconry technique. Both were an awful lot of work.

Peregrine fostering was first used in 1974. We found two cracked eggs in the eyrie at the Royal Gorge in Colorado. Jerry Craig and I took the eggs and gave the parents a couple of prairie falcon chicks to keep them busy until captive-bred peregrine chicks could be flown out from Cornell. Jim Weaver showed up with the two duck hawks and American Airlines paid the tab. We swapped those chicks for the prairie falcon youngsters. The prairies were taken back to their home, no worse for wear. A few weeks later I saw the young Cornell peregrines soaring high over the gorge.

Imagine how pleased we were with ourselves. We then dreamed of what could happen. Given a supply of young, all we would need were wild adults to accept them. No matter that some wild pairs laid eggs with weak shells. We could replace those with beautiful egg replicas until our youngsters were ready.

We stole eggs from several pairs. Those eggs went to the safety of an incubator. Next, we replaced the originals with excellent fakes. A couple of weeks later we crawled back to the eyrie and swapped the dummy eggs for three or four robust youngsters hatched in captivity. In a kind of payment to the old falcons for their inconvenience, we usually placed a half-dozen thawed quail on the ledge.

Actually, the quail were an important food supply until the male could get his act together. He suddenly needed to catch lots of food. One time we showed up at the Paradox eyrie with four big young for the old birds, but no quail. Craig and Berger had forgotten to bring quail. I happened to have a vintage Colt .44-40 Frontier Six-Shooter along. It was part of an old gun collection I wanted Craig to see. Now it was pressed into service. I loaded up and walked into the vast Paradox Valley. That evening, the four adopted meanies were fed fresh rock squirrel by the old birds, courtesy of Samuel Colt.

Only rarely did things go wrong. Once a horned owl killed an adult female who had fostered young. To lessen the burden for the male, we provided an endless supply of domestic quail for the chicks. He learned to anticipate the handout and caught thawed quail thrown to him. At a difficult eyrie, Craig fell while carrying eggs down a snow-covered slope below the cliff. Three eggs were broken. Another time, the chief of the CDW nongame wildlife program came along to verify our skills. He managed to drop the lid of the egg box and cracked an egg. Fortunately, I was able to repair the damage with a bit of Elmer's glue. Cal Sandfort, who was in charge of the incubators at the Peregrine Fund, eventually coaxed a healthy chick from that egg.

EGG THEFT   At first we had trouble transporting stolen eggs by car. Thermostats were not made to be hauled about the high country. When we drove up mountain passes, the thermostats interpreted the thinner air as warmer air and shut off the heating element. Sometimes the heaters broke. Once we were forced to stop beside a busy highway in a San Luis Valley sandstorm to heat a water bottle on a Coleman stove. What did those motorists think as they drove by?

At about that time I invented an ill-fated incubator. I replaced one side of a Styrofoam box with a thin sheet of heat-conducting copper. The plan was to strap the thing against my chest during the drive home. Body heat would flow through the copper, keeping the eggs inside the box safely warm. Field trials were terminated because perspiration caused the copper to corrode, leaving a huge patch of bright blue-green skin.

It was fun stealing peregrine eggs. Sometimes I think it almost a pity the old sport died out. We took all the eggs we could reach. In 1979–1983, the few wild pairs laid a total of twenty-nine sets of eggs. We took twenty-eight. Those pairs fledged eighty-one fostered meanies in those years (a little less than three each, on average). In that era of DDE, each pair we fostered produced on average at least one youngster more than they would have without fostering.

Fostering was sometimes harrowing. The danger took different forms. Craig found himself obliged to ascend up *through* a huge overhanging cornice of snow with a box of peregrine eggs. His rope had cut deeply into the lip of snow as he hung below it. After he made it to the top, a helicopter plucked us from the cliff-top in a sudden snowstorm. Only by flying vertically down the face of the four-hundred-foot cliff of Hermosa limestone could we find our way safely to better visibility.

Jeff Rucks was on his way to see if the pair was incubating at Gateway, Colorado. Driving at a good speed on a moonless night, he was astonished to see four white rabbits hopping in the road in his headlights. A moment too late, he discovered a black steer with white feet walking in the road. In a cloud of dust the little truck was the loser.

Dan Berger, suffering from the heat and dehydration, mistakenly descended twenty-five feet below the eyrie where dummy eggs awaited a replacement with three-week-old peregrine chicks. Realizing his error, Berger shouted to Marcy Cottrell (Houle) and Ann Potter, the observers. "Why didn't you warn me I had gone too far?" The reply: "We thought you knew what you were doing."

En route to the spectacular eyrie on the Conejos River, we stopped at a delightful little bakery in Chama, New Mexico. For reasons of geography and roads, the shortest way to the Conejos country in Colorado from Pagosa Springs is via Chama. Berger and Craig preceded me into the shop. Especially attractive in the glass case near the door was a tray of huge freshly baked glazed cinnamon rolls. These would come in handy on our long hike to the big cliff. We sat down as people do in cafés. Presently, a drop-dead-gorgeous breath-of-spring waitress appeared. She was anxious to have our orders. Berger and Craig mulled over the menu. She looked at me. "What would you like?" Thinking only of the grueling hike ahead, I blurted out, "I'd like two of your big sticky buns." Complete silence; I was mortified. Then we all roared in laughter.

Early in the fostering work, we sometimes tossed monster firecrackers over the tallest cliffs to flush out adults. In that way, we knew the route the climber must take to reach the eyrie to make off with the eggs. One day as we peered over the edge a violent wind rushed up the face of the cliff and into our faces. Pebbles as big as marbles were blown up the cliff and over our heads. Berger taped an explosive device called an M-80 to a fist-sized rock, lit the fuse from his pipe, and tossed it over. We leaned over to watch. To our horror, the firecracker came hurtling back to us, borne on wings of tape that once held it to the rock. The fireball, only a few feet away, was the size of a basketball.

THE HACK   Centuries ago, European falconers found a way to increase the strength and flying skill of peregrines intended for falconry. Several falcons, stolen from nests and too young to fly, were placed on a covered platform on a pole or tree. Food was supplied daily. When the young developed, they were free to venture out and return for food. Gradually the falcons became strong and swift. When they began to catch their own prey, those that had not flown away were netted and trained.

Early trials with hacking as a means of releasing peregrines where no wild falcons occurred were performed in New York by Heinz Mcng, Tom Cade, and Jim Weaver. The simple idea was to supply food until the young birds became completely independent. Unlike the case in falconry, the young falcons would not be trapped back into captivity.

Early results were mixed. The birds were held in boxes with bars in front and were placed on cliffs once used by blue meanies, or on a building. Horned owls at rural sites ate the young on the cliffs after the bars were removed. In the urban setting owls were few, but the new aeronauts required rescue from people and traffic.

A PLETHORA OF BOXES   By the late 1970s, hack boxes for the release of peregrines were appearing across the continent. Their distribution dotted the land from which peregrines had disappeared. More than two hundred of them were eventually built. Some boxes were in the wilderness and some were urban. The boxes ranged along the length of California, up the Colum-

Hack box with bars removed to liberate the forty-two-day-old juveniles. Because no adults were present in hacking, attendants camped nearby to feed the youngsters. From a photo by M. Robert.

bia Gorge, eastward to the mountains of Idaho, Montana, and northern Wyoming, and south to the salt marshes in northern Utah.

The sturdy plywood cubes, four feet on a side, with a removable front panel of steel bars and two hundred pounds of pea gravel in the bottom, were scattered in the central Rockies south almost to New Mexico. Boxes were set on tall buildings from Edmonton and Calgary eastward across southern Canada to Montreal.

In the Midwest, a few appeared by the mid-1980s in the countryside. Later on, most were in cities such as Minneapolis and Milwaukee. Hack boxes were secured to ledges on buildings and cabled to Appalachian cliffs. In a deliberate attempt to avoid killer horned owls, some were bolted to towers made from telephone poles stuck deep in the sand or marshes of Atlantic barrier beaches. Sometimes the poles, sharpened on the end, were dropped like giant darts from helicopters, avoiding the messy task of digging postholes.

Most interesting was a box placed on an old tower at Aberdeen Proving Ground in Maryland. Artillery pieces were once mounted on the tower, pointing straight down, the better to test their projectiles. Boxes could be reused year after year, and some saw service lasting more than a decade. Others were abandoned early, either because peregrines released there returned as adults and harassed the young, or because of predators. The box in the Royal Gorge in Colorado was used but once, in 1985. Owls ate all of the young meanies. That box, like most, still sits tightly anchored to its ledge. It is in full view of the tens of thousands of tourists who peer into the canyon each summer. It goes unnoticed.

Steve Petersburg and Joel Hogan oversaw the hacking operation in Dinosaur Monument in Colorado. They and their coworkers took the direct approach to the owl problem. At sunset, a predator call simulating a rabbit in agony was played on a loudspeaker near the hack box. Any owl coming in for the kill fell to a shotgun. Apparently the grisly task saved peregrines, and the releases were usually successful.

Hacking proved versatile. In Montana and Utah, towers were built in open marshes far from the threat of marauding golden eagles. In middle and eastern North America, no wild peregrine pair offered an opportunity for fostering. All the eyries there were vacant. Hacking was the only option.

Boxes were often set on tall buildings in cities such as Montreal, Toronto, Baltimore, New York, and Saint Paul. These became popular with city folks who watched them via closed-circuit TV. Most were unable to spell *peregrine*, let alone see one. More recently, hack boxes were placed, by popular demand, on buildings in smaller cities, a boon to Boise, Cedar Rapids, and Indianapolis.

Few of us anticipated the degree to which released peregrines would return to their old boxes to breed in later years. Of course the birds were welcomed back, but more boxes had to be built for new releases. Returning falcons did not take kindly to new squatters in their old homes. In Colorado, where big cliffs abound, hacked peregrines seldom returned to the boxes to breed. They much preferred the natural outcrops. Only one box was later used for nesting. It sits to this day in Rocky Mountain National Park.

The problem with hacking was the effort required. Boxes were built and transported to the sites. We put all of ours, a couple of dozen, on cliffs. Sometimes helicopters made the lifting easy. Two attendants camped out near each site. They fed the young through tubes or small doors, keeping out of sight so the young remained wild. Quail were stored in freezers at nearby ranches.

The attendants bore the brunt of bad weather. But biting gnats were the worst because they paid no attention to mosquito lotion. The caretakers at Adobe Creek near the prison at Florence, Colorado, were evacuated because of escaped convicts hiding out in the area. Many attendants eventually made

Newly hatched captive-bred peregrines waiting to be fed on a heat pad, ca. 1979.
Photo by Jeanne Konkel.

OPPOSITE PAGE: *Brian Walton gently removes the eggs from a wild peregrine on*
a tall building in Los Angeles. Dummy eggs kept the pair busy until young, safely
hatched in captivity, could be given to the pair. Photo by Jim Jennings.

good, including Jamie Clarke, who became director of the FWS. A few failed
the course, including a chap I fired for drunken driving in an official vehicle.

Eagles and other predators had to be kept from the hack box. Blank shot-
shells fired into the sky often did the trick. When the big owls were a problem, blank shells were traded for the real thing. Despite their heroic efforts,
attendants occasionally watched young falcons snatched by eagles, or found
remains by means of the little radios the released falcons sometimes wore.
On average, only four in five peregrines placed in the boxes attained the capa-
bility of catching their own prey.

The cost of hacking was steep. Attendants stayed on-site for about six
weeks. They had to be equipped, and the travel was considerable. Across the
continent, managers saw to the training and other needs of the attendants.
A manual for hack site folks was published. Federal and state land agencies
funded a large part of the hacking programs. The Bureau of Land Management
(BLM) and the U.S. Forest Service (USFS), for example, funded several sites
each year in Colorado in the mid-1980s at a cost of about $10,000 per site.

NUMBERS FOR BEAN COUNTERS   Far and away the most amazing aspects of the story to be told of peregrine falcons in the twentieth century are their sudden massive production in captivity and their release to the wild. Never before, or since, was so much done so quickly on behalf of a wild animal.

In 1974, Brian Walton and Carl Thelander drove out from California to visit my breeding project. They had great enthusiasm, the stuff of good things. They teamed up with Jim Roush at the University of California at Santa Cruz, commandeered a nearby abandoned rock quarry, begged for money, and built breeding chambers for peregrines. In a few years the Predatory Bird Group, headed by Walton, was releasing captive-bred peregrines and young hatched from wild eggs. When their work was finished in the 1990s, they had turned loose nearly eight hundred duck hawks, mostly in California.

The Peregrine Fund dumped more than twelve hundred duck hawks bred in captivity into the eastern United States by 1990, and another two thousand or more into the west by 1995. Most releases were in Colorado, Utah, Wyoming, Montana, Idaho, and Washington. The Peregrine Fund gets the gold for sheer numbers placed into the wild.

The Canadian Wildlife Service project at Wainwright, Alberta, did mighty well too, thanks to Trefry, Ursula Banasch, and Harry Armbruster. They produced 1,500 peregrines in the two decades following 1974, and most were released. In eastern Canada, a project headed by David Bird produced more than 60 falcons for release in the period 1979–1990. In central Canada, Lynn Oliphant's team at the University of Saskatchewan hatched more than 250 peregrines.

Even more remarkable, in a Herculean effort beginning in 1981, Bud Tordoff and Pat Redig at the University of Minnesota rounded up *twelve hundred* peregrines from at least twenty-eight backyard breeders and released the falcons in the upper Midwest. The falcons were put out by hacking, sometimes in cities or from structures such as grain elevators or smokestacks at power plants.

An interesting innovation in the Midwest was to use a hack box more than once in a season. When the first gang of up to ten young falcons was strong on the wing, a second set of young was released. The two broods usually got along well, the older birds flying top cover should a hawk come by. You can only imagine all those young did not tidy up the place before they flew off. Such hack sites resembled a landfill of domestic quail remains.

It was easy to lose track of the totals. By 1995 about seven thousand peregrines had been produced in captivity. The feat was all the more impressive in light of the slow rate of reproduction normal to falcons compared to captive game birds or waterfowl. By the beginning of this century, at least a thousand more should have been added, even though breeding for restocking had nearly ceased. A few years before, all the major projects had turned off the incubators, unplugged the brooders, and put the old birds out to pasture.

Peregrines were released to restore populations in other parts of the world. Pesticides decimated peregrines throughout central and northern Europe in the 1950s and 1960s. Nearly 50 falcons were turned out in Sweden under the guidance of ecologist Peter Lindberg, and nearly 250 were released in Germany after the pioneering captive breeding directed by veterinarian Christian Saar.

In all, about sixty-five hundred blue meanies were released to the wild in North America by the mid-1990s. The young falcons flew from hack boxes, or from eyries into which they had been fostered, across North America from the Yukon to Georgia, from Maine to the Pacific. In the late 1980s upward of five hundred were turned out *each year*.

We can only wonder, in light of these figures, what happened to them all. It may come as a shock to understand that by now, all but a handful have perished. Perhaps a very few of those falcons released in the mid-1990s are still out there, and possibly a very few from the early 1990s persist. In the extreme, a wild blue meanie may reach fourteen years. But not many become that old. The average life span is on the order of three or four years.

It is the legacy of their progeny that matters now. In a later chapter we will see what they have brought.

XI » SEARCHES IN FAR PLACES

GRAND CANYON PEREGRINES   "Get back in the damn boat,
Bucko," shouted the boatman. Only moments before, Tom Cade, distinguished professor, scientist, and peregrine expert, was sitting next to me in
the big raft on the Colorado River. He was musing at a little flock of phalaropes whirling on the calm water a few feet above the ugly rapids that roared
in our path. Now he was gone! "Bucko" Cade was simply gone. Then, in one
giant easy motion, the burly and irreverent boatman stood up in the violently
pitching raft, leaned far over, hand still on the tiller, grabbed the submerged
"Bucko" Cade by the scruff of his shirt, and dragged him from the drink. As
quickly as he departed, Cade was back on the raft, spitting water as the rapids coughed us out below. Obviously the boatman had fished folks from the
Colorado River before.

People have been dumped from boats into the Colorado in the Grand
Canyon ever since John Wesley Powell first shot the turbulent river in 1869,
a year after his search of the tributaries of the Des Moines River in what is
now Iowa. No doubt Powell was not paying much attention to the bird life.

We were looking for peregrines. Our party of twoscore observers had
been organized by Bryan Brown to carefully search the inner canyon for falcons. Brown had found pairs nesting commonly on the cliffs at the rim of the
Grand Canyon and supposed that cliffs along the river's edge, five thousand
feet below, also housed blue meanies.

The inner canyon, mainly hidden from the rim, is lined with one cataract after another, not the best setting for thorough searching. Brown hit on
a system we later adapted to helicopter surveys elsewhere. In the case of the
river, two rafts were used. The first raft would go ahead, dropping off a pair of
observers with provisions every two miles or so. The first raft remained with
its last team. The second raft remained upstream.

About noon the next day, the upstream raft would pick up the teams and
drop them off below the first boat. Day after day, this leapfrog process was
repeated. In nine days my son, Ritt, and I ended up just above Lake Mead,
having camped at eight locations along the river. The quiet solitude was
interrupted at seven of our eight campsites by the calls of peregrines tending
to their broods. It was peregrine city.

The great sandstone walls of the Colorado Plateau have numerous potential nest ledges so that the same ledge is seldom used in successive years.

Actually, it wasn't all solitude. During our free time, we searched the rubble under the rocky walls for a well-known example of the effect of selection on isolated populations of animals. Ritt found the creature we sought, a small rattlesnake colored pastel rusty pink. It was a perfect color match to the sandstone. This variant of the otherwise widespread, greenish prairie rattlesnake is found only in the Grand Canyon. Selection enabled this creature to better fit its world, and the high walls of the canyon precluded mixing with ordinary upland forms. The beautiful snake goes by the scientific name *abyssus*.

There is really no way to know how many peregrines nest in the Grand Canyon. Quite likely pairs are spaced a few miles apart on the rims on both sides of the canyon. The same is true for the cliffs forming the inner canyon. What about the cliffs halfway up, two thousand feet above the river? With scopes, we saw blue meanies there, but they were too far and often concealed by intervening buttresses. The amount of falcon habitat defies description. The river course is over a hundred miles long in the park alone.

So how many? No hedging. Most of us who floated through the place in 1991 would guess something like a *couple of hundred pairs* rear their young on those countless miles of walls. If this were poker, I would up the ante fifty pairs.

The Grand Canyon is quite likely home to the greatest mass of peregrines on earth. This is because of the enormity of the chasm and the presence of a boundless food supply. No falcon need go to bed hungry. Just wait until evening, and then rush a flight of bats flitting for insects. Take two; they won't be missed.

THE COLORADO PLATEAU   The Grand Canyon is sheer proof that the drainage of the Colorado River is bounded by high ground built of layer after layer of sediments turned into rock. The plateau extends eastward to the west flank of the Rockies, north to Snake River basin, and west to the mountains of central Utah. Below the mountains that surround its basin, the Colorado River and its tributaries drain the Colorado Plateau. The main stream clears the mountains near Grand Junction, Colorado, and this is where peregrines begin in earnest.

In the early 1980s very little was known of the falcon on the plateau. There were several old records from the country that is now inundated by Lake Powell. Then one day an advertising scheme required videos of an automobile perched on top of a three-hundred-foot spire emerging from the lake across from the Glen Canyon Dam. The big helicopter that was used to set the gutted auto onto the spire blew a fledgling peregrine into the lake.

Fortunately, a passing boat rescued the soaked youngster. The authorities were alerted. The following year, Ron Joseph of the FWS followed up on the report and found two more eyries a few miles upstream. An early conclusion was that the advent of the lake, flooding half the length of the gorge of the Colorado between the Grand Canyon and Moab, Utah, had turned the plateau into blue meanie country.

Of course peregrines were on the endangered species list at the time. Under a contract from the National Park Service (NPS) to the Peregrine Fund, I hired ten veteran peregrine observers and a helicopter, and set out for the plateau in the spring of 1984. It was a glorious time. I was living the dream of those who are hooked on the quest for peregrines. The helicopter would allow us to place teams of two observers in strategic locations along the river where they could scope the best terrain. Further, we could search Lake Powell from the water; a fast boat was at our disposal. If peregrines were on the plateau in good numbers, we would find them.

Best of all, we were not restricted to Lake Powell. Many of the "crown jewels" of the NPS lie on the plateau: Zion, Bryce Canyon, Capitol Reef, Canyonlands, and Dinosaur. A few pairs were known to nest in Dinosaur at that time, but only one other pair had been found in each of the others. Larry Hays, naturalist at Zion, had been watching a pair. They nested at Angel Landing, a spectacular cliff of Weber (pronounced "wee-ber") sandstone and a favorite tourist destination. This pair was in addition to the three pairs known then at Lake Powell.

ZION   I had been instructed to coordinate our activities on NPS lands with the appropriate officials, usually the park naturalists. The Denver office of the NPS had given me all of their names, of course, and unofficial advice that most personnel would be easy to work with. A possible exception was Larry Hays at Zion. It seemed to me at the time a bit strange that a person who had taken it upon himself to keep close tabs on the Angel Landing pair would be "difficult."

As it turned out, Hays was a keen observer and could hardly have been more helpful. That year he had in his employ a very competent and energetic field biologist by the name of Tim Tibbitts. They set the stage for our arrival.

We showed up with teams of young men and women, and a helicopter. Hays and Tibbitts broke out the big maps of Zion and we soon had a plan based on their experiences. We chose twenty-five observation points on the tops of massive cliffs. All were remote, and many were not accessible on foot because the mesas were sometimes rock islands formed by five-hundred-foot vertical walls.

Obviously, the helicopter was the key. Rather, the helicopter pilot was the key. Richard Dick had flown in Vietnam. He had learned to take a custodial interest in the people he dropped off in remote places. In Zion, he would sometimes fly out of the way to an observation post just to check on one of our crews.

The closest thing to a mishap in the two field seasons of daily flying was a pair of lost meanie watchers. Zion exceeds sixty square miles of cliff mazes. The canyons are deeply cut. The massive monoliths all appear the same. Dick flew out to move a team to a new lookout. After a short while he returned, too soon to have finished his mission. I walked out to the running chopper with the map of the sites we had chosen. A sheepish grin marked his face. "Can't find them," he shouted over the roar of the rotors. "That Parunaweep country is a real puzzle." I showed him the location of observation post fourteen, three miles west of the Virgin River. He grinned, buckled up tight, released the friction lock on the collective control, and was gone in a cloud of dust and the deafening whine of the jet turbine.

Another potential problem was averted by strong character. Team members were first matched at random, and they rotated with a new teammate at each park we visited. No one paid any attention to who was paired with whom, man or woman. All were eager to find peregrines. So much for theory; now for the practice.

John and Martha (names changed to protect the innocent) were dropped off on top of a great wall in complete isolation in the back of the Zion wilderness. The staccato *slap-slap-slap* of the rotor blades had barely faded in the distance when it was replaced by the staccato *cack-cack-cack* of a defensive peregrine. The two observers had been set down practically on top of an active eyrie, complete with protesting parents.

They watched for a while, and then Martha walked back to where the chopper had off-loaded their tent and other gear. An hour later, in the gathering darkness, John found the exact location of the nest ledge. He then hiked up through the piñon pines and Utah junipers to the drop point. To his shock, he found Martha standing at fireside, stripped to the waist. John was a married man, and he was deeply grateful to his wife for agreeing to his participation in work he loved so much. "This just isn't fair," he said, in gross understatement. Then he turned and walked away. She got the message. Nothing came of the incident.

We found eight new pairs in Zion, nine in all, counting the old site. Hays reckoned there was room for one more, if each pair defended a territory a mile or two in diameter. Zion was about packed with blue meanies, or so we thought. Once again we "experts" misjudged. In the year 2001, Zion held *eighteen* active eyries. Grand Canyon will long be known for sheer numbers

Adult male feeds half-grown young, bit by bit. The loss of the adult female at one Colorado site did not cause the loss of the young. The male supplied adequate food.

of peregrines, but Zion is number one for extreme peregrine packing. Moreover, Zion provided evidence that by the mid-1980s, peregrines were abundant on the high walls of the plateau.

LAKE POWELL   Glen Canyon Dam is just south of the Utah line at Page, Arizona, and backs up the Colorado River for seventy-five miles, halfway to Moab. What was once a spectacular cliff-rimmed gorge is now an immense lake, its hundreds of sprawling arms branching and branching again. The total shoreline is said to equal the west coast of the United States. The taller reaches of the great cliffs loom high above the clear water of the lake.

Lake Powell has three properties. Most people identify it with fish, houseboats, and beer. These have made Lake Powell famous. But the geological and biological prizes are deep cold water, untold miles of cliffs on countless side canyons, and, above all, peregrine falcons.

Right off, my crews began to find eyries on the tall walls jutting straight up from the lake. On its first flight from such a site, a young peregrine must find a ledge on which to land, or otherwise slide down the smooth red sandstone into the lake. No doubt some young are lost in this way, but most delay that first jump until they have grown strong. They become powerful by flapping and jumping about on the nest ledges before they fly.

Lake Powell can easily hold forty or fifty pairs, and we found about twenty by 1987. NPS folks were quick to suggest that the controversial lake, which buried forever-untold pre-Columbian ruins and artifacts, actually created habitat for the peregrine. The argument seemed plausible until we moved our helicopter searches northward into Canyonlands, upstream of the calm waters of the lake. We found blue meanies there, spaced every few miles. Lake or not, falcons like the plateau.

DINOSAUR   "Okay, lean over and kiss the Tiger Wall," ordered Petersburg. "What for?" I demanded. Steve Petersburg, head naturalist and veteran river boatman, explained that the ritual would bring good luck for what lay ahead. We were looking for eyries deep in Dinosaur National Monument in extreme northwest Colorado. Rafting the Yampa River, above its confluence with the Green, seemed the direct approach.

The Tiger Wall is a perfectly smooth surface of yellowish sandstone marked by vertical bands of dark amber brown "desert varnish" alternating with the yellow rock. The stain is prevalent in the arid Southwest where exposed minerals in the sandstone react ever so slowly to the presence of rainwater. The beautiful wall actually leans out overhead, so the sky above was blocked when our big "donut boat" bumped up close.

A few hundred yards downstream from the spectacular wall is a notorious place called Warm Springs. There, the Yampa drops forty feet into a narrow channel under a huge fractured cliff. From time to time, big hunks of cliff fall into the river, so that the cataract there is usually violent, and always unpredictable. I kissed the wall and off we went. Surely, Petersburg would pull out above the rapids and walk down to have a look. Nope! Ahead, the river seemed to disappear. If only I had kissed the wall with more emotion. Suddenly an appalling hole in the river sucked us to the left. No chance now of keeping to the smoother water on the right.

In a flash we were upside down, the six of us, the twenty-two-foot raft, and all. It was cold and dark under there. My life jacket brought me up clear of the capsized raft. The boat floated by, its contents still strapped underneath. Fast water downstream threw me backward onto a submerged boulder field. Finally I got enough nerve to stand up and wade ashore.

I sat down to gather my wits. Overhead a lone bat jerked along. Here was a bat out in broad daylight! "Pretty risky," I said aloud. Never mind that I was a poor one to speak of risk. Quick as an arrow, a kestrel, smallest of the falcons, flew in, grabbed the bat, and was gone.

In the end, all that we lost at Warm Springs was a box of oranges and my Ray-Bans. Floating oranges were later reported by rafters scores of miles downstream in Utah, but the Park Service was never able to recover my glasses. Even if they had, my days of rafting for peregrines were over.

We plied the plateau for peregrines and found them everywhere. We also managed to set fire to Dinosaur with a gasoline stove. European cheat grass had colonized much of the intermountain West, and Dinosaur was no exception. When dried, the grass is explosive, especially if an unattended stove is plunked down in the middle of it. I think we burned about twenty acres before the firefighters arrived.

BRYCE CANYON AND CAPITOL REEF   Bryce is high ground overlooking the Paria River on its way to Lake Powell. We found three pairs of peregrines there among the wonderfully sculpted orange rock columns. The eyries were no real surprise; we were not far from Zion. Much more interesting was the discovery of a pair of merlins, a small falcon not normally nesting nearly so far south.

Late one afternoon, Bill Heinrich of the Peregrine Fund, Ron Joseph of the FWS, and I flew from the long smooth runway at Bryce, bound in my Bonanza for Capitol Reef, a hundred miles to the northeast in south central Utah. The idea was to spend the night, then to fly over the area in the morning to see where to later put down survey crews with the helicopter.

Before takeoff, Joseph stuck an airsickness patch behind an ear. Apparently the medication is absorbed through the skin. As it turned out, he would need it. We picked up a tailwind halfway to the strip called Wayne-Wonderland near Capitol Reef. The breeze soon became a roaring gale. The sky grew rough. Heinrich sat beside me, seemingly unconcerned. Joseph fell quiet in the back.

We arrived at Wayne in the gathering dusk to find a beautiful long runway of new black asphalt. The only problem was the wind was blowing *across* the runway at about forty miles an hour. I lined up for a landing only to find the drift to the side was far too great. A second pass, much lower, confirmed the long runway could not be used. Because of the side wind, the plane would have been pointed far to the left of the centerline at touchdown. The wheels would have skidded sideways on the new, hard surface. The silence from the backseat continued. We faced the prospect of returning to Bryce in the darkness against a fuel-consuming headwind. There was probably enough fuel, but flight over rough country in the dark is not for amateurs.

Then we noticed Wayne-Wonderland had what seemed to be an unpaved crosswind runway intersecting the asphalt from the south. The crosswind strip appeared poorly kept. But if we could land directly into the gale, the ground speed would be about thirty miles an hour. A couple of hundred feet would accommodate the Beechcraft. My plan was to set her down on the asphalt at the intersection of the two strips and then roll on into the grass. There was no sound from the backseat.

Touchdown on the asphalt went as planned. But ahead the grass strip suddenly disappeared. In its place was a prairie dog town. We weaved among the mounds, and slid to a halt a few feet short of an aluminum irrigation pipe. A guy by the name of Henderson from the NPS took us to headquarters. What I remember most clearly about that sketchy affair was that when Joseph climbed out of the airplane, he had airsickness patches behind *both* ears.

BIG BEND   West Texas has always had a sprinkling of peregrine eyries. Small ranges such as the Guadalupe and Davis mountains held a few pairs. Only in the canyon of the Rio Grande River in the Big Bend country is falcon habitat really extensive. The river cuts a thousand feet through ancient limestones that form high walls on both sides of the border. The beauty is matched only by the danger. The rock has weathered into ridged surfaces, the edges sharp against nylon climbing line.

Grainger Hunt and his helpers scoured the canyon and the nearby Chisos Mountains for blue meanies in the 1970s and were able to locate eight pairs or so. Oddly, the little enclave of peregrines seemed to produce fewer young each year than reported elsewhere. The pairs averaged a bit over one young per pair; elsewhere peregrines ordinarily produced roughly one and a half young per pair. Hunt suspected that pesticides were somehow getting to the birds, perhaps from Mexico. Tests showed substantial DDE in a few of the bird species the falcons ate, but the cause of the seemingly low rate of reproduction remained a mystery.

In 1985 I took the plateau crew to Big Bend under invitation from the NPS. We stayed at Barker House, a white, thick-walled hacienda owned by the Brewster County sheriff in the 1930s. The Mexican village of Boquillas sprawled a stone's throw across the shallow Rio Grande. After a hot day on the cliffs, a cold Corona could be had by wading the knee-deep river. Burros brayed through the night.

The scheme of setting teams down near likely falcon cliffs with a helicopter worked well in Big Bend. We found a few new eyries, bringing the known total to eleven or twelve. We also noted several of the pairs were not nesting and may have lost eggs or young before we found them. I mentioned those observations in our report. They triggered a minor controversy that continues to this day.

Everyone knows a viable falcon population must over time produce enough youngsters to replace adults lost by inevitable attrition (see Chapter I). Field-workers, quite naturally, have focused on the reproductive performance of raptors because it is easy and fun to watch. The mortality of adults is very difficult to measure because it happens at all times of year, and in obscure places. The pitfall is the assumption that reproduction must be excellent year after year. It is not fun to see a nest fail. But reproduction need only match mortality in the long run, offsetting the losses. If mortality is low, a low reproductive rate is not ominous. The difficulty is in measuring mortality.

Given that problem, the fallback position is to wait and see if the population is holding its own. After 1985, the NPS hired more surveys of peregrines in Big Bend, and at last count a few years ago, fourteen pairs were known. Compare that figure with the eight or so known in the 1970s. Naturally, the more recent number is not all actual increase, but partly more search and discovery.

In the meantime, all sorts of restrictions on visitor access to parts of the park became official policy because of the notion that the bird was in trouble. For example, the Santa Elena Canyon trail was closed even though the falcons always nested at least several hundred feet above it and hardly noticed the hikers. North of the river, trails in the Chisos Mountains were also closed.

In the few years prior to the removal of the peregrine from the federal endangered species list in 1999, the Big Bend peregrines were repeatedly offered as evidence the species was still in trouble. Perhaps the falcons there will continue to have fewer offspring than is typical of peregrines elsewhere. But there is no evidence of a decline in breeding pairs.

When we waded the river and headed for the little cantina and a cold beer in Boquillas, we paid no heed to the international border. Neither do duck hawks. In fact, not far south of the canyon of the Rio Grande, in full view of the Chisos Mountains eyrie, a massive escarpment called the Sierra del Carmen trails off to the vanishing point a hundred miles into Mexico. The spectacular red walls are surely a mecca for blue meanies. Perhaps those birds belong to Big Bend as much as to the Sierra. I like to think peregrines disperse both ways across our boundary, resulting in population stability in the region.

SCOTLAND   "I think it's dead." Ian Newton and I stood in the misty spruce plantation peering at a tiny one-day-old chick lying motionless in the palm of his hand. Newton was in the midst of a study on the ecology of the sparrowhawk in Scotland. The species is a pigeon-sized bird-eating hawk. He had brought me to the cold wet grove of dense spruce to show me a nest. The eggs had just hatched and the brooding female, in her haste to leave, had accidentally kicked her tiny youngster from the nest. I had watched helplessly as the white downy bit of fluff tumbled from branch to branch to its death.

Newton had never seen such an event before and dismissed it as insignificant in terms of the total reproductive effort of sparrowhawks in the region. I could not help but blame myself for the death of the bird. If I had not wished to see an active sparrowhawk nest this wretched thing might not have happened. The year was 1976 and I had gone to Scotland to help Newton and the young Richard Mearns trap and band peregrines at their eyries. The visit to the sparrowhawk nest was a diversion from the business of trapping blue meanies.

As a youth, Newton stumbled onto a sparrowhawk nest. The event shaped his future. He was to become a celebrated raptor biologist and always provided guidance for me. A couple of years ago, Queen Elizabeth officially recognized Newton for his work on the conservation of birds of prey.

Newton discovered that the small bird-eating sparrowhawk was governed by the same ecological principles that influence the lives of peregrines, even though the falcon is three times heavier than the hawk, and the two are as different biologically as dogs and cats. They belong to separate bird families. Both species eat mainly birds, and females are much larger than males (see Chapter I). Like female peregrines, female sparrowhawks are dependent on their mates for food. They do little more than eat, sit, and produce eggs in the early weeks of nesting. To be successful in nesting, the main thing a female sparrowhawk needs is a male who owns a territory rich in small birds to eat. The small size of the male comes in handy here, the better to match the evasive maneuvers of prey under pursuit. In such a vast area, females must explore to find such a male and his woodlot. Females dare not be content with waiting for mates to find them.

What is required if a male peregrine is to win in reproduction? Like Newton's sparrowhawks, a male must find and hold a nest site (cliff) against competition from other males trying to do the same thing. For Scottish sparrowhawks, the nest site is in a woodlot or forest of middle-aged trees, not too young and dense nor too old and open. For peregrines the need is the safety offered best by a tall cliff. The males of both species need nest sites not too remote from prey where it can be caught. In the light of Newton's work, we saw that males and females of both species are ecologically very different. However, the sexes are at the same time crucially complementary, so that collectively they contribute to the rearing of the young.

In all, Great Britain may be home to thirty thousand pairs of sparrow-hawks and fifteen hundred pairs of peregrines. The difference in numbers is no doubt related to the great abundance of woodlots compared to cliffs in Britain.

Mearns and I raced among the deep green hills in the uplands of southern Scotland. He drove a very small station wagon with a wooden body. As a passenger, I sat on the *left* side, inches from the windscreen. Normally there would have been a steering wheel to grasp. Imagine narrow tortuous roads bordered by rock fences in fog, all seen in terror at high speed from the left of the centerline. The nimble vehicle had two speeds: stop and wide open.

We hiked in the upland heather moor. Out of the mist came the figure of a huge man. He carried a shepherd's staff and wore a heavy brown wool cape over a kilt, protection from the chill and dampness. The calves of his legs were the size of fence posts, shaped by the mountains no doubt. In a deep brogue he directed us to the ground nest of a merlin, a small falcon. Four reddish-brown eggs lay hidden under a shrub of heather.

Mearns had completed university and was pondering his future. His father had urged him to give up playing around with birds and to "get a proper job." The lad persisted and published, with Newton, his findings concerning replacement and movements of blue meanies. It turned out that only about one in ten peregrines failed to return to nest the next year. About 90 percent survive to nest again. Living is easy in the gentle glens of Scotland. Moreover, the birds tend to stay in the region where they were born, especially the males. Seldom was a falcon found more than seventy miles from where it was first banded as a nestling.

Somewhere in the Southern Uplands is a quiet, beautiful glen near Tala Reservoir. The surrounding mountains are low and nearly treeless. Everything except a small stone farmhouse and the stone fences is some shade of soft green. Newton pointed to the peregrine eyrie on the slope, a half-mile from the farmhouse. Scarcely visible was a low outcrop of rocks in a shallow ravine a hundred yards above the valley floor.

We climbed up. I checked twice, but Newton was carrying no rope. A visit to almost any eyrie in Colorado would be impossible without a rope, a very long rope. Not so in southern Scotland. Most of the falcon ledges were reached by hand-over-hand climbing; the lush grass provided the handholds.

Once at the level of the ledge, Newton gestured to the opposite side of the tiny ravine. White down dancing in the wind caught my eye. There,

Bands from racing pigeons litter the eyrie of this thirty-seven-day-old peregrine on a crag in the uplands of southern Scotland.

crouched on a level place in the green, was a thirty-seven-day-old peregrine. She was mostly feathered, but tuffs of white down still clung here and there. In a week she would be on the wing. I worked horizontally toward her. She reared back, ready to make a last stand. On one leg she bore an aluminum band, fitted by Mearns nearly three weeks earlier.

"Do you see any pigeon bands?" queried Newton. Now that he mentioned it, six inches in front of the lone nestling was the dark red foot of a racing pigeon with a bright blue band still in place. Bands (the Brits call them "rings") were everywhere. Soon there were twenty-two in my pocket, including one from a pigeon banded in Belgium. Mearns had picked up all the bands he could find three weeks earlier, when he banded the nestling. Now the place was once more littered with bands.

Pigeon remains were common in peregrine eyries in Colorado. They were not someone's homing pigeons, but only common pigeons like those in cities. What was going on in Scotland? Newton confirmed that racing (homing) pigeons were indeed a big part of the fare of peregrines in Britain. A great fondness for pigeons had grown among the common folks in the industrial heartlands of Britain. At the same time, overgrazing of the mountains by sheep, together with widespread "afforestation" projects to create pulp and lumber on what was once open moor, changed the landscape. Tree plantations are notoriously poor in bird life. Overall, the effect of these land-use practices right across the uplands was to drastically lower the natural food supplies of falcons.

Now enter the blokes in cities like Glasgow, Liverpool, and Newcastle. Pigeon racing, no doubt involving many a wager, has become a major pastime. Every weekend, whole lorry-loads of pigeons, tens of thousands of birds, are shipped to southern Scotland. There they are set free. The pigeons must then fly the gauntlet, hundreds of kilometers, back to their lofts. Apparently some never make it.

The advent of this new major source of food was a boon to blue meanies. In fact, Newton believes that peregrines have increased well above their former natural level. The falcons were able to colonize even marginal crags because of it. In recent years the peregrine population has grown to over fifteen hundred pairs in Britain, half again those expected in former times.

The folks who race the pigeons know why some of their prized birds vanish. (Actually, the proportion of pigeons caught is tiny.) No doubt retaliation is directed at nesting falcons in the spring. The birds are weakly defensive and can be shot if the gunner employs stealth. Eggs and young are easily destroyed, greatly curtailing the need for fresh pigeons.

The racing-pigeon issue is just another twist in the way people have reacted to peregrines in the British Isles. In feudal times, at least certain pairs were protected so nobility could use their young in falconry. With the rise of shotguns and the hunting of red grouse, gamekeepers were employed by landowners to destroy all predators. At the time of World War I about twenty-three thousand gamekeepers were in the field.

Early in World War II, extensive programs to destroy peregrines were initiated by the War Ministry. The goal was to reduce interference with military homing pigeons carrying messages inbound from the Continent. As a result, the peregrine population was reduced 30 percent. Much of the devastation was on the south coast of England.

The British population recovered quickly after the war, only to be decimated again by the chlorinated pesticides such as dieldrin and DDT. Perhaps only a little more than 40 percent of the falcons remained in the early 1960s. By 1970, following reductions in the use of offending pesticides, a slow recovery began. Conservation sentiment ran high, and raptors in general were protected with great zeal. Guards were posted at many of the better-known eyries to head off foul play.

There's more to the story. Aside from the current concern by pigeon people, illegal persecution of falcons by gamekeepers is probably on the rise. Thanks to Newton and Mearns, the peregrine in Scotland is among the best studied of its kind anywhere. In a cruel twist, their data strongly implicate peregrines in significant loss of red grouse in certain regions. Grouse hunting is woven in the fiber of the people who own the hills of Scotland. Now, not only the ever-present falcon threatens hunting. More ominous is the loss of heather moors and grouse, victims of schemes to produce more sheep and to grow pulp and lumber.

No one can predict how the peregrine will fare in the next few decades in the United Kingdom. The ominous factors are habitat change and increasing ill feelings by grouse and pigeon people. Taking all this together, Newton feels the falcon population may decrease significantly in the coming decades. The direct causes would be loss of habitat capable of producing a variety of natural prey on one hand, and purposeful interference with nesting on the other. Of course there are people who work to protect the population. If the opposing sides finally draw a line in the sand, I would feel more encouraged were there a strong group of falconers ready to stand alongside conservationists to take the case for the peregrine.

CORNWALL   The southwest coast of England is drawn out into a peninsula roughly eighty-five miles long. The place is called Cornwall. This finger of land persists against the North Atlantic because it is made of hard black shale. Facing south, towering headlands overlook the clear blue-green sea. The man who best knows these seawalls and their peregrines is Dick Treleaven.

Treleaven has studied the blue meanies on the sea cliffs of Cornwall for nearly fifty years. Imagine a towering man, a mix of the late film director John Huston and the late actor Gregory Peck. But add, if you will, plenty of white hair. This man has studied his falcons for a long time.

The proper costume in spring in Cornwall is a pair of oilcloth trousers and a matching jacket. It seems to rain most of the time. The Brits ignore Gore-Tex, much preferring the dark green, waxy rain gear made by Barbour. A pair of rubber Wellington boots completes the costume.

The trail along the top of the sea cliffs allows good access to the eyries. The spacing between pairs varies, but some nest within a couple of miles or so of each other. Often the nest ledges are on steep grassy slopes. Because of the many ravines cutting down to the surf, you can sometimes find a point where it is possible to nestle down in the grass, out of the wind, and watch the young falcons through a spotting scope.

Treleaven is interested in all of the things the Cornish peregrines do through the year: pairing, choosing a ledge, rearing young, and so on. But his

Peregrines often roll over to begin a power dive.

claim to fame rests on his passion for watching the falcons hunt. He first saw a peregrine catch prey in 1955, and has been consumed by watching hundreds of successful hunts ever since. No living person has seen more attacks on prey by wild peregrines.

Hunting by Cornwall blue meanies takes several forms. Sometimes the falcons attack birds flying inland, over the neat farms (now off-limits because of mad cow disease) with pastures bordered by hedges. Most often, Treleaven has watched attacks over the sea. Often the quarry is a pigeon. Sometimes smaller birds such as petrels are knocked to the water, then plucked up and carried off.

In the classic style, the perched peregrine spots its prey flying along the coast a few hundred yards from shore. The falcon takes wing and climbs into the wind, sometimes over land and not at all directly toward the prey. All the time the falcon climbs full power to gain a height advantage in the stoop, which will surely follow. Often pigeons show no response to the peregrine at this point, and may even fail to take notice as the hunter hurtles down in a long shallow rush from behind.

In his book, *In Pursuit of the Peregrine*, Treleaven maintains that pigeons sometimes do not see the falcon at all, especially the singletons. Sometimes a bird may be taken from the rear of a small flock, and no one but the victim seems to notice. Of course the hunt is not always easy, even when the falcon is trying in earnest. Sometimes pigeons dodge at the last moment and roar off in the opposite direction, leaving the falcon in a stall.

In 1986, Treleaven took Bill Heinrich and me, and our wives, Beth and Betty, to his favorite eyrie on the south coast. We sat in the light rain watching snow-white breakers pound the black rocks far below. Nesting was over and the adults were not motivated to hunt. Searching for conversation, I suggested to Treleaven that he was really a falconer at heart, and that the need to see one more hunt might be totally compelling. A slight smile broke on his ruddy face. I realized he was really one up on us falconers, not needing to care for a captive bird yet having his hunt whenever he wishes.

ZIMBABWE   In 1989 Bill Heinrich, Jim Weaver, and I went to Zimbabwe (formerly Southern Rhodesia). Our purpose was to help Ron Hartley, and his students at a private boys' school called Falcon College, organize a long-term survey for peregrines and Teita falcons. The latter species (pronounced "ty-ta") is very much like a pigeon-sized peregrine. At that time, neither falcon was well known in Africa. In fact, Teita falcons had been found nesting on only a few high cliffs scattered from Ethiopia south to Zimbabwe, a distance of eighteen hundred miles. In all that country, less than a dozen pairs had ever been found.

Hartley is tall, lean, dark-haired, and bespectacled. He has enormous energy and enthusiasm. Although he is a strict disciplinarian, sometimes resorting to a stick to achieve compliance from his helpers, he is greatly respected. He is an ardent falconer and flies any kind of raptor he can obtain. He hunts all sorts of quarry. I expect he has even caught a mongoose or two with a hawk eagle.

The first night of our meeting we sought hares in the headlights of a truck from which his enormous hawk eagle could be launched. This unorthodox scheme worked very well, if you watched out for cobras while retrieving the eagle and prey in the dark. In fact, the second night I awoke to the sound of gunfire. The revolution that displaced white control of the government had occurred nine years before, yet I feared malcontents were still afoot. Not to worry! It was only Hartley seeing to a cobra in his chicken coop with his Webley .455.

We talked about the possibility that DDT might have decimated peregrines and other bird-eating raptors in south central Africa, as in the United States. In the years following our meeting, Hartley and his boys were able to find a few dozen pairs of peregrines and several pairs of Teita falcons in Zimbabwe. Pesticide tests and eggshell measurements did reveal some effect of the chemicals in peregrines. In fact, eggshell thinning was pronounced, but apparently not so serious as to jeopardize the population. It turns out that peregrines are fairly common in mountainous country in central and east Africa. Blue meanies extend right down to the Cape in good numbers.

The Teita falcon is more obscure, perhaps because it is small and is hard to find on the big rock walls. It may actually be quite rare, perhaps because of competition with peregrines, which could easily displace the trim little falcon if it attempted to nest nearby. A few pairs of Teitas nest in the gorge of the Zambezi River below Victoria Falls. But a thorough search for falcons there is ill advised. The river was the war frontier between Zambia and Zimbabwe; people forgot where most of the land mines were buried. Hiking the rim of the gorge was discouraged.

Heinrich, Weaver, and I decided to follow up on a report of Teita falcons at a place called Songwe Gorge. Things went poorly from the start. There was an incident with the vehicle on the first day. The little diesel pickup was not at fault. The problem was a goat. I was riding in the back, sprawled on a duffel in a camper shell filled with dust. Boom! I sat up and stared at Heinrich through the dirty rear window of the cab. It was apparent we were going faster and faster. We were unable to communicate. After several minutes of high-speed careening, the little yellow truck came to a stop. Weaver got out from behind the wheel, came to the back, and opened the tailgate. "We hit a goat" was his only comment. I had read somewhere that goats were worth a lot in Africa. Goats could be used to buy a wife. I suggested to Weaver that we not linger here long; the locals might have wheels.

That night we camped in a grove of huge old trees, a stone's throw from the Zambezi. The campground had several other campers: a young Austrian couple and their tiny child pitched a tent a few yards upstream, and below, a Swiss lad had pitched a flimsy nylon tent beside a termite mound only forty yards from us. The heads of a couple of hippos were barely visible in the slow water a few yards from the riverbank. On the far shore, two hundred yards further on, a half-dozen Cape buffalo wallowed in belly-deep water.

Weaver decided to sleep in the cab of the truck. It promised to be very cramped (but safe). Heinrich elected the camper shell, the glass up and the tailgate down to provide ventilation. I rolled out my bag on the plywood carrier above the camper shell, fully seven feet from the ground, exposed to the African sky.

My sleep was not very deep. There was a sound. I sat up in my bag and half twisted onto an elbow, the better to see the river. The view was blocked. In the near-darkness, far more obvious than I might have wished, was a mature bull elephant. I recoiled, and he bolted back a foot or two. Eye to eye, the distance was fifteen feet. What could be done? Nothing. Moments passed, then he slowly turned and walked upriver, stepping within inches of the Austrian family in their tent. My heart pounded.

As soon as the first light was apparent, I went off into sound sleep, assured all was well. It turned out there were fresh hyena tracks in the deep dust, inches from Heinrich's head in the back of the truck. The tracks were set on top of those of the monster bull elephant who appeared earlier in the night. Hyenas are well known for their fearless acts of predation on sleeping humans.

First thing in the morning, the Swiss chap, who was oblivious to our nocturnal visitors, headed for the small brick building that housed a spigot useful as a shower. He had no sooner left than a small band of baboons bent on mischief appeared. Quick to spot an unattended campsite, the dog-faced crowd helped themselves. I shouted and threw sticks at them. A big male, grasping a handful of dry spaghetti, walked deliberately toward me, lifting his eyebrows in a jerking motion, the better to flash pale patches of skin on his eyelids. When he had fully intimidated me, he sat on a termite mound a hundred feet away and slowly ate the dry spaghetti, stick by stick.

We arrived at the dry bed of Songwe River at about three in the afternoon. Weaver parked the truck off in the bush to conceal it. The cliff we were seeking was four or five miles up the gorge, so we planned to spend the night. It would be the most terrifying night of my life. The going was easy at first. The riverbed was mostly a pavement of dry, flat bedrock. In places the rock had eroded into depressions the size of bathtubs. Some still held stagnant water useless for drinking. But we soon resorted to soaking our clothes at each pool. In that way we endured the blazing heat.

We had walked about two miles when Weaver casually mentioned there were elephants ahead. Sure enough, about eight huge gray shapes moved slowly three hundred yards off, quartering toward us to our left. In my binoculars it was clear they had seen us. I felt very tiny and quite alarmed. Park rangers had mentioned only the previous day that elephants had recently killed two people. One was a photographer who tried for the ultimate close-up photo. The other was an experienced hunter found with rifle unfired. He had been rubbed into the dirt over a considerable area. Instead of coming down the gorge to us, the little herd turned into a side canyon. We presumed they could continue up the draw and leave the drainage.

We arrived under the big cliff at dinnertime. The gorge was about two hundred feet wide at the bottom. The cliffs on both sides dropped to the river bottom, which was strewn with huge boulders. The cobbled pile of rounded rocks was evidence of its ancient one-way journey down the gorge. We camped on sand opposite the cliff so as to gain a better view of its face.

Heinrich spotted a falcon flying across the gorge toward the cliff. "Peregrine," I said to myself. It seemed as if the falcon would fly over the top of the four-hundred-foot precipice. To my complete surprise, it landed on a ledge only halfway up. "Teita," said Weaver. The bird seemed to have the same shape as a peregrine, but the small size had made it seem much farther away. Perspective is everything when sorting out the falcons. The Teitas were nesting on the same ledge where Heinrich had found them the year before. He pointed out the tree on top to which he had secured his rope. No wonder so little is known about these small elusive falcons that nest so far away and so high up.

Our little campfire glowed in the sand as darkness came. I remember thinking how special it was to be camped in that remote canyon under a Teita falcon eyrie in central Africa. We slept in the increasing chill of the night. The gorge was quiet except for the mutterings of a troop of baboons that had climbed a few dozen feet up the cliff opposite us, seeking refuge in the night.

Suddenly, minutes before midnight, I bolted straight up. The noise was a penetrating trumpet of an elephant only a few paces downriver. I jumped up, expecting a charge at any moment. Fire! We needed a big fire. In a few seconds I had gathered an armful of brush and fumbled for matches. Another trumpet!

The herd we had seen on our way into the gorge apparently came back upriver. Now they wanted passage through our camp. The huge round boulders on the other side of the gorge were too treacherous for safe passage. Elephants are cautious about their footing. Inadvertently, we had blocked the elephants' path. More trumpeting. It was very close. The fire caught and flared up. At the limit of the firelight I could barely make out the great gray shapes. I put more wood on the fire and the huge animals retreated a bit. Weaver was the least concerned. I noticed, though, that he had his shoes on, ready for a sprint if necessary. There was only one tree in sight, and it surely was too small to hold the three of us beyond the reach of an elephant trunk. I threw more wood on the fire.

The elephants made another approach, seeking a way past us in the darkness. Apparently the fire had discouraged them. The breaking of sticks in the brush subsided, and the herd retreated. After a while I lay down and watched the constellation Orion move slowly overhead. There was small comfort in the knowledge that the sun was on its way at the same speed. I kept the fire burning till halfway to dawn. At about three o'clock in the morning, the elephants returned. This time there was no fanfare. They simply walked by us, so near that their low grunts and groans were heard over the roaring fire. Early the next morning, the baboons and we humans left the Teitas in peace. The evidence that people had camped there was mainly a pile of ashes in the center of a large area devoid of anything flammable.

IN REVIEW   Beginning two decades ago, first in the canyon and plateau country of the western United States and then in Scotland and Africa, I gained a sense of the vastness of peregrine country, and of the potential for countless numbers of the bird we had once considered rare. The better part of the fun of those travels was to be in the field with so many fine people. By 1990, those of us who had seen the blue meanie in the different settings knew the falcon had regained its place in the landscape.

Amazingly, in all of the survey efforts involving boats, planes, and helicopters, and hiking in dangerous places, no one was hurt. Some of us got wet, but Bucko Cade, and yours truly, did dry out.

If there are lessons from the searches described in this chapter, they are these. The Grand Canyon and the Colorado River upstream are sanctuaries for duck hawks whose numbers defy counts. Add to this falcon wellspring the upland canyons of the national parks and monuments on the plateau. Don't forget the hundreds of miles of big walls in the Indian reservation country. In all, the region comprises the core of peregrines on the continent south of the northern forests.

Scotland was a reminder of just how much punishment blue meanies can tolerate. The population made two major recoveries unaided. However, in Britain today the species still faces significant threats from humans because not everyone holds this magnificent bird in great esteem. But some Brits do, and I have to believe the peregrine will always be safe in Treleaven's Cornwall.

XII » PEREGRINES REGAIN THE SKIES

DELIVERY TO YELLOWSTONE   "Good night, y'all." I reached for the switch, shut off the light, and settled into my bed in the motel in West Yellowstone, Montana. It was 1983, or maybe 1984—there were so many trips to Yellowstone that they blend together. I had arrived that afternoon with five partly feathered duck hawks from the breeding barn in Fort Collins, Colorado. The following day they would be placed in a hack box on the Madison River in the park. The flight in my 1952 Beechcraft along the backbone of the Rockies had required only a little more than two hours. But such flights were always a bit of a strain, no matter how good the weather.

Bill Heinrich of the Peregrine Fund and Bob Oakleaf, a biologist for the Wyoming Game and Fish Department, were sharing the seedy little room. Oakleaf, who bears a striking resemblance to the cowboy actor Lee Van Cleef, wasn't sleepy. He talked on in the darkness about our meeting with the two college kids in the morning. They would camp at the hack site and care for the falcons until they could fly and hunt. Oakleaf pointed out the difficulty of rafting to the south side of the swift Madison River with the young birds. He mentioned the important gear Heinrich must produce. He wondered if the pine martens would raid the cache of frozen quail again this year. And don't forget the pepper spray, because this was grizzly country.

None of it concerned me. I had done my part. The meanies were safely delivered. In the darkness I noticed an orange glow in the bowl of Oakleaf's pipe. My wife Betty affectionately calls him Stovepipe because of the ever-present pipe. Pop! Off came the tab from a can of beer. Heinrich had given up on sleeping. The two talked of the next day far into the night.

CALIFORNIA COMEBACK   In the early 1980s, Ed Harrison, founder of the Western Foundation for Vertebrate Zoology, and his right-hand man, Lloyd Kiff, had taken to having lunch on the top floor of Harrison's high-rise office building in Los Angeles, enjoying the spectacular skyline. One day while sipping a second margarita, Kiff said, "Wouldn't it be nice to have peregrines nesting nearby so we could watch them during lunch?" No sooner said than done. Thanks to Brian Walton, peregrines were hacked from the top of the building three years in succession. The urban meanie came of age. Today, twenty pairs nest each season in Los Angeles.

By the mid-1980s, releases in California by the Santa Cruz group, headed by Walton, were in full swing. And the new birds flying off were paying off. At the time, the number of pairs nesting in California had grown to sixty. My friends Monte Kirven, Janet Lithicum, Kurt Stolzenburg, and Rob Ramey (the last two were superb on long ropes) were responsible for much of the fieldwork, along with Jeep Pagel. Early on, Jeff Monk and Merlyn Felton were essential to the releases, and Lee Aulman saw it through until the work was finished in the early 1990s.

The Santa Cruz operation originally had about a dozen pairs of captive peregrines. They could produce only about fifty young each year, far fewer than needed to jump-start the pitifully small wild population in California. So Walton and his colleagues began what was surely the last great egg robbery in the civilized world.

By the mid-1980s, up to eighty peregrine eggs stolen from as many as twenty-eight pairs of wild falcons were brought to the incubators in the Lower Quarry at the university at Santa Cruz each year. Over all the years, about five hundred falcon eggs were gathered up. Perhaps one in four were bad when collected, and many others could not be hatched because of severe shell thinning caused by DDT. But well over two hundred of the chicks hatched in captivity were fostered back to wild peregrine parents.

Soon Kiff and Harrison would have their meanies and margaritas too. But not everyone was happy to see the explosion of West Coast peregrines. A coastal colony of California least terns, a seriously endangered species, ended up in the hunting range of a few pairs of duck hawks. The rare terns were being eaten. Not long after the endangered peregrine was declared out of risk in 1999, the FWS actually began a permit process to allow the *shooting* of peregrines in the region of the tern colony. Folks who had worked to see the falcon restored were outraged; the permit process was canceled. (But several falcons were trapped and "relocated.")

Los Angeles is the home of many pigeon fanciers. This spelled trouble from the start. Imagine a flock of rollers or tumblers, both of which plummet from the sky in fits of nearly uncontrolled aerobatics, demonstrating their death-defying stunts anywhere within a thousand yards of a male blue meanie. Sometimes the displays were rudely interrupted. In retaliation, pigeon folks in California have shot at least fourteen peregrines.

Peregrine encounters were sometimes sorrowful. Dan Berger was watching a pair of duck hawks on a tall building near Pasadena when a bright green parakeet (budgie) flew by, obviously someone's escaped pet. The bird fluttered down the street and around a building, out of view. Presently, Berger noted the male falcon was gone. He thought no more about it until the peregrine returned, carrying a small bright yellow-green object.

Recently I learned other budgies had met the same fate. Between 1986 and 1991, Utah wildlife biologist Bob Walters tallied a long list of prey of the falcons nesting on the Hotel Utah and a nearby building in downtown Salt Lake City. It included two budgies, a cockatiel, and a monk parakeet. And just to show how really versatile they were, the pair also managed to catch a couple of hummingbirds and allegedly a male *goshawk*. The hawk is a formidable hunter in its own right.

THE RECOVERY TEAM   Thirty years ago the Endangered Species Act became law. It was a "flower child" of the growing awareness, by people in general, of a widespread lessening of the quality of the environment. Earth Day was first observed in the spring of 1970. Clay White and I, both at Cornell University for the year at the invitation of Tom Cade, sat on the library steps and watched the excitement. Longhaired students, the women sometimes in indecent attire in the form of thin T-shirts, sang and danced in celebration of their discovery that there is a natural world after all, and that it was getting beaten up.

At the time, Richard Nixon's administration was about to invent the Environmental Protection Agency. The first administrator, Ruckelshaus (see Chapter V), would soon ban DDT. Further, in 1973, Nixon signed into law the act that provided shelter for endangered species, including the peregrine; the act became the engine we used to drive the falcon's recovery.

By 1975, blue meanies, along with 435 other species, were on the endangered list. The act decreed that "endangered" meant there was a clear risk the species would become extinct before long without human intervention, and "threatened" meant there was a high likelihood the creature would become endangered. The subjective nature of these definitions has been an annoyance ever since. One person might claim that a species was about to go down the tubes, and another would claim its relative well-being.

The endangered species legislation bestowed broad powers on federal agencies to map out and protect habitat critical to a stricken species. This aspect of the document turned out to be of minor importance to the recovery of peregrines, except perhaps in California and parts of the eastern United States. In many places the provision was irrelevant to peregrine recovery. The only real estate that could be closely linked to duck hawks was the nesting cliff. Because most cliffs had been abandoned at the time of the act, only a limited number of places in the United States were actually declared critical.

The best part of the act was the directive for federal agencies to cooperate to assist species in dire shape. This meant that powerful bureaus such as the USFS, BLM, and the NPS would all work together on behalf of peregrines. Further, the act said they should consult with state wildlife departments. This was new ground, and would be of major importance in speeding help for the falcon.

Not long after the act became law, a chap in the FWS by the name of Gene Ruhr dreamed up the idea of creating a committee to draft a plan for a species' recovery and to oversee its application. Thus was created the "recovery team." By 1975, fifty such teams had been appointed by the FWS, each usually dealing with a different species. Canada had no equivalent act, but administratively devised a recovery plan and then realized that a recovery team would be needed to implement it. The team first functioned in 1986.

Among the teams designated was one to become guardian of the peregrine in thirteen states making up the Rocky Mountain and Southwest region. I was invited to come aboard. The years ahead would be a wonderfully productive time. Imagine the task. Our region extended from North Dakota to Idaho, south to Arizona, and southeast to Texas. In all, nearly one and a half million square miles were included, amounting to about 46 percent of the coterminous forty-eight states. Of course, huge hunks of the region were not meanie habitat, especially Kansas and Nebraska, and large parts of Texas. But to the west, where the ground was rugged, lay half a million square miles where peregrines had once been scattered.

Keith Schreiner, the new chief of the endangered species program for the FWS, appointed the entire team, nine of us in all. There were my old friends and fellow falconers, Morley Nelson, Jerry Craig, and Frank Bond the attorney. Bond had been a student at Colorado College in my first few years there. He played lacrosse and was Bob Stabler's protégé. Stabler taught zoology and coached lacrosse as well.

Other team members were biologists Richard (Dee) Porter of the FWS, Joel Kussman of the NPS, Dale Wills of the USFS, and the late Al Heggen of the Utah Game and Fish Department. The ninth member was Gene Knoder, a pilot and survey biologist for the National Audubon Society. So there we were, the first team to tackle the decimation of peregrines on the continent.

Only Craig, Porter, and I had done serious research work with duck hawks; the others were mainly staunch enthusiasts. Except for me, all were skilled politically, either as bureaucrats themselves or as those who had dealt with government folks. Looking back, we were all green for the task ahead. Most surprising, the thing that made our little group work was an early camaraderie. We fell in like a gang of thieves, all bent on saving the blue meanie.

Schreiner summoned us to Denver and told us up front what we could and could not do. The others may have been familiar with taking orders, but not me, I joked. I was a college professor, not accustomed to such things. In my fifteen years at the college, no one had told me what to do. Nevertheless, Schreiner's directives made sense and we all agreed.

He pointed out that as an official recovery team, we were autonomous. We were to build a recovery plan based on the best biological information, and the draft plan would be exempt from the freedom-of-information provision. We were allowed to be a consultant to agencies other than the FWS, and we could oversee the implementation of the plan, once the regional director of the FWS approved it. Approval would come only after full public review.

There were a lot of things we could not do. We could not act in a political manner, nor could we designate or change the endangered status of the falcon. We could not seek funds for the recovery program or become an activist group. Schreiner wanted us to keep out of court and not to "jeopardize our professional scientific position." We had no role in carrying out field studies, and we could not put the finger on people or agencies that were ignoring the act. We would receive no compensation; this task was a public service. I was proud to be a part of it.

Craig was the team leader. He kept us on track and saw to the busywork. His go-between in the FWS was Bill White, who was a very competent asset. We worked on the recovery plan from early 1976 through spring 1978. Some of it was very boring. There was a big section on the establishment of a public information system. Ultimately, nothing came of it, partly because no one was interested in bringing the bird into the limelight. A long section on protecting "critical habitat" for meanies went largely unnoticed; only seventeen nesting areas were eventually proposed for critical-habitat status in the Rocky Mountain region. The service took the list to the point of publishing it in the *Federal Register*. Then the list was canned because of the supposed risk to the falcons if the eyrie locations were made public.

I had no interest in the budget section and left it to the agency folks on the team. No one paid attention to the actual details of fund allocation anyway. Budgets for recovery were seldom realistic. Money seemed to appear when it was really needed. The plan projected a cost of restoration amounting to $2 million in the first five years; less than half of that was actually spent.

THE RECOVERY PLANS   Our scheme for the recovery of peregrines in the Rockies and the Southwest centered on captive breeding and hacking, and on egg removal, hatching in captivity, and fostering the young back to wild pairs. This was no surprise to anyone. Bond and I had strong connections with the Peregrine Fund, which had just established a major breeding facility at Fort Collins, Colorado, with the help of Craig in the Colorado Division of Wildlife. At that time, this facility of the fund was on the verge of producing several scores of meanies each spring.

We finished the Rocky Mountain/Southwest plan in late 1976. In due time it was approved by the top folks in the agency. The FWS threw a coming-out party for the decree in early 1978. Almost fifty scientists and agency people from the affected states gathered in Denver to speculate on what we had wrought. Craig explained what the plan was all about. I discussed ways to search for peregrines and talked about the pesticide situation. Bill Burnham, who was then in charge of the Fort Collins breeding facility, explained hacking and the role of landholding agencies in that endeavor.

It can be said that the 1978 Denver meeting was the wake-up call for state wildlife agencies. Most important, they became aware of the need to enter into written coopcrative agreements with the FWS in order to receive matching federal money for meanie management. As with everything else, things happen only when funds are available.

MORE TEAMS   In what might seem government extravagance, the FWS soon appointed three other peregrine recovery teams, and each team drafted a recovery plan. Actually, the regional situations of the falcon required different approaches. The Alaskan plan focused on keeping track of the northern nesting birds, which had declined to perhaps a third of their former numbers. The plan also sought to stamp out the use of DDT and similar pesticides in Mexico and countries farther south; little came of the latter effort.

The Pacific states team developed a recovery plan that embraced captive breeding and release, and also the hatching of wild-taken eggs in captivity. California, Oregon, and Washington had lost most of their peregrines and were anxious to get them back. By the way, Nevada was in the region served by the Pacific plan, but apparently that state has always been meanie-poor. The Santa Cruz group in the old stone quarry worked mainly in California in the early 1980s, but later released birds in Oregon. (Eventually, the Boise facility of the Peregrine Fund dumped scores of falcons in Washington, Idaho, and Montana.)

If the Pacific plan had a fault, it was the specification of the numbers of breeding pairs required in each of a dozen subregions before the species could be declared safe. As it turned out, peregrines came back in big numbers in the West Coast states, but the birds failed to read the plan and sometimes were too scarce in certain areas and adequate or plentiful in others.

Believe it or not, when it came time to remove the peregrine from the endangered and threatened list, some people argued that since the precise prescribed pattern of recovery had not occurred (even though total numbers were adequate), the peregrine should not be removed from the list. This absurdity was a good example of how the FWS was held hostage when formal expectations suffered from excessive detail.

The eastern team devised a plan that sought to establish a new population of duck hawks on landscapes where the original birds had been totally eradicated by DDT. That enormous region included the Appalachians, New England, and the Midwest.

Actually, Cade's group at Cornell had released about two hundred peregrines into the central Appalachians and Atlantic seaboard by the time the plan was officially approved in May 1979. The eastern plan, like the Pacific plan, also specified fairly precisely how many pairs must nest in each of several subregions. This provision would also ultimately work against delisting the falcon.

FAMILY PLAN FOR RECOVERY   "Come in, y'all." Standing before me, nearly filling the doorway of his poor little house, was Ralph Rogers. His wife, Missy, peered around him and renewed the offer. The year was 1969. The scene might have been set in a Steinbeck novel. The box house with a low pyramid roof sat squarely in the center of a recently picked cotton field near New Deal, Texas. The Rogerses became schoolteachers, she in grade school; he taught high school biology.

It was early October. I was on my way to trap and band peregrines on Padre Island. Rogers, whom I had not actually met, was to follow me from his home to the beach. But he needed help. The two enormous airplane wheels that would be bolted to the rear of his fenderless Volkswagen Beetle could not be transported inside the tiny car. The big soft tires would provide much-needed flotation for travel over soft sand. It was a dune buggy, Rogers-style. The tires filled my station wagon. We made off for Padre Island with a couple of paper sacks filled with hot tamales wrapped in cornhusks, a gift from Ralph's Hispanic neighbor.

Thoughts of blue meanies on the barrier beaches seemed to compound the journey through the endless expanse of Texas. There should be signs to encourage weary disheartened motorists. The signs might read: YOU ARE LEAVING WEST-CENTRAL TEXAS, or maybe WELCOME TO THE NORTHERN PART OF SOUTH TEXAS. We drove for hours without a sense of progress. Fortunately, we had the tamales.

In 1976, Ralph and Missy left Texas for Montana. Their goal was to find and settle in the best grouse country where peregrines could be flown. They built a breeding barn and begged for falcons to fill the chambers. In 1979, ten fertile eggs were laid at their place. The local game warden thought it necessary to check on the operation every two days to be sure the falcons were really breeding in captivity.

Early in the 1980s, the first hack sites were set up in Montana. At that time, the state had lost all of its wild peregrines, so far as anyone knew. The Rogers family took to operating hack sites each summer as soon as the falcons in their barn finished making homegrown peregrines. In 1981, I flew a load of four falcons, *and* a puppy, to them at a hack site on the spectacular Red Rocks Wildlife Refuge just west of Yellowstone Park.

In 1984, the Rogers family took a break from seeing to falcon success at hack sites. They spent the season pounding nails into the new falcon-rearing barns of the Peregrine Fund in Boise. The land for the facility was purchased with donations from falconers. The following year, in a truly unique and

Ralph Rogers and his wife, Missy, with the pale South American form of the peregrine. Photo courtesy of Ralph Rogers.

heroic move, Ralph and Missy decided to hack *their own* homegrown peregrines.

From 1988 to 1999, they spent every summer in a tent in the Judith or Moccasin mountains in central Montana, or near the Missouri River. They saw to the survival, and eventual independence in Montana skies, of the birds they had bred in captivity. The BLM helped make it possible. In all, the Rogers family hacked sixty-five of their homegrown duck hawks and sent another twenty to hack sites in the Midwest and East.

Their son, Scott, and daughter, Andy, knew summertime meant a tent in the wilderness and the wailing of young falcons learning to care for themselves. Both children became biologists, she a specialist on releasing California condors in Arizona, and he working to restore endangered fish in the Grand Canyon.

A couple of years ago, Betty and I sat beside a fire ring near the Breaks of the Missouri River in the heart of the Blackfoot country in central Montana. Ralph and Missy sat on the other side of the flames. We talked of the wonderful increase in pairs of peregrines in Montana, from *none* in the 1980s to nearly fifty now. We could sense their pride in the restoration work.

I leaned back and looked up. Overhead, thirty-two lodgepoles converged at the peak of the teepee. Encircling the interior, seven yards across, was a canvas lining richly painted in Indian symbols fit for a Lakota chief. But that teepee belonged to Ralph and Missy. In the years of the recovery work, we tended to think only in terms of the falcon as the subject of our presence, and of the ways we might influence its future. The Rogers family knew it was also the other way around.

"PURE" PEREGRINES   The recovery plan for the eastern United States caused a major flap. The problem centered on the simple, irrevocable fact that pesticides had wiped out the original duck hawk. To some people, this meant that the act could not apply, and government funds should not be used to support work on alien peregrines. Since the population was now gone, how could a recovery occur? The conclusion to be reached from that notion is that any peregrine released would be a foreigner.

Perhaps a bit of clarification is in order. Three subspecies of peregrines were recognized as native to North America. By definition, subspecies are *geographical* populations that seem more or less distinct in details of size or color or other genetically based features. Because peregrines nest widely in a great range of environments, slight variation in form was indeed present. With some difficulty, it was possible to sort the meanies on the continent into a marine group in the Pacific Northwest (the Aleutian birds are most distinct), tundra-nesting falcons ranging from Alaska to Greenland, and a type scattered very widely in the continent's interior. As you might expect, this last group (given the Latin name *anatum*, meaning "of the ducks") was, and still is, quite variable.

If you look carefully at individual falcons, some are distinctive. But the variation is often subtle, and by no means holds true for every individual bird from a given locality. I like the variation. It's fun to notice the peculiarities in Colorado peregrines. In some broods of fledglings, the youngsters may be quite different; some may be pale, others dark, and others in between. Adults are different too.

The most graphic example of variation I recall was a pair that nests to this day in full view of Interstate 70 in the mountains of Colorado. The male was small and pure white underneath, with only very faint gray transverse bars; the mask through his eyes and cheeks was no wider than your little finger. His back was pale blue-gray. He would fit, unnoticed, among males nesting on Baffin Island in the Arctic. He seemed the perfect tundra meanie. His huge mate was the opposite. She had a very heavily barred orange-tinted belly, solid black head, and dark slate back. She looked like specimens of the extinct eastern duck hawk I had seen in museums. The differences between sexes did not matter; they fledged two ordinary young on the first try.

Peregrines everywhere are not all cast from exactly the same mold. The genes responsible for shape and color are not always expressed in the same way when they finally end up together in an individual. Genes often mix and blend in unpredictable ways. There is a good deal of genetic variation in some meanie populations, less in others.

And what is more, the variation is really academic, the kind of stuff to be sorted out by those scientists, like my friend Clayton White, who love the variation as much as I do. On the practical side, in the field, virtually no one can say for sure where that duck hawk sailing overhead came from. Most of us are fully satisfied to be certain we are watching a peregrine, and not some other species such as a prairie falcon.

TEMPEST IN A TEAPOT   When the eastern recovery plan was nearing completion, word got out that it endorsed the release of meanies with ancestry from other parts of the world, such as Spain, northern Europe, Australia, and South America. (Most of the birds ultimately released actually had at least one North American parent.) The notion that "foreign" peregrine genes would result in "mongrelization" of North American duck hawks gained momentum. The FWS told Cade to stop releasing non-native peregrines in the East. Cade mounted a major protest. Opposition to the FWS ban came in from the National Wildlife Federation, the National Audubon Society, and the World Wildlife Fund. The FWS hung tight and silent.

In 1979, the highly respected organization of professional ornithologists, the American Ornithologists' Union (AOU), passed a resolution calling for the release of native peregrines only. The pronouncement supported the FWS. The document stated there was a need to "protect the integrity of native ecosystems and gene pools." The incredible resolution went on: "The use of exotic stocks for replacement or augmentation should be avoided to preclude negative impacts on native ecosystems and contamination of native gene pools." This decree was strictly rubbish.

The resolution caused an uproar. Bud Tordoff, then in fact president of the AOU, wrote his disapproval of the resolution in a letter to Warren King of the International Congress for Birds of Prey. Tordoff was embarrassed by the resolution and pointed out that the environment, by "ongoing natural selection," would measure the mettle of each peregrine, no matter its ancestry. He was certain the individuals who made the cut would be those to foster new generations in the eastern half of America.

There was a beauty in what Tordoff said. The New England crags, the Carolina mountains, the nest towers on the Atlantic beaches, and even the cities, west to Cedar Rapids, would shape the meanies of tomorrow and of the distant future. This force would result in peregrine falcons better fitted to their world. Finally, in 1980, the FWS lifted the ban. The agency staff at last agreed with nearly everyone that a peregrine is a peregrine.

Once in a while, I yearn for the eastern duck hawks from the days of the Craigheads and Berthrong, Rice, and Stabler. But even if there had been no DDT, the original bird could not have remained the same. Massive new environmental pressures, caused in part by sprawling society, would have changed the falcon. The old birds would have been in for a real beating. Perhaps they would have slowly adjusted, adapting to nest on buildings and bridges more and more.

In this light, it should not bother us that one of the first pairs nesting in the East, on a Baltimore skyscraper in 1980, had an unusual genetic background. The male was of tundra origins, as determined from leg bands that had been placed when he was released as a youth. The female traced to a parent from California. Her other parent came from Chile. Her name was Scarlet; her mate was Rhett. Their descendants probably fly the eastern skies today.

In the West, from the Rockies to the Pacific, the question of introducing non-native meanies was more easily answered. All the captive breeders held in the West were from that region. The release of only native stock into the Rockies was, for me, not so much a biological imperative as a way to avoid political controversy.

COLORADO TURNAROUND   Colorado entered into a cooperative agreement with the FWS in 1978 and thus had funds for working on peregrine recovery. From then on, Craig hired several field observers each summer. Eventually, over the years about forty workers were students from Colorado College. Most had been in my field classes.

"This is Beth and I think we have found a new peregrine eyrie," said the voice on the phone. Beth Braker blurted out that she and her coworker had just found really fresh whitewash on a four-hundred-foot monolith called the Palisade, overlooking the Dolores River in far western Colorado. At the time only a handful of pairs were known in the state. I pointed out to her, perhaps impatiently, that whitewash does not make a peregrine eyrie. They should go back in the morning and keep their eyes glued to their spotting scopes. When I hung up, I regretted having been so abrupt. Not long before, the girls had rolled a jeep on loan from the USFS. No one was hurt.

The next day a breathless Braker (now a professor at Occidental) assured me there was indeed a pair of blue meanies on the Palisade. This was the first of many pairs that we would discover in the red rock country along the Utah border. We searched intently, but at first the discoveries came slowly. One evening Craig called and said a pair had been found near Durango. The observers (we called them "temporaries" because they worked only in summer) who found the eyrie were greatly alarmed because the female had laid eggs on a ledge where the cliff merged gently with the brushy slope. The eyrie was literally a "walk in," they said. It would be easy pickings for a coyote, bear, or bobcat.

I drove to Durango the next day to see what could be done to save the nest. It turned out the ledge was more of a "crawl on" than a "walk in." It was necessary to crouch under an overhanging part of the cliff to make way along the ledge. Further, the ledge was only six feet wide at its narrowest point. Beyond the lip was a crisp drop of over a hundred feet to the talus below. I knelt in the brush and saw four vulnerable eggs only twenty feet away. Sometimes even meanies choose poorly.

What was needed was a fence. Wire mesh could be purchased in Durango. But wire would be difficult to attach securely to the cliff. My thoughts drifted to the rock walls built by the Anasazi a thousand years before at nearby Chimney Rock. Here was unlimited building material close at hand, big flat slabs of Mesa Verde sandstone, each weighing sixty pounds or more. I worked as fast as possible to minimize the time the female would be kept from the eggs. The resulting barrier was not as well fitted as those made by the ancient wall builders, but it was tight and very, very heavy. The falcons reared their youngsters in safety.

Twenty years ago there were virtually no peregrines nesting in Colorado east of the Continental Divide. Each spring we checked the dozen or so old eyries. The duck hawks were gone. This was a grim time. Would newly released birds discover the old cliffs? The turning point came on the Conejos River. I stalked down through the dense Douglas firs to the top of the cliff. The elevation was ten thousand feet above sea level. Deep melting snow on the north-facing slope made progress slow. The view from cliff-top was among the most spectacular at any peregrine site. I peered into the floor of the glacier-cut valley, at least a thousand feet below. A blue meanie drifted past, wings held stiffly out in a slight downward attitude. He had not seen me. I hid in the rich green conifer foliage, my scope trained on his favorite snag. Sooner or later, he would land there.

A shadow flashed by. I caught another movement through the branches. I glanced through the scope. He seemed to fill the field. Such a close view of a wild peregrine is always a thrill. He was ordinary in regard to plumage, perhaps a bit on the pale side. He reached up and scratched his face with a talon. He was not ordinary at all. He bore a colored aluminum band. He was a released bird. Here was a released peregrine, now grown to adulthood, breeding in the wild.

Reoccupancy of East Slope eyries was painfully slow. In 1975, the pair at the deep canyon called the Royal Gorge on the Arkansas River failed to return. Every year thereafter I searched the chasm, but year after year, nothing. Once in the late 1970s, while I sat quietly searching the canyon walls through the scope, a pair of white-throated swifts, locked together, spiraled down and crashed to the ground within arm's reach. They were either mating or fighting. Either way, before they could regain their senses, I grabbed both with one hand. When I set them free, they flew off like the bullets they are. I may be the only human to have hand-caught two swifts at once.

Without the peregrines, the Royal Gorge lost much of its aura. I once loved the place. Tom Rawles, the old professor and falconer who had figured in my appointment at the college, told me of the site. Now, the spectacular chasm was quiet except when the Denver and Rio Grande train roared in the bottom. Pigeons enjoyed free access to the place; many nested on the thousand-foot walls. Once in a while a blue-gray pigeon would give me a start as it darted by. Often a score of pigeons would race down the middle of the canyon, headed for grain in the distant Arkansas valley. I tried to follow them into the haze with the scope, hoping to see a peregrine attack. The pigeons went unmolested.

In late April 1984 I was back on my rock at the gorge. Almost two hours passed. Something was different. "The pigeons, *the pigeons are gone*," I said out loud. I went on full alert, scanning the opposite wall for a glimpse of any falcon. Nothing. As if it were yesterday, I can remember then lifting my gaze from the spotting scope to rest my eye. I glanced upriver. Coming head on, less than a hundred yards away, was an adult duck hawk. He passed by, black mask distinct from his white cheek. Peregrine falcons have been in the gorge ever since.

One spring I sent Mark Robert down the rope to band a brood in the gorge. Robert (pronounced ro-*bear*) worked tirelessly on the restoration in Colorado for several years. In this instance I failed to take into account the distance down to the eyrie, the heat of the day, and the demands of return up the rope. Robert was exhausted on the ledge, so I got on the radio and asked for assistance. Two climbers gave us a hand. We laughed when the sheriff's deputy in charge hiked down the dry rocky slope above the eyrie wearing black dress shoes, which surely went to the trash.

THE FIFTH TEAM   By the late 1980s the rebound of the blue meanie in the United States surprised even those, like me, who were card-carrying optimists. In Alaska, the number of known pairs had doubled in a decade. To the south, in California, in Colorado, and in the East, where surveys for nesting pairs had been ongoing and extensive, even better gains were reported. In some areas, the decade prior to 1988 had seen three- and fourfold increases, in part the result of the release of thousands of youngsters (Chapter X).

In 1988 the Cornell University facility of the Peregrine Fund was disbanded. Some further releases were done in the East with birds from the Boise headquarters. At that time, recovery had only begun in the northern tier of the western states, and there was interest in speeding up releases there. There was even talk of sending young to Alberta to assist the Canadian program.

By 1988, the original recovery plans had been in effect about a decade, and although there were minor revisions, the plans were clearly outdated. Further, squabbles had erupted over issues such as "genetic purity," the advisability of releases of peregrines in cities, and which states should get the limited number of youngsters available for release. The demand for releasable peregrines had exceeded the supply.

Beyond these relatively simple biological questions, the human factors in falcon recovery had changed. The change was ominous. Inevitably, the recovery plans generated a great deal of interest and activity related to peregrines. At that time, hundreds of federal and state wildlife and land management officials focused much of their professional attention on the falcon. Because of the vastness of the western recovery region, the general lack of leadership, and the increase in differences of opinion on how to proceed, something had to be done. The Portland office of the FWS called for a planning session in Las Vegas in August 1988.

About forty key people showed up at Las Vegas, Nevada. Ten were from the FWS, including the recovery programs manager for the West, Andy Robinson. There were five folks from the NPS, four from the Peregrine Fund, and a dozen from the various state wildlife departments.

I glanced around the room. Many present were friends I had known for so long: Petersburg from Dinosaur; Craig from Colorado; and Burnham, Heinrich, and Clay White. Walton from the Santa Cruz group was there; Oakleaf from Wyoming; and Butch Olendorff, now deceased, from the BLM in Idaho. Nearly all the others had worked on the recovery effort in one way or another. Most of us knew each other. It was an impressive group. Members from three original recovery teams were there. I hoped great strides could now be made in finalizing the return of the species. This was not to happen.

The meeting had two goals. The first goal was to summarize the gains made by the blue falcon throughout the West. The news was very good. Across the board, reports of increases in breeding pairs left little doubt that a true recovery was under way. The second item on the agenda was to see how the group would respond to an FWS proposal to combine and revise the old recovery plans for the Pacific states and the Rockies/Southwest. A new recovery team could be assembled to do the work. The new document would be called an addendum.

The FWS people seemed enthusiastic. They had gone to the trouble to suggest in some detail how the West might be divided into "recovery regions." When the population in a region reached a safe level, it could be removed from the endangered list separately from those in the other regions. My friend Olendorff and I sketched where these regions might be; we came up with very different maps. This was the first red flag suggesting differences of opinion might develop.

Nothing happened for *one year*. Then in August 1989, the FWS appointed the western recovery team with five members: Kiff, White, Hunt, Al Harmata (a respected eagle researcher), and I. I was named leader. We were eager to get to work and set the final course for the recovery of the blue meanie.

First off, there was laundry to be washed. The FWS told us to first recommend whether or not urban releases should be encouraged. Next off, the FWS needed to take a position on the genetic issue; should only falcons with known roots in the western United States be released there? Finally, where should future releases occur? We were also told to provide a draft addendum in six months.

We responded to the questions in November 1989. We urged that future releases be made mainly in the northern states, where the falcons were few, and that some urban releases could be made if necessary, and that only western peregrines should be released in the West. This last decree was based on the great progress of recovery thus far using only western birds. Why introduce outsiders now and stir people up?

The team then met with regional biologists in nine states to learn what the local concerns actually were. Our little group finished a draft plan based on FWS guidelines at the end of 1990. We felt the falcon merited delisting in the Southwest, but recommended it be retained on the list as threatened in the far West and northern Rockies. Our last meeting took place on the eve of Operation Desert Storm. The draft addendum was sent out for review.

In September 1991 a variety of agency folks from the Southwest region met to discuss our addendum. The accord that the original plans had enjoyed disappeared. From that point on, and to this very day, no peregrine policy proposed by the FWS, whether drafted by the service itself or by an independent group such as ours, avoided scathing reviews.

In the span of a decade, a great diversity in viewpoint on how to "manage" peregrines had erupted. For me, and I think for the rest of the team, the most unfortunate aspect was a loss of perspective. By 1991, peregrines released by fostering or hacking had clearly shown they could survive and reproduce. Field reports unmistakably indicated widespread increases in breeding pairs. The rate of annual increase was then about 5 percent. But for many, success was a bitter pill. Perhaps some people had too much at stake in terms of livelihood to let go of the blue falcon.

I will spare my readers the details of what happened to the addendum. The general events went like this. In late 1991 the western team submitted a revision of the draft addendum to Marvin Plenert, the current FWS director for the western region. Then, in the summer of 1993, nearly *four years* after my team was appointed, the service sent out a revised draft for wide review. Comments ranged from complete agreement to total disdain.

One *year* later, Dave Harlow, the point man on the peregrine for the FWS in the Reno office, advised my team that the agency was rethinking the addendum because of public comments. He wrote that the FWS was having second thoughts about changing the status of peregrines on a regional basis as opposed to the entire range of the species. (Incidentally, the FWS soon ignored this new position in the case of the bald eagle, which was delisted except in certain regions in the southern forty-eight states.) Five years had now passed since our group was first summoned.

Anyway, this is where things got very weird. In the spring of 1995 the service called a meeting of agency people to review the addendum once more. Unfortunately, the document under review was counterfeit. Someone in the FWS had rewritten our document. The fake used our well-documented narrative but substituted different recommendations. It mainly soft-pedaled our interest in getting the species off the list and on its way. The bogus addendum proposed minimum standards for wild peregrine nesting productivity that my team felt were ridiculous.

I sent a registered letter to Mike Spear, the new regional director of the FWS (staff changes were frequent), protesting the counterfeit addendum that bore the names of FWS officials Harlow and Pat Zenone. There was no response. I can only imagine that Spear was ignorant of the deed, and, furthermore, helpless.

There was no further action on the part of the FWS in regard to the western team. We were never officially disbanded or further acknowledged. So far as I know, our team still exists. Four years later, in 1999, the Department of the Interior finally removed the peregrine in the coterminous states and interior Alaska from the list of threatened and endangered species. There was a great deal of opposition to the delisting. The same naysayers were on hand. The same axes had to be ground.

As usual, the comments against delisting included "the data are inadequate." Never mind that the bird was declared endangered (rightfully so) on far weaker evidence than was available in the mid-1990s for delisting. Some people insisted we needed a few more years to see if the bird could make it on its own. The ability of the *anatum* population to sustain itself, free from the influence of massive releases of falcons a full decade before, was then obvious.

The final absurdity in this saga was procedural, the stuff of which some agencies are made. People were actually convinced that the falcon could not be directly delisted, but that it must reside for a while on the list of species that were only *threatened* with extinction. No fair leapfrogging the less grave category. You can't go from "endangered" to "delisted" without touching base at "threatened." Perhaps the neat thing about that idea for some folks was the additional busywork of someday having to remove the bird from the threatened list.

A NORTH AMERICAN COUNT   In 1995, Bill Heinrich, Lloyd Kiff, Clayton White, and I were given the opportunity to summarize the gains peregrines had made across North America. We based our report, presented at the 60th North American Wildlife Conference, not so much on information already published, but more on direct contacts with field people who were counting blue meanies or had done so in the past. In most regions, peregrine aficionados were counting their prized breeding pairs every year or two.

No one failed to report substantial gains compared to the previous decade. The phenomenon held true from Greenland west to northern Alaska, south to Baja California, and east to the Appalachians. From 1980 to 1994 the number of pairs of meanies that people had found tripled. It was no surprise to learn from the tallies that the arctic migrant meanies had increased as well. Counts in the fall, at a ridge in Pennsylvania called Hawk Mountain, showed the increase. So did observations on the sand at Assateague on the eastern seaboard, and on Padre Island, Texas.

The information from field surveys, given to us so generously, was interesting in two special ways. First, the rates of increase of nesting peregrines, region by region, were pretty similar. Once the growth of populations had started, momentum gathered, slowly at first. It was as if the meanies had found the land and needed only a little time to make new falcons to claim it.

The growth in numbers did not start at the same time everywhere. In the United States, the population in the East was refounded in the late 1970s, but it was almost a decade later before that happened in the Midwest. The difference owes to the later release program in the upper Mississippi River country compared to that in the Atlantic states.

So how many peregrines existed in North America and Greenland in 1995? Fools rush in. We mulled over all the field reports, considered the difficulty of finding all the birds in the actual areas surveyed, and then added a fudge factor for all the blue meanie country not surveyed at all. Most important, we listened to the opinions of the folks who had spent time in the field. This, of course, was not hard science, but was at least an informed estimate.

Anyway, we came up with an estimate of over *seven thousand* breeding pairs. Such a high number was a big surprise, even to us. The figure might seem to some like a gloriously wild guess, because it included the estimate of over four thousand pairs nesting in the northern forests and on the tundra of North America and Greenland. We recognized that people on the beaches were counting migrant youngsters each year. Those northern brown meanies came from paired adults. All those youngsters amounted to irrefutable evidence of the vast numbers of the adult pairs that produced them.

I think everyone (except the pigeon people) was thrilled to hear the news of the great gains meanies had made. But there were skeptics. Most offensive to me was the grumbling that our wildlife conference report had not been "peer reviewed." This was an indirect way of questioning the truthfulness, or at least the validity, of our report. It was a devious way of casting a stigma on the evidence.

I had, from time to time in my long past, told minor falsehoods. (This was not so in the cases of Heinrich, Kiff, or White.) Joking aside, our report had not actually been sent out to anonymous reviewers, as is the practice of editors of most scientific journals. However, the editors of the conference transactions were wildlife scientists. They had read the paper and suggested revisions before we went public.

We did not doubt the accuracy and broad scope of what we had written. Between us, we four knew all of the *twenty-six* peregrine field people who gave us their findings. We trusted them completely, and that trust was the basis of our report.

Within two years of our report, the FWS set in motion the legal process to remove the interior peregrines from the official federal list of threatened and endangered species (the tundra falcons had already been delisted). In 1999, amid both grumbling and cheering, the now-famous falcon was officially erased from the United States list of endangered or threatened plants and animals. As we shall see in a later chapter, the peregrine did not then fall from the limelight.

SUMMARY   This chapter recognizes the dedicated work of private people and oft-maligned officials in applying the power of the Endangered Species Act to the restoration of the blue meanie. In the 1970s, when the act was new, the common goal was to see peregrine populations revitalized. The members of our recovery team, at least, came together to work; the spirit of cooperation was pervasive.

By the early 1990s, the peregrine had made a very speedy reestablishment on most of the land it formerly held. Further, it flourished once those gains were made. At the same time, the falcon attracted great attention, both within the agencies charged with the care and keeping of wildlife and among the public. In the latter case, urban hacking exposed the magnificent falcon to folks who would otherwise never have heard the word *peregrine*. The falcon became a public darling.

Beginning in the last decade of the twentieth century, the FWS found its collective self in a morass of differing opinions regarding the well-being of peregrine populations. Part of the confusion was self-inflicted. Only because of overwhelming evidence of the security of duck hawk populations did the service just manage to remove the bird from the list.

Some said the FWS needed a "victory" to establish the credibility of the endangered species program. If that were true, it would be a matter of common sense, and commendable. But in my opinion, most of the force behind the delisting was the sheer pressure of evidence that reasonable people could no longer ignore. In retrospect, I believe the first ten years of operation of the recovery plans were both crucial and sufficient. It was also the time, the decade following 1978, when people seemed to love the blue falcon, and worked together to see it saved.

XIII » THE BETTER-KNOWN MEANIE

FALCON WATCHERS   All of the programs designed to restore peregrines to former ranges in North America went beyond the work of simply turning birds loose. Observers tried to keep track of the new falcons by the use of colored leg bands. In many cases, the color on the bird's leg alerted even casual observers to attempt a closer look. Usually a colored band with big numbers or letters was put on one leg. An ordinary FWS band, anodized black for contrast, went on the other. Thanks to the effort of Scott Ward, colored bands were available early on, and many living peregrines were rediscovered after they left release sites or nests, sometimes after many years.

Follow-up searches of old nesting haunts were crucial to see if new birds were staking claims. In some places in the western United States, searches were systematic. Monte Kirven annually checked most of the historical nests in northern California. Bud Anderson did the same in Washington. Every year, Bonnie McKinney visited the old eyries in Big Bend Park, Texas. At least these watchers had birds to count.

In Montana, Jay Sumner and Ralph Rogers worked for a few years without seeing a meanie, and then in the mid-1980s, like all the others, they were rewarded with the discovery of recolonization by the duck hawks. Bob Oakleaf discontinued the hunt for peregrines in Wyoming in the 1980s, simply because there were none to be found. In the 1990s he resumed the quest—and scored. At the Great Salt Lake, Don Paul and Phil Wagner watched peregrines develop a tradition of nesting on hack towers in the salt marshes. These folks hung in there, year after year. Sooner or later, they struck it rich.

Elsewhere, the searches took different forms. In Arizona, biologists visited historical eyries in the early 1980s and found active eyries were few. As a follow-up in the 1990s, the Arizona wildlife people sent out observers to a sample of eyries, rather than attempt a complete survey of all historical sites every year. By then, there were just too many pairs to allow a total count.

In the Midwest, east of the Great Plains, the paucity of cliffs precluded numerous eyries on natural sites. But bird-watchers and local citizens reported new pairs nevertheless. Many of these were nesting on bridges and buildings. This new falcon "culture" resulted from the remarkable fidelity of birds released as youngsters at hack sites in cities. Pat Redig, Bud Tordoff, and Mark Martell at the University of Minnesota in St. Paul tallied the field reports and saw to it they were verified. Their data set is unparalleled. Incredibly, nearly all of the birds nesting in the Midwest were identified from their leg bands, so each could be followed for life. The peregrines had no secrets.

In the East, Willard Heck, Marty Gilroy, and Jack Barclay of the Peregrine Fund kept track of the discoveries of new pairs. Elsewhere, fieldwork was intensive. Bill Mattox oversaw the work in western Greenland for twenty-five years. From the late 1970s onward, Jerry Craig, Dan Berger, and I followed the Colorado duck hawks as closely as possible given the difficult terrain. We saw the Colorado population increase from a few to more than 130 pairs. Because of rapid increase in the population, annual visits to all occupied eyries became a massive undertaking.

The Canadians were a bit more relaxed, but nonetheless thorough, in documenting the return of peregrines. They mounted a nationwide survey every five years (the last one was in 2000). This was a good plan, given the size of Canada. Geoff Holroyd and Ursula Banasch coordinated the regional surveys. Local studies spanning several years were also important. For example, Wayne Nelson studied the Queen Charlotte Island Peale's falcons, and Gordon Court recorded a very dense group of nesting tundra peregrines at Rankin Inlet on the northwest shore of Hudson Bay (Chapter VIII).

All in all, the peregrine is now extremely well known in North America, Greenland, Europe, and Australia. It has also been studied widely in Africa and in South America. One cannot imagine that major revelations in the ecology of this prince of predators will emerge in the future.

In a 2002 summary profile of the species drawn up by Clayton White and coworkers for *The Birds of North America*, more than three hundred scientific papers dealing with peregrines are listed. Most date back less than thirty years. In the remainder of this chapter, I want to review a few of the most interesting newly discovered aspects of peregrine recovery and ecology.

DID WE REALLY SAVE THE PEREGRINE? Like so many other people, I have wanted to believe that human intervention, in the forms of the release of captive-bred falcons, fostering young from wild-laid eggs to new parents, road closures near eyries, and game warden surveillance, did indeed prevent the total loss of the bird. In the end, about seven thousand new blue meanies were deliberately added to the fauna of North America. That immense chore must account for something.

Several times in the four years since the falcon was deleted from the list of endangered species, people have told me how great it must feel to have helped "save the peregrine." Who knows, maybe there is a lifetime achievement award bearing that testimonial. Actually, claims that we saved the falcon are embarrassing and unfounded. We did no such thing.

Bud Tordoff, University of Minnesota, who with raptor veterinarian Pat Redig and others reestablished and studied the large and growing population of falcons in the Midwest. Photo by Steve Wilson.

Several species of birds of prey were in deep trouble over major parts of their ranges in North America and elsewhere as a result of DDT/DDE and other chlorinated pesticides. These included bald eagles and ospreys (both fish-eaters), merlins (small falcons), and Cooper's hawks (bird predators). A few eagles were bred in captivity and released, and a few osprey eggs were taken from regions where DDE was not much of a problem (mid-Atlantic states) and given to pairs (in New England) that could not lay normal eggs. Neither the merlin nor the hawk was managed in any way.

All four species have rebounded to full force in the last twenty years. Bald eagles reclaimed much of their former habitat in the East and expanded to reservoirs and river valleys in the arid West. Only politics have kept the southern population of bald eagles on the federal threatened list. Ospreys made phenomenal gains, and new ground was taken as well. In Colorado, typical of western states, ospreys are now found widely near lakes and reservoirs.

Except in the Southwest, the ubiquitous Cooper's hawks became scarce in the 1970s. They are now back. Dan Berger reported a nearly fivefold increase of migrant Coops at Cedar Grove, Wisconsin, by 1986. The hawk now nests commonly in Colorado, where it was nearly gone twenty-five years ago. In the 1990s, merlins migrating at Cedar Grove in the fall were over nine times more abundant than in the mid-1970s.

You may have recognized that these examples of help-free recovery did not involve peregrines. Consider the case of the United Kingdom. By the late 1960s, peregrines there were down to less than half of their prewar numbers. By the end of the 1980s, they had regained full strength. There was *no* management, other than posting wardens at vulnerable sites to keep villains away.

One last bit of evidence suggests that the big blue falcon would have made it alone without all the excitement created by the Endangered Species Act. Take the case of tundra peregrine falcons in North America. None were released on the Arctic tundra. There was no management. Nonetheless, there is plenty of evidence from nest surveys and counts of migrants to suggest this race of peregrine is at least three times more abundant now than in the 1970s.

Those of you who were caught up in falcon restoration in the 1970s must surely be thinking that the arguments I have made amount to hindsight. That is true. We did not know then what would happen next. Perhaps the bird might crash into utter extinction. Action was the safe course. Apparently Peter Lindberg in Sweden and Christian Saar in Germany felt the same way; they initiated effective release programs in their respective countries in the early 1980s.

THE EFFECTS OF THE RELEASES   What can we claim for all the falcons set free in temperate North America? What were the effects of so many youngsters being released on the landscape? Field reports paint the following picture. Across southern Canada, from the Rocky Mountains to the Atlantic coast, the releases accomplished by Fyfe in Alberta, Lynn Oliphant in the central provinces, and David Bird in the east, established thinly spaced breeding pairs of duck hawks by the late 1980s. The species had been nearly lost in that enormous region in the 1970s. Most of the new pairs were urban, nesting on buildings, this behavior owing to their fidelity to the types of places where they were released. Cade's group at Cornell founded almost a hundred nesting pairs in the eastern United States by the early 1990s. Many were on buildings, bridges, and hack towers. Tordoff, Redig, and Greg Septon began releasing peregrines in the upper Midwest in the mid-1980s. By 1993, about 50 pairs had been established there (including Canada adjacent to Lake Superior). In 2003, the count reached 160. The urban peregrine, now so widespread, was a lasting result.

All of the work mentioned thus far was in regions where the bird had been *totally* lost. In less than two decades those efforts jump-started populations that surely would have taken many decades to build on their own by immigration from remaining populations to the north and west. We now know that nesting peregrines sometimes disperse a few hundred miles from where they were hatched. Eventually, blue meanies would have colonized the eastern half of temperate North America. The natural process would have been very, very gradual. Most of us could not have outlived it.

In the West, the falcon had not quite disappeared. So far as we know, California was home to fewer than a dozen pairs. The remaining known pairs, no more than thirty in all, were mainly in southwestern Colorado, New Mexico, Arizona, western Texas, and northern Mexico.

Because DDT, converted to DDE, is transported far and wide in the body fat of migrant birds, it seems unlikely that peregrines anywhere in North America escaped the thin-eggshell syndrome. In fact, Kiff and Peakall examined peregrine eggshells from many regions of the world. They found only one place where meanie eggshells were always normal: western Australia.

In the wilderness of the Colorado Plateau and the Colorado River basin, duck hawks surely suffered significant reduction in numbers. Recently I asked an FWS biologist if he was certain the poor success of his searches in Arizona in the late 1970s owed to the simple fact that the birds were gone. He was sure that they were indeed very scarce. Years later, searchers found pairs where they had not been able to find them before. Perhaps the mountainous core of Mexico was the only real refugium for the falcon south of the Canadian forests. However, a great deal of DDT was used to protect cotton south of the Rio Grande.

Two population changes began in the 1980s. Peregrines in New Mexico, Arizona, and on the Plateau in Utah began to increase and expand as a result of receding DDE in their prey. Second, the numerous releases in California and Colorado established outlying enclaves beyond the Plateau. The many hundreds of peregrines set free in the northern tier of western states established more outliers, and blue meanies there are still increasing. In the 1990s the western population coalesced as it grew. Incidentally, some of the early releases in California probably augmented the expansion in Oregon, and perhaps northward into Washington.

What if there had been no releases? One can only imagine that peregrines in California and the Southwest would have gradually increased, and then would have painstakingly retaken the vast lands to the north. After all, peregrines in New Mexico and Arizona regained their land without aid, once DDE was diminished. Once the chemical subsided, slow dispersal by peregrines into vacant habitat was inevitable. Without intervention, recovery in the West, as in the East, would have been much slower. Many, many people were not willing to wait to see if the falcon would recover unassisted. I was among them.

LIKE FATHER, LIKE SON   A peculiar result of the releases in the East and Midwest was that young falcons acquired a mindset in regard to movements and places acceptable for nesting later on in life. Jack Barclay studied the pattern of dispersal and nesting in the eastern peregrines. Remember, some birds turned loose there were descendants of tundra falcons with strong migratory inclinations.

Barclay, Heck, and Gilroy found that the tundra birds tended not to hang around the chilly cities in winter, but moved south to the Gulf Coast and Mexico. They were snowbirds of sorts. But when it was time to nest, no matter where they spent the winter, they usually returned to their home areas. Those from coastal towers returned to the towers or other coastal sites such as buildings or bridges in New York City.

Falcons released in the Appalachian region tended to return there to nest. A few of those birds moved west, in one case as far away as LaCrosse, Wisconsin. Barclay found that falcons fledging in New England often spent winters in the relatively balmy central Appalachian region, just as did the original population of duck hawks they have replaced.

A goal of the eastern recovery effort was to release birds in cities and from coastal towers, the better to avoid horned owls. Later, it was hoped, the falcons would move inland to use cliffs once held by the original duck hawks. It was disappointing that no strong tendency for the coastal falcons to disperse inland to cliffs was evident.

In the Midwest almost every bird was, and still is, known by its distinctively marked colored band. It was unlikely duck hawks could nest there without being discovered and identified. This was because roughly 75 percent of the eyries were on buildings, bridges, or power-station smokestacks. In the last case, the eggs were laid on a ledge placed by workers well short of the top. Cliffs are not abundant in the Midwest. Those on the upper Mississippi and on Lake Superior are the most numerous and were checked for falcons every year. These traditional sites were clearly prone to predation by great horned owls, but they too have been slowly recolonized.

Tordoff and Redig found that Midwestern blue meanies kept, in later years, pretty much to the kind of nest site from which they fledged. Falcons that grew up on buildings tended to nest on buildings. Sometimes the birds had to go far to find what they needed. Males were homebodies and moved, on average, about a hundred miles to a new home, half the distance traveled by females.

CITY MEANIES   Before the time of the DDT debacle, peregrines rarely nested on human-made structures in North America. Most famous was the case of the female and her three successive mates that reared twenty-one youngsters on the Sun Life building in Montreal from 1938 to 1952. Of course tall buildings are relatively recent in the New World compared to Europe. In the Old World, peregrine falcons nested on castles and cathedrals for many centuries. There is even a record of a nesting pair on the Vatican.

Duck hawks in North American cities are still learning. In his book *City Peregrines*, Saul Frank left little doubt that they sometimes had big trouble. In New York City, good nest ledges were hard to find. A network of volunteers anticipated the shortage in several cases. Workers erected ledges or boxes with gravel floors to accommodate the eggs of pairs bent on nesting.

The understructures of roadways on high bridges often have ledges covered with a thick litter of pigeon excrement, the perfect place for meanies to scrape a shallow depression for their eggs. Unfortunately, when the young falcons make their first flight, they sometimes end up in the river. Falcons on the half-dozen or so bridge sites fledged as many young as pairs on buildings, but fewer bridge youngsters reached independence.

More than a dozen pairs of falcons nest in the Big Apple. We must think the place is reaching full capacity, given the fact that peregrines do not tolerate near neighbors. Just a few years ago a pair took up housekeeping on the Palisades on the Hudson River, a bit upstream from the city. Perhaps they were escaping urban crowding. Little did the falcons know they were reliving history. Those cliffs of shale on the west side of the Hudson were the traditional home of peregrines before World War II, at a time when city birds were mighty rare.

What will become of the peregrines in the Midwest and East? The future holds a wonderful opportunity for natural selection. The bloodlines from diverse geographical regions in those populations will gradually mix into

*Female successfully
incubates in a snowstorm on
a building in St. Paul, Minnesota.*

obscurity as the birds interbreed. The tendency to migrate south in fall will almost surely wane as the tundra-falcon contingent is diluted. Although urban nesting now predominates from Iowa to the Atlantic, wherever cliffs occur, more and more of them will be used. In a strange paradox, falcons that prefer human structures will likely be crowded by their own kind and will resort to the country. Eventually, the urban falcon will be numerous on the land, owing to so many high buildings, long bridges, tall smokestacks, and grain elevators whose owners will make peregrines welcome. Those birds will persist forever if the human sympathy that brought them there in the first place persists.

FAMILY LIFE   Most of the new discoveries about blue meanies have been made in the nesting season. That is when the falcons are most accessible. In the Rocky Mountains, cliffs are required for nesting. There are almost no urban birds in the region. In forty years of looking for the falcon in the West, I have found peregrines away from the vicinity of their eyries fewer than a dozen times. (I have never seen a peregrine in a city.)

   "Do they mate for life?" The question is second in popularity only to "How long do they live?" Somehow, people in general are curious about these things. These two related matters are actually of basic ecological importance. The second question is more important. The longer a peregrine lives, the more youngsters it is likely to produce in its lifetime.

Blue meanies do appear to mate for life, but life is short. If a mate disappears the survivor accepts another. The attraction is much less to a specific mate than to the nest site. This does not seem very romantic. By means of bands affording identification, Tordoff and Redig found that once a peregrine settles in at a nest site (usually at the age of two years), it is very unlikely to move to another eyrie in a later year.

Because of this remarkable site fidelity, shown by both sexes, the same mates tend to remain together from one year to the next. This phenomenon is probably characteristic of peregrines worldwide. What is not so predictable, perhaps, is how long they live. A good estimate of the *average* life span of an adult duck hawk, once it chooses an eyrie, is three years. Reports from some populations (Scotland and Australia) suggest very low death rates for adults, but high rates are reported for other populations (Sweden and Germany).

Nesting adults on territories were recognized year after year; this male had a distinctive bar behind a normal black mask.

The differences found may relate to technique: the low rates were from birds banded and later retrapped at the nest, whereas the high rates were estimated from band recoveries reported by the public when dead falcons were found. Even if death rates could be measured easily, they could shift if conditions such as crowding or food supply change.

If eight in ten adults survive through a year to nest again, odds are about two in three of the original pairs will be present the next year. Perhaps survivorship is better in some regions, but I doubt if the odds of the same falcons showing up *together* the following year in any population are ever much better than three in four. You can now easily see why peregrines seldom remain paired for many years. The usual case is that one or the other vanishes before long, and is replaced.

Because one or the other adult is often replaced before the next breeding season, it follows that one of the adults in a pair is often a replacement, a novice at the task of making new falcons. Sometimes *both* adults are new. Furthermore, replacement adults are likely only two years old. I guessed that new adults might be inept and have fewer young. I was wrong.

Jerry Craig and I compared the average number of young produced by first-time males to those reared by males that had nested at the cliff the year before. We also did the same for females, and for cases where both male and female were new at the cliff. We found no difference in success at making youngsters. Even when both adults of a pair were nesting at an eyrie for the first time, they did as well on average as experienced pairs. If you think about it, that result makes sense. Much of the behavior related to reproduction in birds is written on their genes. Learning fine-tunes inherited behavior. Generally, birds act instinctively, and the critical things they must do require little learning.

This is the best way, because life is too short for trial runs. There might not be a second season in which to get it right. These notions, if true, make sense throughout the animal world. There surely is a strong pressure to breed just as soon as practical, for tomorrow one may not get the chance.

UNPLANNED FAMILIES   How many youngsters does a peregrine make in its lifetime? There are different ways to approach the question. One approach is to realize that each adult, on average, must produce enough offspring so that when it dies, at least one will still be alive to assume the role of adulthood. This means that every adult will have assured its replacement. Thus, the population will be perpetuated.

This view reveals the importance of the survivorship of youngsters before they can become adults at age two. As you might expect, it is not easy to estimate how well young peregrines survive those first two years. They tend to be scattered all over the landscape. One method has been to band a bunch of meanies in the nest, and then wait for reports of the discovery of dead banded falcons. The number of falcons that died *in their first year* can be compared with the number of reports of death in *all* their years. This approach requires the banding of huge numbers of nestlings, because relatively few are ever found later and reported. You can imagine the rate of reports of band recoveries is very slow. Decades pass before a reasonable sample is available.

Anyway, estimates using the band-recovery method suggested fully half or more of the young that leave the nest do not live to their first birthday. Perhaps only 40 percent make it. Life is risky in the early business of being a peregrine falcon.

In the Midwest in recent years, many yearlings (with no home territory) are actually seen loitering about like teenage humans. The youthful falcons are seen because there are so many people in the region. The one-year-olds can be compared with the total number of young known to have fledged with them in their "nestling class." On that basis Tordoff and Redig claim that a minimum of about one in four lives at least one year. Actual survival is surely better. Some yearlings undoubtedly avoided detection and are therefore not counted among the living one-year-olds.

Once a blue meanie approaches its first birthday, the survivorship rate is probably nearly as good as that in later years. The yearlings have proven in their first year that they can deal with the vicissitudes of living a free existence. Perhaps three in four of the yearlings make it to age two and the time of breeding. Incidentally, some yearlings do breed. We have only a few records from Colorado, but in the Midwest, at a time when the population was expanding rapidly, about 11 percent of nesting peregrines were yearlings.

It will now seem obvious that all the youngsters that leave the nest do not endure to breed. If only 40 percent of the first-year birds survive, and three in four yearlings survive to age two, then only 30 percent of the original fledglings reach adulthood. What is more, only about two in three of all breeding attempts are successful in producing young. All this means that roughly only one in five fledgling duck hawks reaches sexual maturity (age two years) and achieves parenthood then. Compare that low rate to the human situation.

Further, the breeders suffer attrition after their first crack at nesting. On average, adults last only about three years at an eyrie. A very few, like the female on the Sun Life Building in Montreal and the one-legged male at the Royal Gorge, finally produced a score or more of fledglings. They were rare exceptions.

Craig and I have determined the payoff, in youngsters, to an adult when it returns and breeds another year. On average, the gain in lifetime family size is about one and one-half fledglings for each year of nesting. Some beat the odds; a female in Colorado produced eighteen young in seven years. Others lose bigtime. A female failed completely in all of six successive annual attempts.

The record for reproduction by a wild duck hawk is actually twenty-two young, recently achieved by a female in the Midwest. She gets the gold medal. The silver goes to that female on the building in Montreal who produced twenty-one young, even with a war going on. A male in the Midwest gets a bronze for seeing to the fledging of twenty young. Each of these venerable falcons lasted long enough to outrun the competition.

The interesting result of all of this is a simple conclusion. Very few of the young that fledge in a given year in a region, or from a particular nest, contribute importantly to the next generation. More surprising, few *adults* contribute importantly. Instead, the future of any peregrine population rests on the brown wings of a small portion of young that win the survivorship lottery by chance and skill, grow up, and then breed year after year, "time true and tested."

UNRECOGNIZED RELATIVES   In the spring, adult peregrines are intensely attracted to cliffs. Pairing is more likely when both sexes seek cliffs rather than scouting the vast countryside, in which case potential mates would be thinly spread. The cliff serves as a magnet, calling in the blue meanies to a blind date. After the encounter, each mate must respond to the behaviors of the other in an acceptable way. Beyond that, there is no identification check. Neither falcon knows the pedigree of the other. No background profile is made.

Tordoff and Redig have recently shown just how blind the dating can be. Because nearly all the breeders in the Midwest are banded, it was no trick to check the birth certificates of each pair. Shockingly, in seven instances, pairs were made up of near relatives. Sometimes the mates were brother and sister, or half-brothers or -sisters, or parents and offspring. Collectively, those pairs attempted to nest seventeen times, amounting to 4 percent of all nesting attempts the researchers saw.

To everyone's great relief, there seemed to be no ill effects. None of the thirty-seven young that were ultimately produced showed any sign of abnormality, and the near-relative pairs produced as many young as pairs without closely related members.

Close inbreeding is more likely, by chance, in small populations than in big ones. Peregrines are always few compared to many other kinds of birds, and the species may have been exposed to inbreeding for a very long time. If so, bad genes shared by family members would have long since had the opportunity to come together. And when they did, the individual bearing them would have disappeared, ridding the population of the unwanted genetic baggage. In that way, today's peregrines may simply carry few bad genes.

POWERFUL PARENTS ALL   Way back in the 1970s, we began to look for environmental conditions that might work for or against successful nesting by peregrines in different parts of Colorado. One of the reasons for do-ing this was to be able to designate certain places as critical habitat for the falcon. We used as the measure of nesting performance the *average* number of young produced by all pairs that showed up each year to nest, whether or not they actually succeeded. The average includes pairs that produced young and those that failed. Bear in mind there is no magic number in this regard. Chance plays a role. For example, a cold, wet spring in a region at the time of egg incubation or tiny hatchlings works against pairs who choose open nest ledges.

Our work was fruitless. Pairs nesting high in the mountains (up to ten thousand feet) were as successful as pairs that nested in the foothills, or on the edge of the Colorado Plateau. Production of young did not vary by the kind of habitat within hunting range of the eyrie. Pairs whose eyries over-looked piñon-juniper woodland did just as well, on average, as those over oak brushland. And we could not classify certain types of cliffs as better places for eyries. In fact, only a few cliffs harbored pairs that routinely did less well than the others; one of those cliffs seemed to have no good ledge for a nest.

Overall, duck hawks everywhere in Colorado have done well in making new falcons. They have usually averaged, year to year, between one and a half and two young fledged for all pairs that show up to nest. Janet Lithicum and Brian Walton have reported that California meanies have done about as well in recent years.

Jerry Craig went to a lot of trouble to see if duck hawks in Colorado tend to choose cliffs that face south, the better to cope with springtime in the Rockies. Of more than eight hundred different cliff faces used by peregrines at least once since the 1970s, there was only a slight preference for those with a southern or eastern exposure. Lots of faces used by the falcons had a northerly view, especially at the lower elevations. Whatever the view, nesting attempts at different elevations had about the same success.

WHAT NOW OF DDE AND EGGSHELLS?   DDT (especially its by-product, DDE) was the dragon slain by Ruckelshaus in 1973 (Chapter V). Other persistent chemicals used to poison insects were also banned. Because those chemicals are very durable in the environment, we had good reason to keep track of them.

We did that by saving unhatched peregrine eggs stumbled upon in our comings and goings from eyries, and by collecting small birds the falcons eat. I had the gruesome task of homogenizing those poor prey birds into a pink puree (to mix all tissues bearing different amounts of DDE) in a blender. It proved less messy if I first plucked all the feathers and removed the feet and beak. Far worse was the job of opening rotten eggs so the contents could be bottled and sent off to the laboratory.

It turned out there was a lot of variation in the amount of DDE in birds peregrines eat in Colorado. For example, some robins were pretty clean, others not so clean. Different kinds of birds were more or less contaminated. Mourning doves had little DDE; Brewer's blackbirds were fairly dirty. So were white-throated swifts, the favorite food in Colorado. The variation probably owed to different diets in different places, age, and body fat condition.

It was no surprise to find that birds that eat insects had more DDE than those that eat mainly seeds. And birds that migrate had more than those, like Clark's nutcrackers (a kind of jay), which remain in Colorado the whole year. Because our falcons ate a great variety of birds, most females did not get enough of the dirty ones to load up on DDE.

The spoiled eggs we collected showed that as well. Some falcons laid eggs whose contents had stiff amounts of DDE, but others laid eggs that had little. This was especially true at the end of the 1980s, compared to the 1970s.

Inevitably, DDT and DDE will be slowly purged from the food supply of peregrines, some of the loss caused by chemical breakdown, and some the result of runoff from the surface to places where falcon prey cannot acquire it. The DDE molecules that remain intact will become distributed on fat molecules everywhere on earth.

The unhatched eggs Craig and Berger collected in Colorado over the years tended to have thinner shells if the egg contents tested high in DDE. However, the relationship was not very tight. There is a possible explanation for the loose relationship. Female falcons build egg yolks (where most of the DDE resides) several days before laying. Hence the yolk probably reflects general amounts in the falcon over that time. But shells are made in a matter of hours. If a female ate a highly contaminated bird just before the shell formed, the shell could end up thin, even though DDE in egg contents was low.

The presence of clean and dirty prey in the diet of females that are building shells in a whole set of eggs apparently causes thin shells and more normal shells. Because DDE is quick to act, the thickness of a shell may depend in part on what food the male brought to the female.

We found the usual case is the presence of both thick- and thin-shelled eggs in the same set (clutch). One eggshell from the clutch did not represent the rest. Further, shell fragments picked up on the ledge after the eggs hatched naturally showed the same bewildering variation in thickness. These vagaries of DDE and shell thickness confounded our attempts to link them with the number of young that successfully flew from the nest.

There is good news in this shell game. Because DDE is declining, we have seen a general improvement in shell thickness in Colorado in the last three decades. Thinning is roughly half that typical in the 1970s, and is far less than might interfere with production of new youngsters. This is the case in many regions of the world today.

MORTALITY   There is little doubt that collisions with obstacles cause many deaths of blue meanies. Steve Sweeney reported that about 80 percent of the nearly 170 falcons found injured in the Midwest in recent years suffered broken bones or damaged soft tissue. In most cases the peregrines could not have made it without medical care. It is no surprise that nearly 80 percent of the falcons brought in were less than one year old. Young peregrines seem to have a problem dealing with their speed.

In Colorado, Craig found that about 20 percent of banded birds found dead had crashed into some object. Wires were the problem in half the cases. Three were killed in collisions with vehicles. A state trooper actually saw one of the hits. Craig did not learn if the pilot of a jet fighter on the runway at Buckley Air Base in Denver noticed the peregrine that collided with his aircraft.

There has been good opportunity to actually witness predation on Colorado blue meanies because they have been watched so intently for over three decades. The field people actually saw eleven falcons killed by golden eagles. Eight of those killed were large nestlings. Three of the young were wearing radio transmitters at the time; two of the radios were traced to an eagle nest a quarter-mile away. Adults are not immune to eagle attack. One adult female was swept from her perch near the ledge where her mate incubated the eggs.

Horned owls are especially nasty predators of young falcons. Five young peregrines were killed in a three-year period at a Colorado eyrie nestled in a small canyon. The site has since been abandoned. Peregrines now safely fledge their broods from a much higher cliff farther upstream.

These conspicuous instances of death tempt me to claim them as the major ways in which meanies meet their end. The difficulty is that collisions may most often occur where the damaged falcon can be found, biasing the conclusion. Further, a broken bone is easy to recognize for what it is. But what of falcons that are lost in bad weather, or are somehow weakened and get too far behind in feeding themselves? Their disintegrating remains are seldom found on the vast landscape.

There is one cause of death that is likely to increase. In 1994, an adult male we radio-tracked in Colorado was found dead a few miles from his eyrie. His back was laid open as if by a talon. I believe he was the victim of aggression by another peregrine, or perhaps a prairie falcon. Tordoff and Redig now see an increase in damaged peregrines, apparently the result of territorial aggression. That sort of thing will probably escalate as peregrines become more competitive for limited nest sites.

WORK REMAINING   So much study has been done on blue meanies that it may seem unlikely anything interesting remains to be discovered. Several important issues are not well understood. Generally, these become important as the falcon finds itself crowding into a finite world.

One aspect of peregrine ecology needs attention. No notion about peregrines has gained so much credibility with so little hard evidence as has the concept of a "floater" component in the population. The idea is simple: not all adult peregrines end up nesting in a given year because most cliffs are already in use by mated pairs. The main support for the floater concept is based on the immediate substitution seen when a paired bird is lost. In one historical case, an adult disappeared. Another peregrine replaced it in a day or two. Before long, the other adult was lost; it was also replaced. The new pair ended up rearing the orphaned young of the original birds.

There is a possible explanation for the prompt replacements, short of assuming a floater contingent. The adult replacements might have come from recently failed nesting attempts nearby. If the mate of a pair were lost early in the breeding season, the survivor might tend to wander, without actually seeking a new cliff and a new mate. If such a bird happened to find a vacancy, it might seem to an observer as if the replacement bird had been waiting in the wings all along. By the way, it seems biologically reasonable for the new member of the pair to help raise young not its own. By pitching in, the new mate gains a stake in the territory and in its new partner that might pay off in descendents the following year.

The floater idea might seem logical in one way. If a regional population were to grow to the point where good cliffs were in short supply, some adults might be *forced* to wander, awaiting the chance to nest at a later time. I do not think it is so simple.

First off, cliffs in western North America, for example, come in a wide array of "flavors." Blue meanies worldwide have shown great versatility when it comes to choosing nest sites. The species has clearly shown it can rear young at eyries on less than massive rock walls. Dinky little cliffs are now used in Colorado. Will blue meanies ever run out of places to nest? Such a circumstance is hard to imagine because there are so many cliffs large and small. But if all the serviceable cliffs were occupied to the limit of territorial spacing, then the population would have reached the "cliff limit." Floaters would then seem inevitable. (A small percentage of cliffs might not be used each season just because no pair happened to find them before the nesting season had elapsed.)

Second, the postponement of making youngsters by mature adults is illogical. As we have seen, if you are a peregrine, life is short. Once certain sustaining skills are acquired, delay of reproduction makes no sense. Why would a perfectly good duck hawk, in the prime of life, not go for it, even if that meant pairing with a mate at a less-than-wonderful cliff? Peregrines in North America will likely reach full population in the next decade or two. Ecologists may then learn if nonbreeding adult floaters are significant.

REVIEW   In the last three decades an enormous effort in the field has been focused on peregrines. Some of the work was incidental to attempts to measure the successes of releases of falcons in regions where DDT had decimated them. By the end of the twentieth century, peregrines were surely among the most thoroughly studied of wild animals.

Intensive restocking quickly built new populations and hastened expansion elsewhere, where no doubt the species would have eventually regained lost numbers without restocking. Other raptor species, once in jeopardy because of DDT/DDE, recovered with little or no help from humans.

Blue meanies have become less affected by DDE, now that the poison is slowly subsiding in the environment. Within the not-too-distant future the species will approach full population in North America. Fieldwork then might center on how the bird is affected by its own crowding. The nature of a proposed nonbreeding floater contingent of adults might best be studied then.

The falcon has shown surprising resiliency in adjusting to a great array of pressures caused by human activities, and lends itself well to hands-on management and research. Banding has revealed characteristics of peregrine ecology as diverse as close inbreeding and the lopsided contribution to future generations by the relatively few old meanies in a population at any one time.

XIV » PEREGRINES AND PEOPLE

FREE FALL   Launched from an airplane, a human drops at a speed of about 150 miles per hour. Skydivers do it all the time, arms and legs held out, and at least one eye on an altimeter strapped to a wrist. After a timely tug on the ripcord, the parachute slows the descent to only several miles per hour. The slowing results from all the surface of the chute dragging in the airflow.

A couple of years ago, a Colorado College student by the name of Seth Layman dropped by my office and handed me a copy of the June 1999 edition of *Parachutist* magazine. The photo on the cover was phenomenal. There, close-up and in color, was a plummeting skydiver. Above the spread-eagle human was a diving peregrine, the two separated by only a few feet. Far below was the rugged Washington coast and Puget Sound.

The idea of measuring the diving speed of a meanie in full stoop by falling in tight formation was the brainchild of Ken Franklin. Layman, whose dad has been a falconer for many years, helped with the training of the falcon. To measure speed, the human needed to record the elapsed time of the fall and the distance fallen. A stopwatch and an altimeter could do the job.

The seemingly impossible task was to train the falcon to dive with the skydiver. To begin the test, the skydiver tossed the peregrine out of the airplane just prior to his jump. The falcon had been taught that the plane signified food and feeding time. The falcon managed to keep up with the slow-flying plane in the moments before the diver bailed out. When the diver jumped, the peregrine focused on an ordinary lure made of leather and held at arm's length. Down they went, the falcon seeking to catch the tightly held lure. The meanie was doing its thing.

Layman showed me a video taken by a cameraman falling with the falcon. The sequence showed the big brown juvenile duck hawk was *loitering* as it tagged along. Of course the bird was pointed straight down, but its wings were not held tight to its body, and its feet, long toes and all, buffeted in the slipstream.

In our work on dive speed at Mount Princeton a few years earlier, Vance Tucker had clocked a hunting male blue meanie at speeds more than 180 miles per hour (Chapter I). Franklin's video suggested to me his falcon was holding back, no doubt impatient with the diver for falling so slowly.

Skydiver with lure in hand; the trained peregrine is not at full speed because its wings are partially extended.

Franklin needed a faster lure. In a move that surely complicated the measurement of rate of fall, he devised a heavier, streamlined lure that could outspeed the skydiver and plummet away when released. The heavy lure did the trick. When the skydiver in the video released the lure under the falcon, the lure hurtled downward like a meteor. In a heartbeat, the falcon responded. Wings came in and were held tight. The feet were tucked into the feather faring under the tail. The head came back and was held straight ahead, rounding off the leading surface of the bird. Lure and falcon accelerated away and quickly vanished below, beyond the range of the camera.

Franklin and his helpers had clearly demonstrated experimentally that peregrines can easily exceed the speed of an ordinary skydiver. Claims of speeds approaching two hundred miles per hour or more now seem credible. It had never before occurred to me that there was any valid reason for a person to deliberately jump from an airworthy flying machine. Now there is one good reason: to dive with peregrines.

BALLOONS AND KITES   Humans are exceedingly clever in broadening the usefulness of the animals they train. So it is with falcons. Regardless of the quarry to be hunted, it is nearly always crucial for the hunting falcon to climb high, to take a great "pitch." Some falcons go up early in their training. Peregrines seem to have a natural eagerness for climbing high, no doubt because they instinctively stoop on prey at high speed.

Gyrfalcons and prairie falcons, and hybrids made by crossing these species with peregrines, are sometimes reluctant to go high up and circle as a speck overhead. This works against falcons if the intended prey is speedy. Without the advantage of a high dive, the hunter cannot often catch up to its prey, or if it does, the falcon may be eluded when the prey dodges. North American grouse such as prairie chickens and sharptails are very difficult catches for a falcon without the speed of a stoop. So are fast ducks, including mallards and pintails.

A couple of years ago Tony Head invited several Colorado falconers to witness the making of a high-flying falcon. Head is a fireman who used his free time to hunt grouse. A powerful falcon speeding from a high stoop is needed. Head's falcon was a male peregrine-gyrfalcon hybrid. These captive-bred crosses are popular because of the great speed in level flight inherent to gyrfalcons. The peregrine part tends to reduce the gyrfalcon tendency to fly all over the countryside. Further, the mix results in a bird more resistant to ailments than are gyrs. In the hands of a good falconer, this kind of hybrid is very effective.

Head and his entourage gathered on a hill on open prairie. We all watched quietly. Head opened the rear door of an enclosed trailer. Inside was stuffed a huge helium-filled weather balloon, perhaps eight feet in diameter. From the back of his trunk, Head produced a reel of nylon line. The reel had a crank handle and was mounted to a heavy base.

When the balloon was secured to the line, he tied a falcon lure to a ring on the line in such a way that the lure would dangle twenty feet under the balloon. A clever clip held the lure under the balloon until the lure was jerked free. When that happened, the lure would be free to slide down the line tethering the balloon.

All was in order. The tether line was unwound, and soon the balloon and its dangling lure were fifteen hundred feet overhead. The lure was not visible to my naked eye. Head brought his peregrine-gyr hybrid from the back of his truck. In the preceding two weeks of training, the falcon had been taught to race to the lure in gradual increments, beginning a few feet off the ground. I was spellbound by what happened. When the hood was removed, the big gray bird with peregrine bars on its belly took a quick upward glance and bolted from the glove.

With the stamina of a true athlete, the falcon pumped out a quarter-mile or more, and then turned in a steep climb. There were two more outruns, one nearly a half-mile into the wind. Then the bird turned and made a climbing rush for the balloon. The falcon was now a mere speck. I could not judge its altitude relative to the balloon.

Suddenly, almost overhead, the speck and the balloon merged. The falcon grasped and held the lure, and, free to descend, set its wings. Falcon, lure, cord, and ring slid down the fifteen hundred feet of nylon line to our gathering of cheering onlookers. Just as it arrived, the falcon slowed its descent with a few powerful wingbeats. It was now clearly time to test this athlete on Nebraska prairie chickens.

Rumor has it that the balloon technique was first used in Germany. Around 1976, Bill Burnham and Bill Heinrich were almost certainly the first to test the usefulness of balloons in North America. Putting caution aside, they used cheaper *hydrogen* instead of helium. They taught two gyrfalcons, among the first bred in captivity, to climb into the windy sky over the Pawnee Grasslands in northern Colorado.

Instead of balloons, big kites work well if there is a moderate breeze. The saving is in the cost of helium. Kite or balloon, there are avid proponents of teaching a falcon to motor on up to a dizzy height. But those of us who fly blue meanies are simply thankful so much extra effort is usually unnecessary.

"FALCONEERS" Cadets who handle the mascots of the Air Force Academy must bear the burden of the name *falconeer*. The word has always been objectionable to me. Members of the press, or just plain uninformed spectators, use it freely in lieu of *falconer*. By the way, cadets, and many others who should know better, pronounce the name of the trained mascots "*phal*-cons," rather than the historically correct "*fall*-cons," as in the word *falling*. And so it is that the cadets are called "phal-con-nears."

Anyway, in 1962, I was naturally drawn to the mascot program at the Air Force Academy just north of Colorado Springs, even though I feared the public display of falcons at football games might create a rush to raptor-keeping. Don Galvin and Hei Heiberg were there in the 1960s, not long after the mascot was adopted. Later a series of veterinarians were in charge. Jim McIntyre was a "blood and thunder" fellow and created much goodwill for the program throughout the top ranks in the Air Force. In 1977, Major Tommy Thomas urged me to become the civilian advisor to the academy program. I lasted twenty-five years. After Thomas left to obtain a degree in public health, Jerry Henningsen was in charge. He soon left for the same reason. Larry Schaad effectively oversaw the falcons and their handlers for over a decade. Then the program came under the able care of Ric Riddle, who ended up at the Pentagon. Tim Wells was next, and then Tim Woodruff. All these men were a pleasure to be around.

Each year, four first-year men or women cadets were invited into the program to replace outgoing seniors. Most had not handled a falcon on the glove. My job was to keep the cadets from inadvertently harming the birds, and to keep the falcons from training the cadets. The cadets were much like the college students I dealt with daily. They were usually keen to learn. I adjusted to being called "Sir."

Beginning in the 1980s, we bred prairie falcons for the lure-flying demonstrations at halftime in the football games. Tiercel (male) prairies were fast and agile. One or two were released from the top of the press box in the stadium, and by the time they reached the cadet falconer in midfield, their speed was impressive. The cadet caused them to undershoot the swinging lure by a quick tug on the line. The falcon would zoom up the far side of the stadium. By this time, only a small portion of the spectators had noticed what was going on.

Each time the falcon stooped, it was made to miss the lure. Experienced birds had learned they would not be allowed to overtake the swinging lure in early passes, so they circled the rim of the stadium while the clock ran down. Sometimes they decided to leave the ball game altogether. They were usually recovered outside the stadium by tracking their tiny radios. Opposing fans loved it. They cheered when a falcon went AWOL. Once a prairie went AWOL at an invitational game in Japan. It was recovered *after* the cadets returned home. The lucky falcon spent the rest of its days in a Japanese zoo.

In the 1990s, peregrines became available. Some were gifts, and some were bred at the academy. Blue meanies were not well suited to a strafing attack on a swinging lure. They preferred greater heights than did prairie falcons. In a way, the high style was to their advantage. Football fans often wadded paper cups or popcorn boxes into balls and threw them at low-flying falcons overhead. These surface-to-air missiles were always too little, too late.

The cadets often took two or three falcons to each away game. Many trips were aboard commercial jets. The falcons were carried on the gloves of cadets riding in the main cabin. More than once, passengers wrote formal complaints to the airline about the mascots after the birds revealed they were not house-broken.

My early fears of a rapid growth of falconry because of the high profile of the academy program were unfounded. Apparently few people actually asso-ciated the midgame demonstration flights with the possibility of personal involvement. After all, few people run out and buy a goat after seeing the Navy mascot at a football game, or a bulldog after a Georgia game. Visitors to the falcon loft at the academy were frequent, yet no one seemed to show strong interest in obtaining a bird.

Much more surprising was the almost complete lack of interest in fal-conry shown by the cadets themselves after graduation. Down through the years, only one cadet I knew actually trained a falcon after leaving the acad-emy. I can only guess why the cadets left falconry. Lure flying was the end-point of the training program. Unlike gamehawking, where every flight is a challenge and its outcome unique, luring sooner or later becomes tedious and boring. Further, cadets were busy in active duty after graduation.

THE NEW FALCONRY   Falconers today take for granted a technological advancement that reinvigorated gamehawking. The development of micro-transmitters and super-sensitive receivers thirty-five years ago made possible the timely recovery of otherwise lost birds. Before telemetry, when a falcon flew away, a new one had to be acquired. The new bird had to be trained, so the loss of a falcon meant starting over. The falconer was back to square one.

A great many perfectly good peregrines were lost before the bird or the fal-coner became proficient. For some, the disappointments were unbearable and they gave up. Nowadays, no one flying a big falcon on waterfowl or game birds would dream of going to the field without a transmitter on the bird. Many fal-coners place one on each leg, the better to insure against malfunction. Modern transmitters are no heavier than a quarter. Some falconers attach them to a central tail feather.

In the late 1980s I was in the habit of flying my female peregrine Dowdy at dusk. The duck ponds were twenty miles from home. By the time my labora-tory was over, the sun was already settling toward the mountains. One evening, Dowdy missed a duck at the first pond. We raced to a second, arriving fifteen minutes after sunset. It was a clear evening. The blue-gray shadow of the moun-tains had by then climbed well above the eastern horizon. Above the shadow, the sun's direct light colored the sky a bluish-orange. Time was running out.

I "snuck the pond," approaching from behind its earthen dam. Dowdy was on my glove. Ever so slowly I peered over the dam, eyes scanning left and right so as not to miss the very first view of a duck on the water. If the ducks were to spot me they would flush because of the close range. I saw several mallards and jerked my head down as if it had bumped a hard object.

A hundred feet back from the pond I removed Dowdy's leash and swivel. Time was short, so I lifted her quickly to the takeoff. She climbed slowly in the dusk. Perhaps my hurry made the climb seem so slow. I rushed to the pond, and before the duck hawk had gained her usual two hundred feet, I raced over the dike. The waterfowl splashed into the air and disappeared into the gloom. I searched the sky. It was empty; no falcon was to be seen.

A brisk hike around the pond revealed no falcon with its quarry. I felt a slight bite of fear; this was horned owl country. I ran as fast as possible to the car. An antenna had to be attached to the radio receiver. I fumbled in the dark, reminding myself to slow down. Once the rig was together I flipped the switch. Antenna held high, I swept the horizon in a full circle. There was no *shup-shup-shup* signal from the transmitter. This was very serious. Had the transmitter failed, had its battery gone dead? "Steady, trust your equipment"—advice I had given others many times. I headed back to the pond three hundred yards away. There was no moon.

Finally at water's edge, I swung the antenna in circles. No signal. Then I rotated the antenna so that the elements were vertical instead of horizontal. Part way through another circle, off to the north, was a very weak signal. The falcon was far away. I started off toward the source. It had grown too dark for haste.

Surprisingly, with every few hundred paces, the signal grew noticeably stronger. It could mean only one thing. The short wire antenna on the transmitter was on the ground, causing the signal to be badly weakened. I wondered how the falcon would react if I walked up to her in the dark. I hoped she was not in the talons of an owl, or held by the teeth of a coyote.

A few hundred yards farther on, and now about a half-mile from the car, the signal became very strong. I reduced the volume, but the directional antenna was swamped. Normally, I would have disconnected the antenna and placed a paper clip in the receptacle on the receiver. In that manner, changes in signal strength could lead me to the transmitter by trial-and-error movement in the way people use metal detectors to find hidden treasures.

All those thoughts are as vivid now as then. What was the chance of actually stepping on my bird in the dark? I continued on very slowly, and then stopped. Eyes wide open and staring, I looked down. A few feet ahead was a faint gray patch of ground in the blackness. The patch seemed to be about five feet in diameter. What on earth was it? Slowly, I shuffled forward, knelt, and touched its edge. It was very soft. What could be so very soft on a dry grassland? I dropped to my knees and lowered my face, the better to discern the grayness.

Those moments will remain among the most memorable events of my life. I struggled to visualize this thing before me. Just ten inches from my face emerged the black mask and white throat of my peregrine, both gray in the darkness. In her feet was a half-plucked mallard. I was kneeling on a bed of plucked duck feathers. The background melody to this drama was the loud *shup, shup* of the telemetry receiver, now only inches from the transmitter.

Across North America in the fall and winter each year, hundreds of telemetry transmitters are activated daily as falconers take to the field. And every day, dozens of trained falcons and hawks that might have been lost without their radios are safely recovered. I hope not just a few of those folks routinely carry a small flashlight in their lure bag. I do now.

PEREGRINES FOR SALE   In the early 1960s I learned that people were raiding prairie falcon eyries in Wyoming and Colorado and selling the birds in the East and Midwest. The deeds seemed all the worse because some of the nests were those I was studying. I became vehemently opposed to the sale of raptors. I've changed my mind.

By the late 1960s nearly all the states had extended protection to birds of prey, thus ending legal sales. Early in the 1970s raptors became federally protected as well, and of course the endangered species law further shielded blue meanies. Qualified falconers could take a limited number of non-endangered raptors from the wild under strict rules. Both Canada and Alaska allowed some capture of young maritime peregrines; they were never considered endangered. All was as it should be.

After 1973 duck hawks in the tundra and interior of the continent could not be taken into captivity for any purpose. Then came captive breeding. Peregrines held in captivity were "grandfathered" (exempted) in 1978 by an amendment to the Endangered Species Act, thanks to the good work of Frank Bond on behalf of falconers. Many of these old birds were paired up in captivity. Further, captive-bred youngsters from the recovery projects were sometimes given to falconers who had donated their falcons to the cause in the beginning.

By 1980, private people held many exempt blue meanies or their offspring. Naturally the breeders wished to see peregrines in falconry. They also wanted to recoup the expenses of breeding the birds. In 1982, Bob Berry and others successfully persuaded the FWS to develop rules that would enable breeders to sell captive-bred raptors.

The proposed rules to allow sale of captive-produced raptors hit the *Federal Register* in January of 1983. Despite claims by opponents that breeders would steal eggs or young from eyries and claim they were produced in captivity, sales became legal. Any youngster produced was fitted with a permanent federal band, and records were kept for all birds sold. There have been very few abuses. Wild raptors were excluded, and only licensed falconers who had passed the falconry exam could keep a captive-bred raptor. In 1985, Berry successfully testified before congressional committees on fisheries and wildlife to counter recurring objections to the 1983 approval.

In the last decade, a handful of companies in North America have specialized in providing equipment to falconers. Hoods, bells, gloves, and so on are offered in great profusion. Complete telemetry outfits can be had for a thousand dollars or so. On the pages of a 2001 catalog, independent raptor breeders posted their ads. Harris's hawks, goshawks, gyrfalcons, and falcon hybrids were available. A deposit would reserve a new bird in the spring. At least *twenty* of the fully illustrated ads offered peregrines for sale. The situation is similar in Europe.

Today, no qualified falconer need be without a peregrine. The cost depends on the sex (females are more expensive because people tend to hunt prey better suited to the larger size). Special handling costs more. Apparently ideal is a youngster that was allowed to fly free ("at hack") for a few weeks to gain flying skills. Anyway, a perfectly fine blue meanie can often be had for the price of a telemetry outfit, sometimes less.

TOWARD A BETTER PEREGRINE   The 1983 ruling allowing the sale of propagated peregrines encouraged people seriously interested in breeding. Now it was reasonable to make costly investments in permanent facilities. A breeder could plan for the long term and think about developing a genetic lineage of peregrines especially well suited to falconry. Such a man is Pete Widener.

Widener and his wife, Lucy, are both falconers. She flies a goshawk. He flies peregrines. In 1977, Widener built a modest loft suitable for blue meanies on their ranch outside Sheridan, Wyoming. He had no breeding pairs at the time. I recently asked him if it wasn't risky to build a loft with several breeding chambers for birds he did not have. "Nah," he said. "I figured if I built a barn, the birds would come to fill the space."

Slowly the stock came. People donated birds to the project. Some of the first pairs he put together were worthless because they were old when taken into captivity or were reared by hand and thus imprinted on humans. In those days, peregrines from the Pacific Northwest were not endangered and were easier to come by. Actually, Widener was most interested in that big, dark subspecies.

By the early 1980s, the Wideners had produced a few peregrines, and they decided to make a better meanie. By artificial selection, they would winnow out, from the falcons they would produce, those that seemed inferior when trained for falconry. The better birds in each generation would form the basis of the next. In practice, it is not always easy to choose the better birds. A big variable is the skill and circumstances of the training. Poor handling can ruin an otherwise superior hunter.

In the intervening twenty years, more than 350 peregrines have been produced on the Sheridan ranch. There have been bad times. All the youngsters in two broods were totally blind. They had to be destroyed. Now, only a few generations into the program, it is perhaps too soon to see clear-cut progress in creating a genetically superior falconry bird. But Widener remains enthusiastic, and falconers want his peregrines. It is important to realize that all of the domestic breeds of animals now in the care of humans began in just this way. Perhaps in the distant future, the Widener Peale's falcons will be the standard against which all others are measured.

Several other kinds of raptors are widely used in falconry in the United States. Red-tailed hawks alone may outnumber peregrines because so much of the land is suitable for hunting with these woodland hawks. Harris's hawks and goshawks are very popular, not to mention the gyr-peregrine hybrids.

In any case, captive-bred peregrines will certainly remain in demand. Evidence that blue meanies are popular in comparison to all the other types can be found in recent issues of the journal of the North American Falconers Association. In a sample of four issues, fully one article in five on the practice of falconry is concerned exclusively with peregrines.

OPERATION FALCON   In 1981, gumshoes in the law enforcement section of the FWS undertook a covert sting operation to entrap falconers in illegal sale and "trafficking" of birds of prey. The key villain working undercover for the feds was a one-time hawk dealer and would-be falconer who had been found guilty of selling raptors taken from the wild. The government hired him for a repeat performance. The agent was to be both a buyer and a seller. He would make a deal, and then finger the unsuspecting patsy.

In all, about fifty-two falconers were entrapped between 1981 and 1984. Some bought birds from the secret agent; others were urged to change federal marker bands to hide exchanges of birds. Eight people were actually *given* illegal birds, mainly gyrfalcons, because the agent had difficulty selling them. Several other falconers, who were offered illegal birds by the dastardly fellow, actually reported the undercover agent who solicited them. Needless to say, nothing came of their complaints.

Operation Falcon went public in August 1984. The phone rang; my wife, Betty, answered. The voice said, "How's Jim?" Betty said I was fine, and that I was not home at the moment. "Did they take his bird?" My poor wife was totally confused. "His falcon is here in the mews." It turned out my friend had heard that federal agents had seized a falcon from a fellow named Enderson. The poor chap was actually named Anderson.

In the end there were just over fifty convictions. No American was found guilty of "dealing" in raptors, and none took a wild bird and claimed to have produced it in captivity. Only two were found to have taken birds from the wild illegally. In all, eight peregrines were involved in the illegal activities. One falconer surprisingly sold a gyrfalcon to the informer; it was the very bird the agent had given to him in the first place.

Early press releases by the FWS, and a formal statement by an associate director to the House Subcommittee on Fisheries, Wildlife, and the Environment (March 1985), claimed raptor dealers had netted profits of three-quarters of a million dollars in the preceding three years. The only dealers discovered were in fact two Canadians, whose transactions accounted for much of the actual total of $180,000 changing hands.

Fortunately, one man studied the FWS news releases, private reports from falconers, and court records. He is Will Shor, a retired Navy systems analyst. I came to know him through our interests in falconry and the biology of peregrine survivorship. When Operation Falcon became public, Shor was editor of the quarterly newsletter of NAFA. He simply could not substantiate the huge profits that the press releases attributed to falconers. At most, the amounts paid by falconers in the United States for birds purchased for their own use added up to $17,000 over three years, amounting to no more than "the value of a used car."

Shor eventually knew more about Operation Falcon than the feds themselves. His greatest contribution was to keep meticulous records of all allegations and the outcomes of the indictments. A wide gulf eventually separated early claims made by the witch-hunters from cases brought fairly to justice. When federal agents raided the homes of falconers in June 1984, they confiscated 106 raptors. Eventually all still alive were returned to their handlers.

There was a very bad aspect of Operation Falcon. Many innocent people were unjustly fingered. The Peregrine Fund was clearly singled out as a target. FWS personnel or their cooperators leaked news of the investigations to the press. The National Audubon Society fell for the propaganda originating with the FWS law enforcement section and published a very derogatory article concerning falconers and the Peregrine Fund in its magazine.

This was at a time when the Fund was the primary force in peregrine restoration in North America. A good share of the program was paid for by private donors who understandably became reluctant to donate in light of the allegations. No case was ever made against the fund or its employees, many of whom were falconers.

In Canada, witch-hunting was simultaneous with that in the United States. My friend Richard Fyfe, who guided peregrine restoration in that coun-

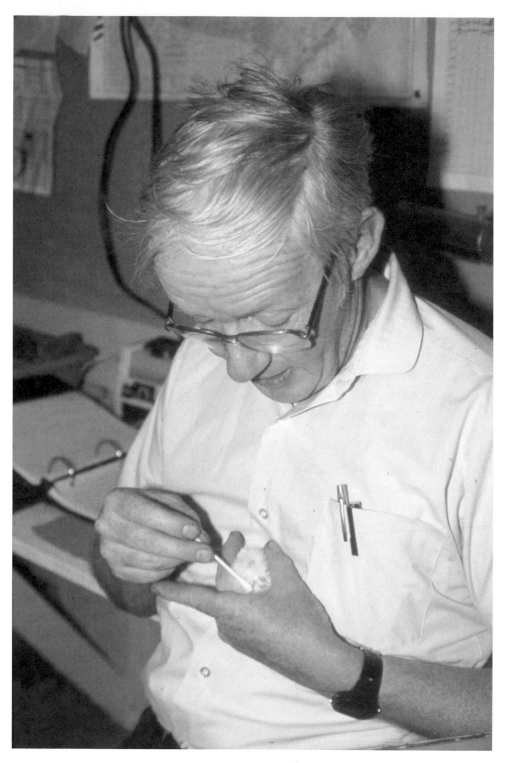

Richard Fyfe, Canadian Wildlife Service, cleans a new captive-bred peregrine chick. Photo by Ursula Banasch.

try, fell under investigation by Canadian Wildlife Service agents simply because he had been handling and breeding blue meanies for many years. Fyfe was employed by the CWS at the time. The mere fact that he was under suspicion, however unjustified, intimidated his supervisors. They gave him little defense or support. We all knew Fyfe as a man of the highest integrity. Of course, no charges were ever made, but the stigma of the inquiry ruined his career.

An interesting theft involved blue meanies. People in the FWS learned that a peregrine eyrie had been found at Lake Powell, Utah, a recreation area administered by the NPS. The FWS sent two agents to Utah, bent on obtaining falcons to use as bait in the sting. When one of the agents rappelled to the eyrie he found three eggs instead of young falcons. They stole the eggs anyway.

The thievery of the eggs at Lake Powell was seemingly in contempt of the Endangered Species Act. Ordinary citizens would have been severely penalized for the deed. The act declares it unlawful when any person commits, solicits another to commit, or causes to be committed certain acts regarding listed species. The agents who lifted the eggs were apparently in violation of the act. As it turned out, the FWS had found fine print that allowed the deed for enforcement activities.

Ever since Operation Falcon I have noted a higher level of vigilance among falconers in respect to unlawful activities. The dust finally settled, and falconers now have a stronger code of ethics. And to those who did break the law in those early years of the 1980s came humiliation and loss of the privilege of belonging to NAFA.

MONITORING MORASS   Only a handful of formerly endangered animals have increased in numbers to the point where they have been removed from the list. A few others were taken off when it was discovered their plight was not as dire as originally thought. In 1999 the American peregrine was delisted because it had made massive gains in sheer numbers, and because no agent or factor, such as eggshell thinning, seemed ominous. The book could now be closed. But it was not to be.

The Endangered Species Act has been amended since 1973. One amendment requires a five-year "monitoring" study after the delisting of any species, presumably to detect any backsliding. The requirement makes little sense in the case of the peregrine.

Between 1990 and 1995, releases of peregrines by hacking and fostering had essentially drawn to a close. A few dozen birds were turned loose after that time, but the work of augmenting natural increase was long past by 1999, when the blue meanie was delisted. The releases were really the only significant recovery actions underwritten by the act.

Nearly everywhere in the United States, counts of nesting pairs were made most years right up until delisting. Annual counts are still made in several areas. In effect, peregrines have been counted for over a decade since recovery management ceased.

It might seem logical, in this case, to waive the monitoring requirement because counts were made right up to the moment. Further, recent counts continue to show expansion except where the falcons were nearing the limit of available nesting sites. Instead, the clamor for a monitoring scheme was as persistent as the delay on the part of the FWS to organize such a process. In 2003 the FWS began to provide funds to a few states for monitoring before a system was finalized.

The dictionary says that *monitor* means to watch over something to ensure "that good order is maintained." In the case of peregrines, the simplest plan would be to designate a fair sample of nesting cliffs around the country and visit them for several years to see if the falcons are still around. Unfortunately, no money was earmarked for monitoring any delisted species (funds are short even for species *remaining* on the list). Worse, biologists and bureaucrats disagreed on how monitoring should proceed.

In an effort to help, the Raptor Research Foundation appointed a group of biologists to develop a counting scheme the FWS might adopt. The committee included Mike Kockert, Ted Swem, Robert Kenward (a Brit), Carol McIntyre, Joan Morrison, Brian Millsap, Gordon Court, and me. All were seasoned raptor biologists, but only Swem, Court, and I had done much fieldwork on blue meanies.

We worked for a few months to find a plan all could accept. The effort was futile. Instead of finding a simple, economical way to count meanies, we ranged from the requirement of a full-blown scientific research project fit for a species still on the list to a plan involving visits to a couple of hundred eyries from coast to coast every few years to see if the birds were okay. I favored the latter.

The folks in the FWS seemed helpless. They had actually taken very little role in overseeing all the regional counts made when the bird was *on* the list. No wonder their role in monitoring was new ground. Other problems included continual change in FWS staff positions, so that no one was in charge for long.

In addition to these difficulties was the pressure from protectionists placed on the FWS to devise a monitoring program adequate to detect the slightest downswing in peregrine numbers. It turns out falconers want to capture a modest number of meanies each year, as they can now do with several other non-endangered raptors. The anti-harvest folks have sued the FWS to prevent a harvest until an ironclad monitoring program is in operation.

Far from fading into obscurity, the big blue falcon remains in the center of a controversy second only to the battle to delist the bird in the first place. When a count system is finally set in motion, the issue of a small harvest by falconers will surely emerge on another battleground. It is as if we have all become captives of our own notions of the falcon. Good-natured compromise is not easy when we are held hostage to personal agendas.

PEREGRINE PRESENT   Whatever the outcomes of the petty scuffles in stuffy agency office buildings or in tastefully carpeted courtrooms, a safe future for the blue meanie seems assured. Anyone who wishes can see and enjoy peregrines. A few folks who have the time can elect to fly the big blue falcon from the glove in what Aldo Leopold called the perfect sport. My children grew up with peregrines. They spent many months in the field looking for what was then rare, but is now common. A few weeks ago, my daughter, Anne, called on her cell phone from the streets of Baltimore. She was walking with her airline flight crew when a familiar scream was heard overhead. The crew had its first look at an urban peregrine.

As of this writing, yesterday morning my son, Ritt, called en route to his office in Mesa, Arizona. A big dark female peregrine, wintering with the snowbirds, was plucking its prey on a street lamp above the freeway. It was the second falcon he had seen perched with prey in two weeks.

Two years ago a cadet took one of the Air Force Academy peregrines home to Phoenix during winter vacation. The bird flew off for a few hours one morning. In the course of radio-tracking the errant mascot, the cadet encountered *four* wild peregrines. They were spending the sunny winter on tall buildings.

In Colorado, a person bent on watching peregrines can fully enjoy the experience. Perhaps a waffle cone on the veranda at the Royal Gorge Bridge suits your style. Blue meanies feed their young below to the tune of live country music. Or you can sip a Chardonnay at a sidewalk table in Ouray. Your spotting scope will be barely noticed by the souvenir shoppers. My favorite way is to savor a hot cup of Kona coffee at the art gallery in Frisco. Expect to be inconvenienced when the flight of the foraging male brings him directly overhead as he glides to Dillon Reservoir on a hunt.

The sweetest victory for me in peregrine recovery came in 2003. In 1952 Vernon Seifert and Bob Stabler (Chapter IV) banded young peregrines on a cliff towering on the crest of the Front Range west of what is now Air Force Academy property. After fifty-one years, peregrines are rearing their young in the old nest long ago abandoned by golden eagles.

RÉSUMÉ   The last century saw people and peregrines drawn closer together. Whether in skydiver speed trials, or climbing to a helium-filled balloon, or in a show of swift flight from a stadium press box at the Air Force Academy, blue meanies have been wonderfully tractable in the hands of the people who love them. Peregrines seemed destined to be of two kinds: some were to be truly wild as before, and some were born into the care and keeping of humans.

Three decades ago a marvelous recovery effort was set in motion in North America. The nearly complete accord among people bent on averting extinction in the early years gave way to strongly divergent opinion. Operation Falcon, an unjustified program of entrapment by FWS enforcement people, revealed the far extreme of distrust.

Ineptness in establishing a post-delisting monitoring scheme by the FWS and inevitable future disagreements concerning a limited capture of wild peregrines for falconry and captive breeding are signs that we are in an awkward period of adjustment. Meanwhile, whatever your interest in peregrines might be, now is the time to enjoy them.

EPILOGUE

Those who have known the blue meanie carry memories of their encounters that are never to be forgotten. I remember two special times that seem indelible. These recollections are of peregrines at the end of the twentieth century. It was a time when the falcons were back in force. In both experiences, wild falcons and their world stood in simple beauty.

DROP THE BLACKBIRD   If you gain a vantage point on the south flank of the San Juan Mountains in Colorado, you can easily see deep into New Mexico. The country was etched deeply by the tributaries of the San Juan River on its way to the Colorado. The surface offered little resistance to the waters; now, in row after row, cliffs of yellow Mesa Verde sandstone perch on eroded talus slopes of soft gray Mancos shale. In places the sandstone is deeply pockmarked like giant blocks of Swiss cheese, or laminated layer upon layer with softer mudstone. Either way, there are countless holes and ledges for cliff-nesting falcons. Off in the haze to the south is the cliff at Stinking Lake where Wetmore tried unsuccessfully to obtain a specimen of a duck hawk for the National Museum in 1919.

The cliffs are miles long, something of a challenge for meanie watchers. The rough, potholed faces of the walls can easily hide a peregrine. A few years ago, one day in July, I clamped my scope to the truck window below such a cliff, well aware of the difficulty. A person just has to be patient. It was late in the day. The sun, low in the west, shone along the cliff and onto the sides of the potholes. Black shadows and yellow rocks stood in sharp contrast. My attention was drawn to a section of the cliff with several long single streaks of bright whitewash. Clearly, falcons had been there recently.

A pothole caught my attention. Inside was a shiny black object that seemed out of place. Was it sunlight on the back of a raven? Then I saw motion. A black-and-white object appeared just to the side; the pattern was that of the head of a peregrine. The shine was its blue-gray back. The meanie was eating some small bird in the quiet solitude of the deep hole. It finished its meal, wiped its beak, and flew east along the cliff into the dusk.

The next morning I scanned the cliff from a greater distance so as to get a broader view. The cliff seemed deserted. A few huge dead ponderosa pines stood on top of the cliff, remnants of a pre-settlement gallery forest that once covered the region. A century ago, eager loggers called these prized trees with orange bark "yellow boys." Exhausted from searching the cliff, I scanned the trees. There it was. Five hundred yards from where the peregrine had been the evening before was the black silhouette of a falcon perched on a heavy branch.

The only thing to do now was to watch and wait. The wait was brief. Slowly the falcon raised its wings, as if in anticipation of flight. Then it lowered them. Again the wings came up, well over the bird's head. The falcon leaned forward and, out of balance, was committed to flight. This was no polished flyer. I was watching a youngster.

The bird flew head-on for several seconds, then veered west and intercepted a second peregrine. The second bird was smaller and much paler; it was the adult male. The adult pitched up sharply and lowered its feet, exposing a fully feathered blackbird. The young falcon had seen the approaching adult in the distance. It had flown out, intent on interception, and then flared up to avoid collision. As it was about to grasp the prey, the adult dropped it.

The juvenile shot out a foot but missed. The prey fell by. Before it had gone twenty feet the adult flipped upside down, dove vertically, and was there. Prey held tight, he climbed on quick, stiff wingbeats in two graceful circles. The juvenile made another rush for the adult. Suddenly *two more* dark fledglings came into the field of my scope and joined the first in the chase. It appeared as if all three were females.

The adult, now well above the top of the cliff and two hundred yards out, decided against an attempt at a graceful food transfer. He must have seen the risk in a free-for-all involving rowdy youngsters and sharp talons. The darkness of the females made them appear much larger than the male. He dropped the blackbird.

I followed the falling corpse in the scope. It did not fall far. A juvenile came from the side, grabbed the prey in midair, and set its long wings in a turning glide. Suddenly it banked sharply and dropped the bird. Another youngster caught it. Soon all three young were wheeling about. Whenever the falcon with the blackbird was approached, it released the food. Then, in a flash, the lifeless prey was grabbed by another dark brown meanie.

The melee slowly lost altitude. No one was paying attention to height. No one seemed intent on keeping the food. Each had apparently already had breakfast. At last the trio was barely fifty feet above the oakbrush. The game was called on account of low altitude. The female with the prey set her wings, caught a thermal, and rose quickly to the level of the cliff-top four hundred feet above. She turned, pumped directly to the wall, and landed near a ledge covered with fresh whitewash. She had returned home to dine.

Obviously, the three youngsters had been out of the eyrie for days. They all seemed practiced, if not graceful, in the air. No one stalled in too tight a turn, and all used the momentum of forward speed to maneuver, rather than resorting to heavy wing flapping to keep from falling. Of course the spectacular aerial display had not been so much a game as a learning session. It was preparation for the not-too-distant time when prey would evade their rushes, and when attempted piracy in the air could be avoided only by evasive aerobatics.

LAST ROCK AT BEAVER CREEK   April in Colorado is a wonderful time. The weather is unsettled, always changing. But there is a certain mildness in the wind. In the mountains, snow showers hang from fluffy clouds as they race by in the flow aloft. Blue sky comes and goes, and sunshine often beams full strength on huge snowflakes.

Such was the day, three years ago, at Beaver Creek. I sat on a huge ledge in ankle-deep kinnikinnick at the edge of the cliff. Before me was the canyon and the river, a thousand feet below. To the north, Pikes Peak was partly hidden in a light gray veil of snow. To the south the gorge opened onto the sprawling basin of the Arkansas River ten miles away. Four hundred yards upstream, the white roof of the old hack box was barely visible on the top of the cliff where the falcons usually nested.

In the bottom of the gorge was a broken-down power plant. Remains of water-driven turbines rusted inside. The plant became defunct in the flood of 1965, when tons of gravel plugged flumes carrying water down a thousand-foot gradient to the turbine blades. Just below me was wreckage of the steep railway tram that had carried men and provisions to the station.

Despite the former human activity, the chasm and surrounding highlands are now a de facto wilderness. Two locked gates bar access from the county road. The trail from the second gate (made of welded iron pipes) has not been maintained since the power station failed. The hike in to the eyrie is a long one.

The touch of sadness I felt on that lovely April morning can, I hope, be forgiven. Peregrines had been removed from the endangered list almost two years before. I knew the field surveys would be discontinued. This was perhaps the last year I would come to this place. I had seen the birds disappear from here in the crash of the 1960s, and had recorded their return in the late 1980s. Dozens of captive-bred youngsters had flown from the hack box in the interim.

Snow squalls came and went. No peregrine was to be seen. A big gray goshawk sailed by in midmorning. It gave me a start because it was so close. Coming head-on, goshawks look a lot like peregrines. A migrating merlin pumped upstream a hundred yards away. There was still no peregrine. For some reason, when I am in the field, my lunch is always eaten by midmorning. That cold day, eating seemed all the more important. About noon, a large granite boulder down the slope in front of me stood up and walked off. Bighorn! The sheep was a perfect match for the color of the granite rubble where it had been resting.

By early afternoon no peregrine had appeared. I began to imagine dreadful things. Perhaps the pair had not returned this year, or maybe one of the birds had been killed and its mate deserted. There had been several nest failures here over the years. The peregrines often nested on an open ledge, I remembered. One year a sleet storm got the tiny young. It wasn't a total loss; dozens of violet-green swallows gathered the down from the dead chicks to line their nests. I shuddered at the notion of swallow chicks warmed by peregrine down.

In a little while, the wind picked up. Another snow squall swept my side of the canyon. I dug my last piece of reserve clothing, a camo rain jacket, out of the rucksack. It would be very easy to miss a peregrine in weather like this, I thought. Then I heard a call, *klup*. It had a hollow resonance only a raven could utter.

Presently, four ravens appeared, flying at my level in the snowflakes. The wind was at my back; the ravens were coming head-on. If they continued, the foursome would pass right by me. Onward they came, half sailing, half pumping into the wind, talking to each other in croaking, guttural tones, muttering quietly under their breath. Slowly they came on without a hint of haste.

Many times in the course of my decades watching duck hawks, ravens have fooled me. In the wrong light, in the wrong wind, it is easy to confuse raven for peregrine. The foursome went by, not ten yards away. They all saw me, but none seemed to take alarm. They were so very black. Wonderful birds. By the time natural selection got around to ravens it had perfected the process.

My time was up. It was late and very cold. I knew the peregrines were not at Beaver Creek. What the hell, I'd go over to the hack box for a last look. Snow had gathered on the north side of the pinnacle that held the box. Somehow the rock was steeper than I had remembered, and wet lichens made for slick footing. Once at the box, I checked the interior. The gravel floor was bare except for fecal pellets of a rock squirrel. I remembered the box when it was full of five-week-old ruffian falcons, all ready and able to repel any rock squirrel.

As a last resort, I shuffled as close to the edge of the cliff as I dared, picked up a twenty-pound boulder, and threw it over. Sometimes the crashing of a rock would cause a falcon to fly out. I figured there was not much chance of that. After all, I had watched the cliff for seven hours.

The falling rock hit a ledge forty feet below. The impact shattered the rock. The breeze up the face of the cliff carried the smell of super-heated rock. The force of the collision on the surfaces where the rock and cliff met must have been enormous. The same odor is produced when flint is struck with a steel to create sparks for a fire.

No peregrine appeared, confirming my conclusion that the site was not in use. I threw another rock for good measure. It went all the way to the bottom and hit with a sharp report. Nothing. I retreated from the edge, worked a few yards to the left, and threw the last rock. I picked it up just because it was handy. It went halfway, struck a buttress, and ricocheted straight out from the cliff.

Out she came. A hundred feet below, the dark blue-gray back of a peregrine flashed out. She flew to a dead spruce, landed, and turned to see the cliff face. Then she ejected a huge slice of whitewash, full proof she had been sitting on eggs for several hours. She had taken no time from her vital task to defecate.

I was overjoyed. I lifted the binoculars for a close-up. She saw the movement and glared at me. She was another dark one, my favorite type. Massive yellow feet held the spruce branch.

The snow came again and she and her tree disappeared in the white. I headed home. There would be no reason to check on them in the future. But despite myself, I have returned every year since then. Peregrines will always lay claim to this piece of wilderness.

The twentieth century hosted the coming-out party for the peregrine falcon. In a matter of a few decades, the bird touched many thousands of people. They came to watch it, to study it, to breed it, to manage it, and to fly it from the glove. Some of us allowed it to cjaculate on our heads. A few even jumped from airplanes with it. Most of us are much richer for it all. I predict that people, in their various ways, will always seek out and be changed for the better by the blue meanie.

BIBLIOGRAPHY

Cade, T. J. *Falcons of the World*. Ithaca, N.Y.: Comstock/Cornell University Press, 1982.

Cade, T. J., and W. Burnham, eds. *Return of the Peregrine*. Boise, Idaho: Peregrine Fund, 2003.

Cade, T. J., J. H. Enderson, C. G. Thelander, and C. M. White, eds. *Peregrine Falcon Populations: Their Management and Recovery*. Boise, Idaho: Peregrine Fund, 1988.

Craig, G. and J. H. Enderson. *Peregrine Falcon Biology and Management in Colorado*. Fort Collins, Colorado: Colorado Division of Wildlife, 2004.

Craighead, F., and J. Craighead. "Adventures with Birds of Prey." *National Geographic* 72:1 (1937).

———. *Hawks in the Hand*. New York: Houghton Mifflin, 1939. Reprint, New York: Lyons & Burford, 1997.

———. "Life with an Indian Prince." *National Geographic* 81:2 (1942).

Frank, S. *City Peregrines*. Blaine, Wash.: Hancock House Publishers, 1994.

Frederick II of Hohenstaufen. *The Art of Falconry*, ca. 1248, ed. and trans. C. A. Wood and F. M. Fyfe. Stanford, Calif.: Stanford University Press, 1943.

Freuchen, P. *Arctic Adventure: My Life in the Frozen North*. New York: Farrar and Rinehart, 1935 (reprinted 2002).

Fuertes, L. A. "Falconry, the Sport of Kings." *National Geographic* 38:6 (1920).

Hickey, J. J., ed. *Peregrine Falcon Populations: Their Biology and Decline*. Madison: University of Wisconsin Press, 1969.

Houle, M. C. *Wings for My Flight*. New York: Addison-Wesley, 1991.

Lascelles, G. "Falconry." In *The Badminton Library*. London: Longmans, Green and Co., 1892.

Meredith, R. L. *American Falconry in the Twentieth Century*. Boise, Idaho: Archives of American Falconry, 1999.

Michell, E. B. *The Art and Practice of Hawking*. Frome, England: D. R. Hillman and Sons, 1900; reprinted, Boston: Branford Company, 1959.

Peakall, D. B. "DDE: Its Presence in Peregrine Eggs in 1948." *Science* 168:592–594 (1974).

Ratcliffe, D. *The Peregrine Falcon*. London: T. and A. D. Poyser, 1980; 2nd edition, San Diego: Academic Press, 1993.

Taverner, P. A. "The Birds of the Red Deer River, Alberta." *Auk* 36:1–21 (1919).

Treleaven, R. B. *In Pursuit of the Peregrine*. Wheathampstead, Hertfordshire, UK: Tiercel SB Publishing, 1998.

Webster, H. M., and J. H. Enderson, eds. *Gamehawking at Its Very Best*. Denver: Windsong Press, 1988.

White, C. M., N. J. Clum, T. J. Cade, and W. G. Hunt. "Peregrine Falcon (*Falco peregrinus*)." In *The Birds of North America*, No. 660, ed. A. Poole and F. Gill. Philadelphia: Birds of North America, Inc., 2002.

INDEX

thickness, 67–68; and Kiff, 70; and
Madison Conference, 63–65; note-
book from, 52
Higby, Warren, 35, 38
Hogan, Joel, 157
Holroyd, Geoff, 204
hood (falcon), 35, 47, 128
horned owl (great), 79, 153, 157, 217
Houle, Marcy Cottrell, 22, 154
Hunt, Grainger: at Big Bend, 170; and
blue meanie, 4; and captive peregrine, 150; falconry by, 140; at Madison Conference, 64; and population
limit, 15, 16; and western recovery
team, 197
Hunter, Don: in Denver (1961), 37; at
Georgetown, 49; and NAFA Meet
(1963), 139; in Queen Charlotte
Islands, 39–47; and Raptor Research
Foundation, 49
hunting: of blackbirds, 114; in Cornwall,
176–177; of ducks at Culiacán, 114;
role of males in, 11–13; of shorebirds,
115; use of feet in, 24
hunting range, 21–22
hunting success, 23–24
hybrid falcons, 223, 229, 230

ice (and icebergs), 75, 82, 85, 97–99, 104
inbreeding, 214
incubation, 95
Indian (burial site), 37
Inuit, 102
Inuvik (NWT), 84, 87
Iowa, 27, 32, 163

Jenny, Pete, 115–116
Joseph, Ron, 165, 169–170
juvenile plumage, 18–19

Kendall, Henry, 147
Kendeigh, Charles, 34
Kenward, Robert, 234
kestrel(s): captive, 28; city nesting of, 29;
compared to prairie falcons, 32, 34;
DDE tests on, 68, 69; in Iowa, 28;
Minelli and, 51; population in Illi-
nois, 33

Kiff, Lloyd: and eggshells for Peakall,
69–70; and hacking, 183, 184; and
peregrine count, 199; and western
recovery team, 197
King, Warren, 192
Kirven, Monte, 149, 184, 203
kite (training), 223–224
Klimes, Bob, 137
Knight, C. W. R., 136
Knoder, Gene, 186
Kochert, Mike, 234
Konkel, Dan, 144, 145
Kussman, Joel, 186
Kuyt, Earnie, 81

Laguna Atascosa National Wildlife Ref-
uge, 119
Lake Powell (Utah): discovery of pere-
grines on, 165; Operation Falcon and,
233; surveys on, 168
Lake Willoughby (Vermont), 146
Lansing (Iowa), 32–33
Laramie Plains (Wyoming), 50, 51
Layman, Seth, 221
lemmings, 98
Leopold, Aldo, 235
life span, 211, 212
Lil (captive peregrine), 51, 128–129, 147
Lincer, Jeff, 68
Lindberg, Peter, 161, 206
Lithicum, Janet, 184
Living Bird (journal), 100

MacDonald, Brian, 120
Mackenzie River (NWT) 73, 76, 82–84;
color of, 85; map of, 74; navigation
on, 83; peregrines on, 88; source of,
82
Madison Conference: attendees at, 63-64;
DDT discussed at, 65–66; and raptor
declines, 71
Maechtle, Tom: in Greenland, 97; on
Padre Island, 117, 122–124
males (role of), 11, 25, 172–173
mallard, 98, 131
map (of North America), 74
Martell, Mark, 204
Martin, Bob, 97, 138–139

Marvin's biscuits, 78, 82, 85
mascot (at Air Force Academy), 34, 35, 224–226
Matagorda Island (Texas), 107–108
Mattox, Bill, 13, 96, 97, 98, 99, 204
McCallum, Bob, 138
McIntyre, Carol, 234
McIntyre, Jim, 225
McKinney, Bonnie, 203
McLeod River (Alberta), 59, 60
Mearns, Richard, 172, 173, 176
Meng, Heinz: on Assateague, 120; and captive breeding, 150; and Cooper's hawks, 31; and hacking, 155
Meredith, R. L.: buried at West Point, 140; and falcon identification, 19; in falconry, 50; and migrant peregrines, 107; in Montana, 54; in Texas, 134
merlin, 174, 206, 239
Mexico: and Big Bend, 170–172; Culiacán, 113–115; peregrines in, 207
Midwest (U.S.): banded peregrines in, 204; city nesting in, 203; hack boxes in, 156; inbreeding of falcons in, 214; mortality in, 217; nest fidelity in, 208–209; population of, 207; population growth in, 199; recovery plan in, 188; releases in, 160, 208
migration: by adult males, 124; in Dry Tortugas, 112; estimates of, 122–123; origin of, 111–112; on supertankers, 113; in world, 111
Millsap, Brian, 234
Minelli, Mike, 51
Mohr, Carl, 30
monitoring, 233–234
Monk, Jeff, 184
moose, 83–84
Morrison, Joan, 234
mortality, 217
mosquitoes, 78, 81–82
Mueller, Helmut, 123
Mueller, Paul, 3, 28
musk oxen, 97, 98
Mutch, Brian, 118

National Audubon Society: Clement and, 151; Knoder and, 186; Operation Fal-
con and, 231; "pure" peregrines and, 192; Yukon study and, 90
National Geographic (magazine), 132, 134
National Park Service, 165, 185, 186
National Science Foundation, 66, 76
National Wildlife Federation, 192
Naval Arctic Research Laboratory, 94
Nelson, Morley: in Boise (1962), 39; in Colorado, 152; and Madison Conference, 64; on recovery team, 186; and trained duck hawk, 135–136
Nelson, Wayne, 151, 204
nest(s): in Arctic, 94; in cities, 209–210; in Colorado, 194–195; northern limit of, 100; in Scandinavia, 16; success of, 212, 215. *See also* eyrie
Nethersole-Thompson, Desmond, 67
Newton, Ian: and future of peregrine, 176; and population limit, 15; in Scotland, 173–174; and size difference, 13; sparrowhawk study by, 172
New York Zoological Society, 151
Nixon, Richard, 185
Nobel Prize, 28
North American Falconer's Association: peregrine articles in journal, 230; first meeting of, 140; formation of, 36, 140; impact of, 141; and Operation Falcon, 231, 233
North American Raptor Breeders Association, 93
northern phalarope, 98
Northwest Territories, 73, 74, 77
Nosgay, Ben, 78–79, 79
Nye, Al: on Assateague, 120, 134; falconry by, 135; in Pennsylvania, 53

Oakleaf, Bob: hacking by, 183; at Las Vegas meeting, 196; Wyoming surveys by, 203
Oar, Jack, 97, 150
Oeming, Al, 54
oil platforms, 118
Old Crow (Yukon Territory), 92–93
Olendorff, Butch, 196, 197
Oliphant, Lynn, 160, 207
Operation Falcon, 230–233, 236
orange-breasted falcon, 19
osprey, 64, 206

Reid, Ed, 132
releases (of captives), 160–161, 183
reproduction, 212–214
Resolution Bay (NWT), 75
Rice, Jim, 120, 193
Riddle, Ken, 129, 138, 139
Riddle, Ric, 225
Robert, Mark, 195
Robinson, Andy, 196
rock ptarmigan, 98, 103
Rocky Mountain goat, 9
Roder, Larry, 29, 38
Rogers, Missy, 189, 190
Rogers, Ralph, 190: and hacking, 189–
    191; in Greenland, 97; in Texas, 189
Rosenfield, Bob, 97
rough-legged hawk, 95, 98
Roush, Jim, 160
Ruckelshaus, William, 70, 215
Rucks, Jeff, 154
Ruhr, Gene, 186
Russell, Bill, 136

Saar, Christian, 161, 206
sale (of peregrines), 228–229
Sandfort, Cal, 143, 153
Sanderson, Milton, 30
Sans Sault Rapids (NWT), 83
Santa Cruz Predatory Bird Group, 160,
    184, 188
Saunders, A. A., 53, 59
Scandinavia, 16
Schaad, Larry, 225
Schram, Larry, 147
Schreiner, Keith, 186
Science (journal), 70
Scotland: peregrines in, 16, 212, 172–175;
    sparrowhawks in, 172
Seegar, Bill, 117, 122
Seifert, Vernon, 235
Septon, Greg, 207
sexual maturity, 213
Shane (captive peregrine), 46, 48, 51, 129,
    147
Shinners, Bill, 138, 140
Shor, Will, 231
Sierra del Carmen (Mexico), 171
Sindelar, Chuck, 63

size: advantage of, 11; and agility, 10; of
    prey, 10; of the sexes, 10–14
skydiving, 221–223, 222
Slave River (NWT), 73, 80, 82
Slowe, Dan, 117, 138
Smith, Hobart, 34
Smith, John, 108–110, 117
Smylie, Tom, 53, 139, 140
snow bunting, 13, 98, 99
snowy owls, 98
Sondrestrom Air Base (Greenland), 97
Southern California Falconer's Association,
    137
sparrowhawk, 172–173
Spear, Mike, 198
speed: advantage of, 9, 21; measurement of,
    7–9, 221–223; and plumage, 15
Spencer, Don, 65, 69
Spofford, Walter: at Lake Willoughby, 146;
    at the Madison Conference, 64; at
    Reelfoot Lake, 31; at Woods Hole, 49
spotted sandpiper, 86
Stabler, Bob: and Al Nye, 53; and duck
    hawks, 193; and Falconry Association
    of North America, 139, 140; and Frank
    Bond, 186; and Peregrine Club, 132;
    and prairie falcons, 50; at Woods Hole,
    49
Stickel, Bill and Lucille, 65, 66, 68
Stoddart, Jack, 51, 56, 57
Stolzenburg, Kurt, 184
subspecies, 191
Sumner, Jay, 203
surveys: in Arizona, 203; at Big Bend, 170–
    172; on Colorado Plateau, 165–170; in
    Grand Canyon, 163; in Montana, 203;
    in Rocky Mountains, 61–63; in Wyo-
    ming, 203
survivorship, 213
Swanson, Ralph, 29, 38
Swartz, Jerry: and DDE in Alaska, 68; on
    Gulf Coast, 108; in Illinois, 29; on
    Yukon River, 90
Sweeney, Steve, 217
Swem, Ted, 234

Taverner, T. A., 53
Teita falcon, 178–182